Guide to College Writing

7th edition

"I meant..."
"But it says..."

Emily Dial-Driver
Rogers State University

Layout by Bryce Brimer.
Cover design by Randy Riggs.

Acknowledgements:
With special thanks to Jeana Driver, Grant Driver Jr., David Schramme, Alan Lawless, Guylene Hull, Claudia McBride, Linda Putnam, Julia Sheppard, Polly H. Dial, Ellen D. Fitzpatrick, Gary Moeller, Phil Sample, Shelly Borgstrom, Cassie Hughes, Sally Emmons-Featherston, Doug Martin, Robin Pryor, Victor Gischler, Jim Ford, Diana Lurz, Hugh Foley, Judy Hubble, Susan Rainey, Laura Gray, Chip Rogers, Lori Butler, Tricia Bugajski, Bryce Brimer, Nat Hardy, Jesse Stallings, Brandon Jones, Laura Smith, Renée Turk, Frances Morris, and the students of composition.

Printed in the United States of America.

ISBN: 1-60250-046-0 (978-1-60250-046-4)

59 Damonte Ranch Parkway, #B-284 • Reno, NV 89521 • (800) 970-1883

www.benttreepress.com

Address all correspondence and order information to the above address.

Contents

Contents

USING THIS BOOK

The *Guide to College Writing* is designed to be accessible, usable, and directive. It is not a philosophical statement about writing. It is a straightforward guide to writing easily-formatted, easily-read college essays. The principles are basic but can be applied to any level of complexity in writing. In addition, the *Guide* gives basic information on a number of other kinds of writing. The instructions are simple, written in a "first do this, then do that" style that should be easy to follow and easy to use.

The *Guide* is divided into sections. The majority of the text is devoted to the writing process and the research paper, including using the library. Other sections include mechanics, business and science writing, and examples of various kinds of student writing.

Examples in the appendices include MLA, APA, and MLA- and APA-endnoted papers. The first page of the appendix has a key to those examples.

Examples in the main portion of this book which apply to all forms of documentation are surrounded by a solid line and unshaded, like this:

Examples in the main portion of the book in MLA format are shaded, like this:

Examples in APA format are surrounded by a dashed line, like this:

WHY BOTHER?

The employer says, ***"I just can't find anyone to do the job."***
The agency asks, ***"What's the problem?"***
The employer replies, ***"Well, I guess the main problem is that I can't find anyone who can communicate in writing."***

Almost every job requires some kind of writing. For example, we may think of police work as "cops and robbers," but police work is more than just action. Police have to write traffic accident reports, investigation reports, incident reports, prosecution reports, information reports, memos, letters, press releases and so on and on and on. . . . You would not survive in a quality police department if you could not write good, concise, complete, understandable reports. And most police work is not considered a desk job!

Another active job that requires writing is nursing. Aside from tending to patient needs, nurses compose both professional and business letters, design professional standards, write research reports and articles for professional journals and professional seminars, complete innumerable patient reports, and more.

So, accept the fact that you are going to have to write. You are going to be held responsible for (and judged on) those "English things" like spelling, sentence structure, punctuation, etc. In addition to being judged on mechanics, you will be judged on how your papers look. You have probably heard that "first impressions are important." This saying is true not only when meeting other people; it also applies to how your paper looks when your boss or customer or instructor sees it. If the paper is neat and looks as if you followed the rules for correct manuscript format, the first impression will be good; this could affect your grade!

Writing is not something you are born knowing how to do. It is a skill, like swimming or riding a bicycle or driving a car (or talking or reading), that you learn to do. Some people write more creatively than others, but anyone who wants to do so can learn to write well.

The best way to learn to write is to write. And in college–in all departments and in many different kinds of circumstances–you will be required to write. Writing is in your future!

TAKING NOTES

One of the ways you write in college is taking notes. Note-taking helps you learn by requiring you to listen, process, and paraphrase before writing. In addition, classroom note-taking is the very best preparation there is for taking "field notes." The quality of the finished report, record, or study is based on the quality and quantity of raw information. The ability to take good notes is the way to get information of the quality and quantity you need.

Taking notes matters.

The style or manner of taking notes is not important. What is important is taking the notes. One method of taking notes is the outline method (see **OUTLINE**). Another method is the "Pearls of Wisdom" method: you listen to the lecture and, every time you hear something that sounds important, you write it in your notebook. If information is written on the board, an overhead, or a PowerPoint slide, you should probably write it down!

One way to take notes is to create a response log, which provides you with a review and study method. It also allows you to take an active part in learning because the act of writing reinforces the concepts. Then the log becomes a visible, permanent record of the class and is handy for review.

Take notes on one-half of the front side of the paper only. Leave the other half blank. Later, when you are studying, cover the class note half and use the other side, preferably the left side, to recall and recite the important information.

EXAMPLE (response log):

#5 26 May 07	Atomic Numbers Dr. Lawless
review main idea here key detail review	CLASS NOTE MAIN IDEA HERE Examples, important sub-points
review main idea here key detail review	CLASS NOTE MAIN IDEA HERE Examples, important sub-points
review main idea here key detail review	CLASS NOTE MAIN IDEA HERE Examples, important sub-points
	VOCABULARY:

ANNOTATING TEXT

The log system can also be used in response to print. You may interact with the text by annotating the margins. Annotating is marking—marking the text with explanations or notes that relate to your own experience or information or to other information in the text. (Yes, you can usually still sell the book back at the end of the semester with writing in it. The next buyer may even be grateful.) Or you may choose to use the log method previously discussed, taking notes about the text selection on half a page, and then responding to that section on the other half of the page.

JOURNALS

Another way you may be asked to write in college is to keep a journal. A journal records your work, your experiences, your impressions, and/or your thoughts. It will help you learn to write. It will help you learn the subject about which you write–whether the subject is yourself, or a subject you are taking in class, or a subject in which you are interested.

A journal should be easily identifiable. Your name and the journal subject should appear prominently on the front cover or first page and on each page. Each entry should be labeled by specific subject and date so that you or another reader can easily distinguish one entry from another.

EXAMPLE (journal entry heading):

- If you are keeping a journal for a physics class, you might write your name, class, class number, time of meeting, and semester on the front cover in the upper right corner and/or in the upper right corner of the inside of the front cover.
- The first entry might be labeled as follows:

#1	Aug 25, 2005	Discussion of Light Waves	Sally Student

HINTS for journals:

1. Put the journal entries in the required type of notebook, spiral notebook, or folder.
2. Turn in the journal when it is due.
3. Complete the assignments, making each entry the suggested length.
4. Write legibly in ink on the front of the pages.
5. Be coherent; stick to the subject.
6. Show good writing skills.
7. Do not use the words *bored* or *boring*. To be bored shows a lack of inner resources to which you should never admit.

Generate ideas using pre-writing techniques.

FREE-WRITING

Free-writing is the technique of letting ideas flow from your head, maybe even from your subconscious, through your pen or through your fingers on a typewriter or computer keyboard. All you have to do is write. Begin by putting down the subject and just keep writing. Usually you will give yourself a time limit of five or ten minutes. Keep writing for the full time. Do not stop. If you run out of ideas, write "I cannot think of anything to say." The physical activity of continuing to write will help you generate ideas and prevent writer's block.

When you have finished free-writing, you can look back over your paper and discover any relationships between ideas or thoughts. You can weed out the irrelevancies and concentrate on the meaty thoughts that you have generated. When you have chosen one idea or a group of ideas from one (or more) free-writings, then you can move on to one of the pre-writing techniques that involve more organization.

EXAMPLE (free-writing):

- The topic is music.
- For five minutes, you write and YOU GENERATE THIS:

I have to write about music which I am listening to and it's good stuff only it's not regular music like country or rock or classical and that's a weird term anyway because classical is only a period in music like romantic or baroque or that stuff that doesn't have music just words like chants and then chants like the Buddhist monks and they toured with the Dead I like rock like the Dead and it's weird that they are funding research into folk music like Pete Seeger and Joan Baez I can't think of anything to say I can't think no like tribal which can be cultural or about emotion like New Age soothing stuff or the nature stuff or wind chimes are they music and what about just drums or hollow logs and even combinations like rock and aborigine where do people get recordings of tribal and who buys that and who buys

- You look at what you have written and find some topics on which you might be interested in writing. Those topics are in bold-face print in the pre-writing below:

I have to write about music which I am listening to and it's good stuff only it's not regular music like **country** or **rock** or **classical** and that's a weird term anyway because classical is only a **period in music** like **romantic** or **baroque** or that stuff that doesn't have music just words like **chants** and then chants like the **Buddhist monks** and **they toured with the Dead** I like **rock like the Dead** and it's weird that they are **funding research into folk music** like **Pete Seeger** and **Joan Baez** I can't think of anything to say I can't think no like **tribal** which can be **cultural** or about **emotion** like **New Age** soothing stuff or the **nature stuff** or **wind chimes are they music** and what about just **drums or hollow logs** and even **combinations like rock and aborigine** and **where do people get recordings of tribal** and **who buys** that and who buys. . . .

- You might decide that you need another free-writing to generate more ideas about one of the topics in the first free-writing, or you may decide to begin working with one of the topics you have already discovered.

BRAINSTORMING

Brainstorming means making a list of all the ideas that occur to you about the subject. The list can be words or phrases related to the subject. Since a list is less structured than sentences, you will be able to explore ideas rapidly.

You may brainstorm by yourself and spark ideas from your own experiences. Or you may brainstorm in a group so the group members help each other generate ideas. If you do brainstorm in a group, do not feel that you must accept their ideas any more than they should feel they have to use yours. Brainstorming is designed to bring you more, not fewer, ideas.

Probably the first brainstorming list will be a random one. Then you can relate and classify the ideas. This process will generate your second list, and maybe the third and fourth!

EXAMPLE (brainstorming):

Change (random list)

amt. money	work	insurance	food	play
lifestyles	computers	crime	malls	space
houses	cars	lawsuits	commitments	shopping
schooling	libraries	information	clothes	environment

Change (grouped list)

Lifestyles
- houses, types
- commitments
- clothes
- car
- food, restaurant--
  - fast, convenient
- shopping--
  - malls/catalogs
- insurance--
  - lawsuits/crime

Work
- number of people in family
- computers
- amount of money--
  - lifestyles
  - work styles
- kind of job

Notice that the second list adds some ideas and that it leaves out a few as well.

MAPPING

Mapping is like brainstorming; but, for you, it may be more creative and less restrictive than lines and lists. Start with putting the subject, circled, in the center of the paper. Draw a line from the subject circle to a major idea about your subject. Cluster any sub-ideas relating to the major idea in circles at the ends of lines drawn from that major idea. Then, draw another line from the subject circle to another major idea about the subject and cluster sub-ideas around that major idea. Continue until you feel you have finished.

EXAMPLE (mapping):

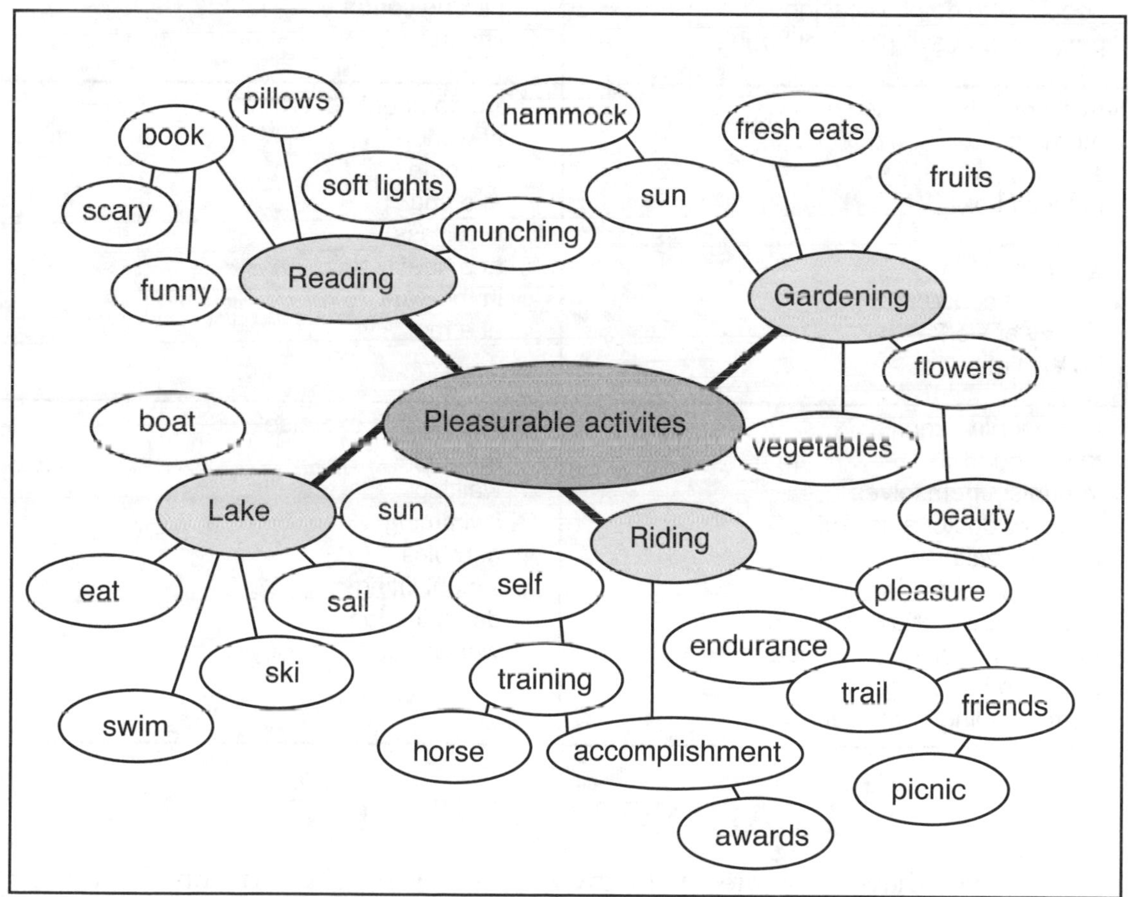

JOURNALISTS' QUESTIONS

The journalists' questions are *who, what, when, where, why* and *how*. Asking yourself these questions forces you to investigate the subject from more than one perspective.

EXAMPLE (journalists' questions):

The subject is **excercising**. Your lists might be	
Who exercises? people under a doctor's care fanatics and body builders people enrolled in classes people who paid good money desperate flabby people people who do physical jobs people who have physical hobbies	**What** is exercising? repetitive movement aerobic weight bearing using weights lifting boxes picking cotton jittering
When do people exercise? mornings after work at lunch hour evenings weekends only on vacation all day at work hobby time	**Where** do people exercise? at work at home at a spa in a class at a health club in the park at a mall
Why do people exercise? to feel good to punish themselves to follow doctor's advice to stay healthy to look good or look young to win a prize or award to make up for eating sundaes to do the job or hobby from a feeling of obligation	**How** do people exercise? running walking swimming aerobics weight lifting doing the job working on the hobby

READING FOR WRITING

After you have generated your own ideas, you might add outside support by reading critically and learning about the subject. However, do not depend only on using other people's words and ideas for your papers. Use your own words and ideas as well.

Sometimes the parameters of the assignment do not allow you to read about the subject. In that case, it is your thoughts and experiences that the instructor wants in the paper.

WRITING FOR A PURPOSE

Writing starts with a purpose: inform, explain, persuade, entertain, or explore.

Writing to inform means giving the audience information straightforwardly; it does not appeal to emotion or to prejudice. Writing to explain is a kind of informative writing: explanatory writing may, however, be more personal than writing to inform.

Writing to persuade means persuading the reader to accept your point of view, perhaps about the validity or invalidity of an action. Persuasive writing may appeal to the audience's emotions but should not appeal to prejudice. In addition to emotional appeal, effective persuasion uses accurate information to convince the audience.

Entertaining writing amuses, frightens, depresses, uplifts, etc., using emotional and psychological devices to appeal to the audience.

Writing needs a reason.

Exploratory writing explores an idea, an emotion, or an experience for the benefit of the writer and of the audience. Writing to explore is probably the most difficult type of writing. As in other writing, word choice is vitally important because the emotional, logical, and psychological impacts on the audience are necessary ingredients of exploratory writing.

Some writing will combine purposes. Some items written mainly to inform the audience will include humor for interest or excitement. Most persuasive pieces will also be informative because people are unlikely to change their minds on the basis of just an appeal for change. They need reasons, good reasons, and solid information on which to base their change of position. (At least we hope they need reasons!) And, a persuasive piece may use humor to get some of the information or some of the persuasion across.

Jessica Mitford's article "Behind the Formaldehyde Curtain" is informative. The purpose of the article is to inform the reader about what goes on behind the "formaldehyde curtain" at a mortuary. But Mitford's selection of details and words make the subject, while still morbid to some, entertaining also.

The article "Self-Defense: Can You Protect Yourself and Avoid the Slammer?" by Arthur M. Miller is mainly informative but is also persuasive. The information about self-defense laws can persuade the reader to review opinions on self-defense and to consider the possible results of self-defense.

Thus, writing may contain multiple purposes. Still, when writing, selection of a main purpose is necessary to decide how to approach the subject. You would approach the subject of the Asiatic cockroach invasion of the U.S. one way if you wanted to inform your reader about that kind of roach and what problems it causes. You would approach it differently if you wanted to persuade your reader that EPA rules against some insecticides should be set aside so Floridians, and others, could defend against the invading roach. You would use another approach to explain to or inform your reader about how to combat the roach. You would approach the subject still differently if you wanted to entertain your reader with stories of the roach that came to dinner and lunch and breakfast and. . . .

Remember that as a college student, you will mostly be writing to inform.

WRITING FOR AN AUDIENCE

Another important decision in writing is deciding to whom the writing will be addressed. The selection of the audience is vital to many of your decisions as you progress through the writing.

College writing is usually addressed to an audience as well informed on a subject as you were when you started writing. For instance, when you write a research paper in microbiology, the audience to which you write will probably be your classmates, who know as much about *staphylococcus* bacteria as you did when you began the paper.

Even though an instructor or professor is going to read (and grade) your paper, and even though you are always aware of that grader as you write, you do not actually write your paper to the audience of the grader. If you kept the grader in mind as the audience, you would have to write to the level of the grader. To inform the grader, a person who is purportedly an expert in the field in which you are taking a class, you would have to use a different vocabulary; include different sentence structure; take a different, more advanced approach; and furnish different, more complex, more esoteric information than you would use in addressing an audience of college students at your level. Choosing an audience of college students to whom to write makes your chore easier.

Professors grade, but papers are written at classmate level.

If you do not choose a college audience, you may choose any specific audience to which to write: four-year-old boys, second-year astronauts, gerontology majors, high school dropouts. Whatever audience you choose, you will have some important decisions to make about how you write:

How much does the audience already know about the subject?

- What is the audience's age and education level?
- How much information can you give them?
- How much do they need?
- How much will they understand?

What kind of vocabulary will you use?

- Do any words you ordinarily use need defining for the audience?
- Is specialized vocabulary appropriate?

What preconceptions do you have to work against?

- Has the audience already made a decision on the issue?
- What do they already believe?
- What arguments can you use that will be persuasive?

Remember that, writing as a college student, you will mostly be writing to a college audience.

THE COLLEGE ESSAY

An essay is a relatively brief piece of non-fiction prose that tries to make a point in an interesting way. Every essay emphasizes content by concentrating on subject, focus, and organization.

1. An essay is fairly brief. Some classic essays occupy only a few paragraphs; and, in a composition course, you may be asked to keep your first essays between 350 and 750 words. An essay generally falls between two and twenty-five typed, double-spaced pages. Below that minimum number of pages, the development typical of an essay would be difficult. Above that maximum, people might be tempted to read the piece in sections.

2. An essay is non-fiction. An essayist tries to tell the truth about the world, an event, or a person or to speculate about possible changes in the world. If the essay contains a story or a description, we presume that the details have not been made up.

3. An essay makes a point. An essay tells or explains a topic, expresses an attitude toward something, or supports or rejects something—an opinion, a person or place, a work of art, an institution, a movement. A poem, novel, or short story may also do these things, but a poem, novel, or short story appeals above all to the reader's imagination. An essay directly addresses a topic or specific subject, and its usual purpose is to win sympathy with or agreement on the point (or thesis) it is maintaining.

4. An essay should be interesting. An essay should arouse curiosity, convince the reader that the main idea is worth bothering about, and move toward a satisfying finish. To be an effective essayist, you must be willing to strike some balances. You will want to tell the truth, but make people interested in reading it; write with conviction, but consider whether your ideas and attitudes will stand up under criticism; supply evidence, but not to the point of boredom; be purposeful, but not follow such a predictable pattern that the reader's attention wanders.

FORMAL ESSAY ORGANIZATION

Essays can be organized in any number of ways. You have seen examples of different kinds of organization in your reading at school, in textbooks, in articles, in magazines, in lots of things. Essays can have an unstated main idea (or thesis), can have very long or very short paragraphs, etc. However, the easiest essay to read and to write is the essay that we discuss in this section: the three-section essay.

The three-section essay (introduction, body, and conclusion) described below is a convenient, easy, easily-followed, simply-structured way to write about almost anything—but, remember, it is not the only way.

Organization

The three-section essay is usually 500-1500 words (and four or five or more paragraphs) but can be of any length, from a couple of pages to twenty-five pages. The principle is the same no matter what the length. The introduction becomes an introductory section, the body becomes a body section, the conclusion becomes a conclusion section. If you are writing a ten-page paper, you will, of course, have more than five paragraphs. You might have three paragraphs of introduction that culminate in the statement of thesis; then have three body sections, each of which has five to seven paragraphs; and finally end with a two-paragraph conclusion. Still, the principle of the three-section essay remains.

INTRODUCTION

The introductory section begins by capturing the reader's attention and ends by introducing the central idea of the paper. For a five-paragraph essay of two to five pages, a paragraph of introduction is generally five to thirteen sentences long.

The introduction may get the reader's attention in any number of ways, including using facts, quotation(s), a personal anecdote, or a story. The introduction may use one or more of these devices, depending on the length of the paper and the writer's decisions.

The paragraph moves from general statements about the topic to specific statements. The culminating specific statement in the introductory section, the last sentence in the section, is the thesis. **The thesis statement announces the main idea of the paper and is usually the last sentence in the introductory section.**

BODY

Begin each body paragraph (which will contain seven to thirteen sentences) with a topic sentence that is an expansion of one of the subject elements of the thesis. Thus, every topic sentence relates to and develops the thesis, and every sentence in the paragraph is related to and develops the topic sentence. (See **PARAGRAPH DEVELOPMENT**.)

CONCLUSION

A paragraph (generally of seven to thirteen sentences for a five-paragraph essay of two to five pages) is needed to unify the theme. The conclusion may summarize the main points and/or restate the thesis and/or tell the significance of what you have said in the body of the paper. It may make a prediction or recommendation; it may refer to the introduction. What a conclusion may **NOT** do is introduce new material.

WRITING HINTS

1. Plan. (See **ORGANIZING PAGE EXAMPLE.**)

Planning and organizing is, along with consideration of the audience, most important. It is vital to know where you are going on a trip before you start, if you want to get there. It is just as vital to know where you want your writing to go so you can decide how to arrive. Make decisions on purpose, subject, audience, thesis, and subject elements before you start writing. Involve yourself in pre-writing activities such as brainstorming and mapping. (See **PRE-WRITING.**)

2. Choose a specific audience and write to that audience.

You may choose to write to someone who is reasonably familiar with the subject or who is as familiar with the subject as you were to start with. If you choose a different specific audience, keep your audience constantly in mind throughout the writing process and make decisions about vocabulary, style, explanation, and detail based on that audience. (See **AUDIENCE.**)

Write to an audience.

STYLISTIC HINTS

1. Underline titles of books and TV shows. Titles of episodes of TV shows and titles of short stories and poems are set in quotation marks. See **PUNCTUATION** for a complete explanation of underlining (italicizing).
2. Avoid using the word "you" unless you are speaking to a specific audience, as I, the writer of this text, am speaking to you, the reader, and to you alone. To say "you" can be disconcerting or offensive to the reader. If you said, "The movie made you feel good" and some readers did not see the movie or did not enjoy the movie if they did see it, they might find the flow of reading disturbed. If you said, "You know that this is true" and readers did not wholly agree with you, they might not wish to read the remainder of the argument, and you have lost the chance to inform or convince them.
3. Avoid using contractions, such as "can't" or "don't" or "I'm."
4. Avoid saying, "This paper will show. . ." or "In this paper, I will. . . ."
5. Avoid using "there" at the beginning of a sentence or "it" as a sentence subject.
6. Be very careful about using absolutes. If you say, "Everyone is . . . ," then you need to be sure everyone includes everyone: babies and people in hospitals and people with mental disorders, etc.
7. Take great care about punctuation, spelling, sentence structure, and other mechanics. Good mechanics make good reading. Poor mechanics are obvious to informed readers and distract them from following your arguments or evidence. It is even possible that readers will take the opposite position from that which you encourage because they are irritated by poor mechanics or they may assume that the writer is not credible or not informed.

8. Concentrate on using active voice rather than passive. Instead of saying, "The beautiful blonde cocker spaniel was attacked by a ravening monster with green slimy fangs" (which is passive voice), say, in active voice, "A ravening monster with green slimy fangs attacked the beautiful blonde cocker spaniel." It is much more effective.
9. In writing about literature, use present tense. Shakespeare's Romeo and Juliet live today in Verona, despite having died at play's end many times.
10. Refer to authors by last names—unless you know them personally. Conventions say they should be referred to by their last names and their last names only, not prefaced by an honorific, such as "Mr." or "Ms."

THE ORGANIZATION PLAN PAGE

An organization plan page allows you to organize a topic by following these steps:

Step 1: General Subject

You will begin with a general topic, which is usually the subject that is assigned to you by the college instructor or professor.

Step 2: Restricted Subject

Then you have to restrict or limit that topic in accordance with the parameters of the assignment. Those parameters include the audience, purpose, time, and length. The audience for a college paper is generally your classmates. It is true that the instructor/professor will grade the paper; but, if you actually choose the professor as an audience, you will have to do much more research and in more depth than you will if you have your classmates as an audience. (See **AUDIENCE**.)

You may choose to inform, to persuade, to entertain, or to explore as a purpose for your paper. Generally, in college, you will choose to inform.

The time and length are parameters generally assigned to you. A lecturer will say, "The paper is due in two weeks and it has to be between ten and fourteen pages." How long you have to do the paper and how long the paper has to be will, to a large extent, determine how much information you need to gather and how much information you can use in the paper.

Step 3: Subject Elements

After you have determined the limited topic, you need to decide on two, three, or more supporting subjects for that limited topic. Those subjects will become the basis for the supporting paragraphs in the paper. These specific subjects are called subject elements; they may also be called controlling elements, elements of control, subject segments, etc.

You should list the subject elements (or at least label them) in the order in which you plan to handle them. (See **PARAGRAPH ORGANIZATION**.) Generally, you will use **spatial order**, **chronological order**, or **order of importance**. You probably learned about these ways to organize previously, but a short review might help you. **Spatial order** means you organize the essay in the way space is organized, left to right, up to down or down to up, clockwise or counterclockwise. **Chronological order** means organizing the essay in order of time, generally from the first event to the last event. When you organize in **order of importance**, you usually organize the essay from the least important to the most important information, from the least amount to the most amount of information, or from the least persuasive to the most persuasive information. You want to leave the reader with the strongest possible image or argument so that the reader carries away your best idea.

Step 4: Title

The next step is choosing a working title. You are not stuck with this title; you can change it any time you want, but you may find the working title an aid in helping you focus on the topic.

Step 5: Thesis Statement

Now you can develop a thesis statement, a statement of the main point of the essay. The thesis may contain the subject elements to provide a focus for the paper and an aid to the reader. You may write a thesis statement that does not include the subject elements, if you can clearly focus the thesis statement without the subject elements, but it is likely that you will need to utilize the subject elements in the thesis.

A thesis statement expresses the main idea of the essay. It is a statement—**one sentence**—which tells the reader what the remainder of the essay will cover. The thesis delineates the central idea in the essay, clearly and completely. The thesis, because it gives the main idea in the essay, limits the essay's range and indicates the structure of the essay, generally by giving the subject elements to be covered in the essay. The thesis may state a topic and give an opinion on the topic, which you intend to support or to prove.

A thesis statement does not use the words, "This paper will show," "I think," "I feel," or "In this paper, I will. . . ." A thesis statement does not ask a question or state a truism (a statement of the obvious, such as "People need education" or "Bears live in the woods.")

A thesis statement should be clear and understandable. The reader needs guidance to the body of the paper; the thesis statement gives that guidance.

One way to form a thesis is to pose a question to yourself. If the subject you have chosen to write about is water pollution, you might ask yourself this question (known as a **research question**): What are the causes of water pollution? Examining the causes provides data for drawing a conclusion which becomes the thesis. That is, examination of the causes of water pollution leads to this thesis statement: *Water pollution is caused by chemical run-off, soil erosion, and excess biological waste.* A discussion of these three ways (which are subject elements) provides the body of the paper. This statement of thesis contains a topic, an opinion, and the subject elements (also known as elements of control).

Examples of thesis statements appear in each of the essay examples in the section on essay development and in the **Appendix**.

Step 6: Topic Sentences

From the thesis statement and the subject elements, you can develop the topic sentences for the body paragraphs of your paper. Each subject element will become a topic sentence. Remember to put the topic sentences in the order you think you will handle them in the paper.

As we said in the section on paragraphs (see **Paragraph Development**), the topic sentence will direct and focus the paragraph and should be clear and understandable. It should not be a question, should not state the obvious (such as "Radio is a medium of communication"), and should not say, "This paragraph will show," "In this paragraph I will," "I think," or "I feel."

Examples of topic sentences appear in each of the paragraph examples in the section on paragraph development and in the section on essay development.

EXAMPLE (organization plan page):

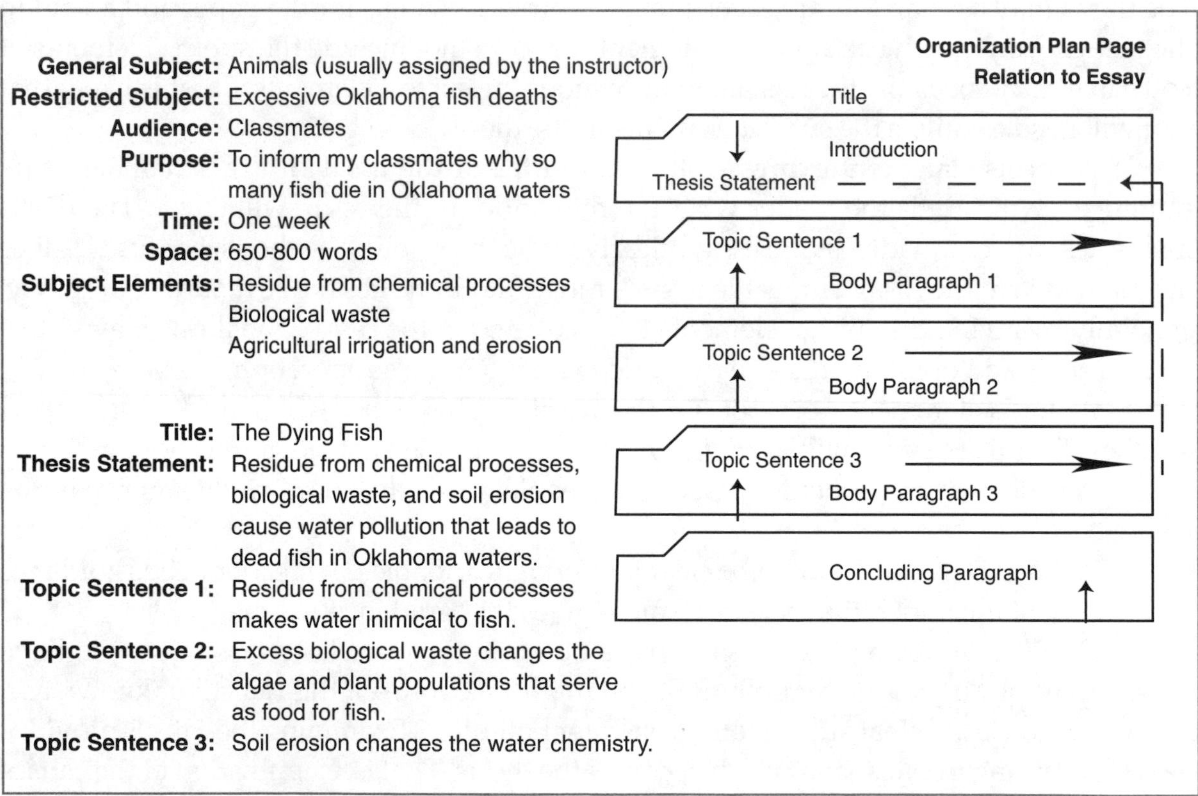

Organization

Longer essays follow the same basic plan as a simple five-paragraph essay: a clearly-defined thesis at the end of an introduction that catches the reader's attention and guides him/her to the main idea of the paper; body sections that support, develop, and explain the main idea of the paper; and a conclusion that ends the essay so the reader feels closure. Below is an example of an organization plan page for a longer essay, followed by the relationship of the organization plan to the essay structure.

EXAMPLE (organization plan page):

General Subject: Animals (usually assigned by the instructor)
Restricted Subject: Excessive Oklahoma fish deaths
Audience: Classmates
Purpose: To inform my classmates why so many fish die in Oklahoma waters
Time: One week
Space: 1000-2000 words
Subject Elements: Residue from chemical processes
Biological waste
Agricultural irrigation and erosion

Title: The Dying Fish

Thesis Statement: Residue from chemical processes, biological waste, and soil erosion cause water pollution that leads to dead fish in Oklahoma waters.

Lead Topic Sentence 1: Residue from chemical processes makes water inimical to fish.
Subsidiary Topic Sentence 1A: Chemical residue leaches into lake water from ground water.
Subsidiary Topic Sentence 1B: Residue from chemicals from agricultural and industrial use runs into waters.

Lead Topic Sentence 2: Excess biological waste changes the algae and plant populations that serve as food sources for fish.
Subsidiary Topic Sentence 2A: Biological waste can originate in factory farm operations.
Subsidiary Topic Sentence 2B: Excess biological waste may originate in sewage systems.
Subsidiary Topic Sentence 2C: Detritus from foliage may result in excess biological waste.

Lead Topic Sentence 3: Soil erosion changes the water chemistry.
Subsidiary Topic Sentence 3A: Prior to inclusion of soil, water chemistry is a result of several factors.
Subsidiary Topic Sentence 3B: Erosion can result from defoliation of various kinds.
Subsidiary Topic Sentence 3C: Soil in water becomes a different chemical mix.

Organization

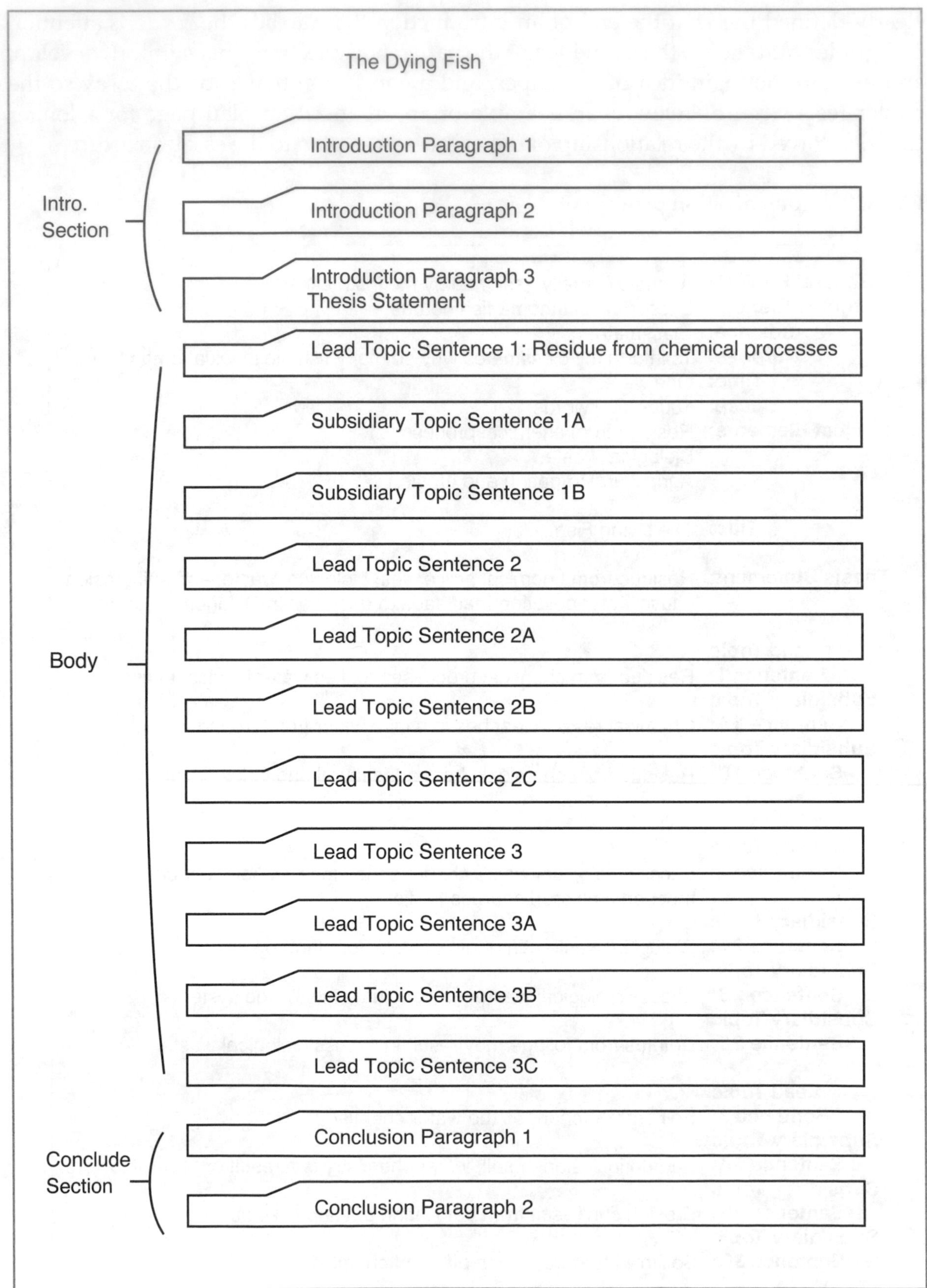
The Dying Fish
Intro. Section
Introduction Paragraph 1
Introduction Paragraph 2
Introduction Paragraph 3
Thesis Statement
Body
Lead Topic Sentence 1: Residue from chemical processes
Subsidiary Topic Sentence 1A
Subsidiary Topic Sentence 1B
Lead Topic Sentence 2
Lead Topic Sentence 2A
Lead Topic Sentence 2B
Lead Topic Sentence 2C
Lead Topic Sentence 3
Lead Topic Sentence 3A
Lead Topic Sentence 3B
Lead Topic Sentence 3C
Conclude Section
Conclusion Paragraph 1
Conclusion Paragraph 2

OUTLINES

For a long paper, you might want to use all the detail possible and add an outline to the organization plan page. The specifics for writing a formal outline are included in the example below.

EXAMPLE (outline):

Topic: Outline
Audience: Classmates [Notation of audience, purpose, and thesis statement may be included either as part of this outline or as part of a formal organization plan page; the outline below would function in place of listing only the topic sentences.]
Purpose: To inform
Thesis: Outlining follows specific rules of formatting and information.

I. An outline follows a particular format.
  A. An outline may use sentences, phrases, or words.
  B. The sequence of labeling is Roman numerals (I, II, etc.), then capital letters (A, B, etc.), then Arabic numbers (1, 2, etc.), and then lower case letters (a, b, etc.).
  C. Labels (letters or numbers) occur only in sets of two or more.
    1. I must be joined by II.
    2. A must be accompanied by B, etc.
II. An outline covers the important points of the material.
  A. Each label type is of parallel importance.
    1. Main points appear with Roman numerals.
    2. Sub points related to the Roman numeral heading appear as A, B, C, etc.
    3. Minor points related to the capital letter appear as 1, 2, etc.
  B. Clarity and precision are vital in entries.

NOTE:

1. Indent the outline parts as in the example.
2. Periods, not dashes, appear after the label numbers or letters.
3. Outlines may consist of sentences, topics, or words. The first word in each entry should be capitalized. If the outline is a sentence outline, it must contain only sentences; and each sentence must end with the correct end mark. Topic and word outlines do not contain sentences and do not end with punctuation.
4. Each entry with a comparable label should be of parallel importance and phrasing. If the heading labeled I is a noun, then II, III, etc., should be nouns. (Clarity is more important than parallelism so you may sacrifice parallelism for accuracy.)

ALTERNATE WAYS TO WRITE AN ESSAY OUTLINE

When you write an outline for an essay, you must include the statement of thesis. One way to do that appears in the previous section on the Organization Plan Page, or you might use one of the following alternatives.

Alternative 1

Topic: Outlining
Audience: Classmates
Purpose: To inform

I. **Introduction**
  A. Possibility: listing the main strategies to use in writing the introduction
  B. Note: Remember that the thesis statement actually appears at the end of the introductory section, even though you will not put the sentence in the outline until Roman numeral II.
II. **Thesis Statement**
  A. Topic sentence of first body paragraph
    1. Main point
      a. Supporting point
      b. Supporting point
      c. Supporting point
    2. Main point
  B. Topic sentence of second body paragraph
  C. Topic sentence of third body paragraph
III. **Conclusion**
  A. Possibility: listing the strategy you intend to use in the conclusion
  B. Possibilities: summarizing the main points, restating the thesis (only in a long paper), or telling the significance of what you have said

Alternative 2

Topic: Outlining
Audience: Classmates
Purpose: To inform

Thesis Statement: Write the thesis statement at the top of the outline. Then make an outline as shown in the *Guide to College Writing* under "Outlines."

I. Main point
  A. Supporting point
    1. Detail
    2. Detail
  B. Supporting point
II. Main point
Etc.

PARAGRAPHS

A paragraph is a group of related thoughts generally longer than a sentence and shorter than a whole composition. A paragraph is a series of sentences developing one topic. This topic is usually introduced in the topic sentence of the paragraph. The topic is developed or illustrated in the remaining sentences of the paragraph. Sometimes a concluding sentence summarizes the topic of the paragraph or re-states the topic sentence. Thus, a paragraph may have a structure something like this:

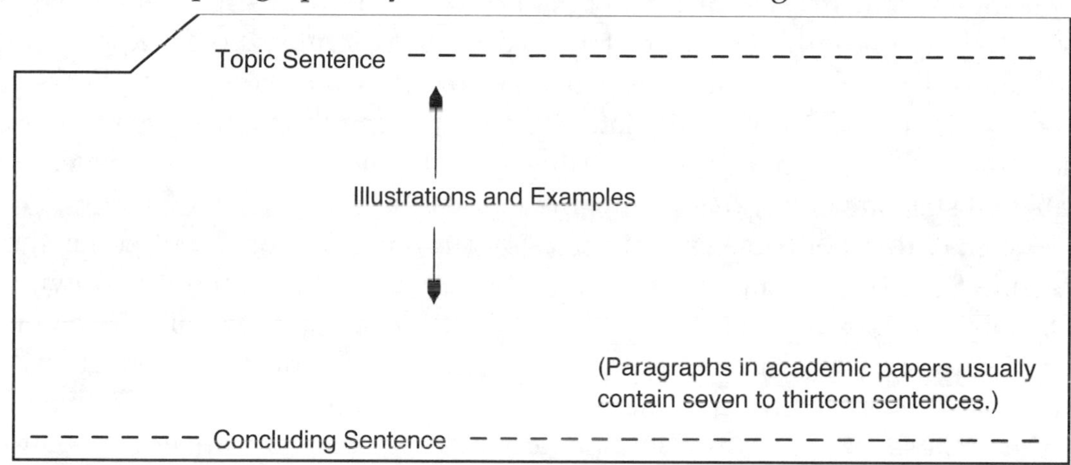

A paragraph in an academic paper is generally seven to thirteen sentences long.

DEVELOPMENT

Paragraphs are not simply collections of sentences. Those sentences are related by topic. The topic is "controlled" by the **topic sentence**. Generally in academic papers, the topic sentence appears as the first sentence in the paragraph.

To develop a paragraph, begin with a topic you know about or can research and find out about. Then you must focus the topic into a controlling idea. How do you choose a controlling idea? First, you need to think about whether you have anything to say about the topic, whether you can elaborate on, or develop, the topic. You need to decide if you can express the idea so that you AND the reader can determine what kind of information might appear in the paragraph. You need to consider whether the idea is both specific enough to handle in only a paragraph and whether the idea is broad enough to need several sentences to support.

Then, from the controlling idea, you create a topic sentence. A topic sentence should direct and focus the paragraph and should be clear and understandable. It should <u>not</u> be a question, should <u>not</u> state the obvious (such as "Radio is a medium of communication"), and should <u>not</u> say, "This paragraph will show," "In this paragraph I will," "I think," or "I feel."

To write a clear, understandable, directive, and focused topic sentence, you need to think about how you want to address your topic. For example, if you were really familiar with cars, you might want to write about the advantages of a standard shift.

Organization

You decide that you have enough information to create at least a paragraph. You also know that you can narrow the topic so that you will need only a paragraph in which to discuss the idea. You select the controlling idea that a standard shift is better than an automatic transmission. Then the topic sentence might read, *Although automatic transmissions are convenient, standard transmissions are superior in three ways.*

After you create a topic sentence, you have to think about support. You cannot just say standard transmissions are better than automatic transmissions, you have to tell the reader why you think they are better. To do that, you must create support for the topic sentence. The topic sentence is a general statement even though it is the focusing sentence. You must include specific statements supporting the topic sentence. For each specific statement of support, you probably will also need details that develop and illustrate that statement.

You may think of these as a hierarchy of support. The topic sentence is the top of the hierarchy, the most important sentence, so to speak. The second step down is the specific statements of support and the third step is the developing details. Based on this amount of support, you can conclude that paragraphs, in academic papers at any rate, usually contain seven to thirteen sentences, even though this may seem a relatively long paragraph to those who read only newspapers and magazines and are not familiar with academic, or scholarly, writing.

EXAMPLE (hierarchy of support for a paragraph):

Topic sentence with focus and controlling idea
- Specific supporting statement
  - Detail 1
  - Detail 2
- Specific supporting statement
  - Detail
- Specific supporting statement
  - Detail 1
  - Detail 2
  - Detail 3

EXAMPLE (hierarchy of support for a paragraph):

- **PARAGRAPH**

Although automatic transmissions are convenient, standard transmissions are superior to automatic transmissions in three ways. First, standard transmissions are more enjoyable for some people to drive. The driver has a sense of power at his or her fingertips and is engaged with the driving experience. Second, engines are more responsive to standard transmissions. This allows more control over the car. Starts can be quicker; downward acceleration allows quick response in traffic. In mountainous terrain, the driver can shift to a lower gear to slow the car. Most important, standard transmissions are economical. Repair and maintenance are less expensive for a standard transmission than for an automatic transmission. A standard transmission also increases fuel economy. Cars with manual transmissions may get one to four miles per gallon better gas mileage than cars with automatic transmissions.

- **LABELLED PARAGRAPH**

  Topic Sentence–Although automatic transmissions are convenient, standard transmissions are superior to automatic transmissions in three ways. **Supporting Statement 1:** First, standard transmissions are more enjoyable for some people to drive. **Detail 1:** The driver has a sense of power at his or her fingertips and is engaged with the driving experience. **Supporting Statement 2:** Second, engines are more responsive to standard transmissions. **Detail 1:** This allows more control over the car. **Detail 2:** Starts can be quicker; **Detail 3:** downward acceleration allows quick response in traffic. **Detail 4:** In mountainous terrain, the driver can shift to a lower gear to slow the car. **Supporting Statement 3:** Most important, standard transmissions are economical. **Detail 1:** Repair and maintenance are less expensive for a standard transmission than for an automatic transmission. **Detail 2:** A standard transmission also increases fuel economy. **Extended Detail 2:** Cars with manual transmissions may get one to four miles per gallon better gas mileage than cars with automatic transmissions.

COHERENCE AND UNITY

A paragraph is not simply a collection of sentences; a paragraph is not even a collection of sentences related by topic and under the control of a topic sentence. Paragraphs also have the attributes of coherence and unity.

Unity means oneness. That means all the sentences in the paragraph work together as a whole. Thus, every sentence in a paragraph must develop and support the controlling idea of the paragraph.

Coherence means consistency and logical progression. It means making the paragraph fit together so that it makes good sense to the reader. The way to achieve coherence is through using organization, repetition, and transitions.

Generally, we talk about three kinds of organization or logical order: **spatial order**, **chronological order**, and **order of importance**.

When you use **spatial order**, you arrange the paragraph (using the support) in the way that space is arranged or ordered. For example, if you were describing a house arranged like this,

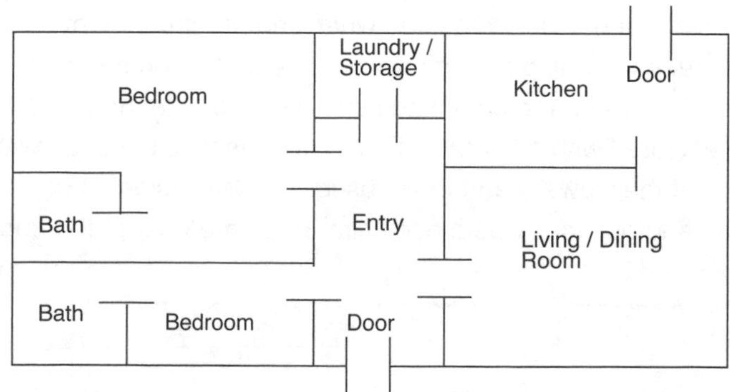

you would not want to describe the living/dining room, one bedroom, the kitchen, the bath, the entry, another bath, etc. It would be too confusing for the reader! Instead, you might want to describe the house by beginning in the entry, continuing into the living/dining room, the kitchen, the laundry room, the bedroom, the bath with that bedroom, the final bedroom, and then the bath with that bedroom. Of course, you might pick other ways to describe the house: by rooms oriented to each direction or by going clockwise, for example. Whatever plan you choose to describe space, it should have a logical orientation to the space itself.

EXAMPLE (paragraph in spatial order):

> My house, like Baba Yaga's, follows the sun. I do not mean that it literally turns using legs as Baba Yaga's house does, but it does have sunshine in every room. My front door faces directly south. My living room, which also contains an area for dining, is to the right as I enter the front door and has many windows on the south side so it is full of sun all winter long. I can walk through the living room to the kitchen, which has many windows on the north side, making the kitchen sunny all summer long. Directly to the west of the kitchen is a small storage area which contains my washer and dryer and which has a set of windows on the north side as well. Directly to the west of the storage area is my extra bedroom. It has windows on the north and on the west so it too is bright and sunny during the winter and summer. Attached to the extra bedroom is a small bathroom. Directly to the south of the small bathroom is my bathroom, which is inside my south-facing bedroom. My bedroom has floor to ceiling windows and is filled with light all seasons. So, although my house does not have legs, all the rooms follow the sun!

Organizing chronologically means organizing or arranging in the order events happen. For example, you would begin by telling what happened first and then what happened second and so forth until the final event—the end.

EXAMPLE (paragraph arranged in chronological order):

> Organizing a film series using a committee can be a rewarding experience. The rewards accumulate with each step. First, the committee must decide on the theme of the series and on what films would appropriately reflect the theme. Then the committee must decide exactly which films to order. The decision means discussing the films themselves as well as film theory and history, and the discussion is enlightening and educational. More lessons follow. After the films are ordered, the committee has to prepare publicity, determine who will introduce or host the films, get information on the films to the hosts, and decide what kind of refreshments would be appropriate. Each of these tasks requires learning to work with people in the committee, learning to negotiate with and work with people outside the committee and even outside the organization, and learning about the specifics associated with each task. Finally, the lessons continue with the showing of each film. The reaction of the viewers and the subsequent discussions, both formal and informal, reveal a range of ideas and opinions about each film. Each member of the committee learns much from the experience.

Organizing in **order of importance** generally means arranging in order of the least important to most important or in order of the least emphasized to the most emphasized.

EXAMPLE (paragraph arranged in order of importance):

> Training a dog requires three major attributes. A dog trainer must understand the reactions of dogs. What does it mean when a dog wags its tail, wrinkles its lips, or rolls over on its back? These may be mixed signals. A wagging tail can mean a greeting or a nervous reaction, a wrinkled lip can mean indecision about whether the dog is threatened or is threatening, and rolling onto the back may mean submission or a desire to have an itch scratched. In addition to understanding actions, a dog trainer must also be consistent. If a dog licks and the trainer scolds one time and praises another, the dog will be confused and consequently unruly. If the trainer rewards the dog with praise and goodies when the dog sits on command and does not scold the dog for doing the same thing, the dog will learn that it is a good thing to sit when commanded, "Sit." Finally, and most important, a trainer must be patient and loving. Dogs, like children and adults, make mistakes. Overreaction and brutality or screaming can cause a dog to lose confidence in the trainer and in self and consequently cause the dog to refuse to or to be unable to learn. A trainer's consistent, calm relationship with the dog will increase confidence and make the learning process much easier.

Repetition is writing something again. Usually when we talk about repetition, we are referring to repeating words. For example, in the paragraph on dog training the words *trainer* and *dog* are repeated. This repetition helps tie the paragraph together.

Transitions are words that function as cues. They serve as connections between sentences, connecting one sentence to a subsequent one. Order words such as *first, second, next,* and *then* are transition words. Other words are actually called transition words; they are connector words, such as *therefore, however, thus,* and *at any rate.* Transition words also tie the paragraph together, leading to increased coherency.

EXAMPLE (coherence, using repetition and transition words):

> In the next paragraph, repeated words are underlined and transition words are **bold**:
>
> Training a dog requires three major attributes. A dog trainer must understand the reactions of dogs. What does it mean when a dog wags a tail, wrinkles its lips, or rolls over on its back? These may be mixed signals. A wagging tail can mean a greeting or a nervous reaction, a wrinkled lip can mean indecision about whether the dog is threatened or is threatening, and rolling onto the back may mean submission or a desire to have an itch scratched. **In addition** to understanding actions, a dog trainer must **also** be consistent. If a dog licks and the trainer scolds one time and praises another, the dog will be confused and consequently unruly. If the trainer rewards the dog with praise and goodies when the dog sits on command and does not scold the dog for doing the same thing, the dog will learn that it is a good thing to sit when commanded, "Sit." **Finally, and most important**, a trainer must be patient and loving. Dogs, like children and adults, make mistakes. Overreaction and brutality or screaming can cause a dog to lose confidence in the trainer and in self and consequently cause the dog to refuse to or to be unable to learn. A trainer's consistent, calm relationship with the dog will increase confidence and make the learning process much easier.

Transition Words:

to sequence
again
also
and
besides
even
finally
first . . . second . . . third
furthermore
in addition
indeed
last
moreover
next
one . . . another
still
then
too

to conclude/ summarize/repeat
all in all
altogether
as a result
as has been said
consequently
in brief
in conclusion
in other words
in particular
in short
in simpler terms
in summary
on the whole
once again
that is
therefore
to conclude
to put it differently
to repeat
to summarize
thus

for timing
after
after a while
afterward
as long as
as soon as
at first
at last
at length
at that time
at the same time
before
during
earlier
eventually
finally
formerly
immediately
in the meantime
in the past
lately
later
meanwhile
next
now
presently
shortly
simultaneously
since
so far
soon
subsequently
then
thereafter
until
when

to narrow focus
after all
indeed
in fact
in other words
in particular
specifically
that is

for comparison (and contrast)
also
but
by the same token
despite
even though
however
in comparison
in contrast
instead
likewise
meanwhile
nonetheless
on the contrary
on the one hand . . . on the other hand
similarly
still
the same way as
though
yet

to illustrate
after all
even
for example
for instance
indeed
in fact
namely
of course
specifically
such as
the following example
that is
thus
to illustrate

to show concession
admittedly
although
certainly
granted
naturally
of course

to show cause and effect
accordingly
as a result
because
consequently
for this purpose
for this reason
hence
otherwise
since
so
then
therefore
thereupon
thus
to this end
with this object

to show place
above
behind
below
elsewhere
far from here
here
nearby
on the other side
there
to the left
to the north
to the right
to the south

to limit/ to state exception
but
however
nevertheless
nonetheless
notwithstanding
while

PATTERNS OF DEVELOPMENT FOR PARAGRAPHS AND ESSAYS

Essays and paragraphs must have coherence and unity (see **COHERENCE AND UNITY**). Individual paragraphs must be coherent and unified, and the entire essay must have unity and continuity. All the sentences in the paragraph must work together as a whole; in addition, each paragraph must contribute to the whole of the essay. Thus, every paragraph must develop and support the controlling idea of the essay, stated in the thesis statement.

The essay must also be consistent, with logical progression. It must make sense to the reader. Just as when you write paragraphs, an essay has coherence through organization, repetition, and transitions. As you may remember, we usually talk about three kinds of organization or logical order: spatial order, chronological order, and order of importance. You should consider the kind of organization you want when you plan the essay. (See **ORGANIZATION PLAN PAGE**.)

Repetition is writing something again. Usually, when we talk about repetition we are referring to repeating words. Using transitions means using words that function as cues, as connections between sentences or paragraphs. Words such as *first, second, next, then, therefore, however, thus,* and at *any rate* are transition words. (See the transition word list previous.)

Just as you can have more than one purpose for writing, you can use different kinds of development in a paragraph or an essay. However, for the purpose of illustration, each pattern of development can be considered in isolation, which we will do here.

NARRATION DEVELOPMENT

Narration generally tells a story (or narrates an incident). It is usually **chronological**, told in order of time. Since it tells a story, narration can be seen as an extended, or elaborate, example. (See **EXAMPLE DEVELOPMENT**.)

EXAMPLE (narration paragraph):

> Going to a play is a traumatic experience for my family. Once we had tickets to see a production in a city about twenty-five miles away. We had plans for the entire evening. First we would pick up some friends and go someplace to eat. After the play we might stop at another place to have dessert. When we started for the play, everyone was ready, almost on time. We were running only fifteen minutes behind schedule. We picked up our friends–who had decided not to eat. So our family stopped at a fast-food place, intending to grab a bite on the way. After we got the food, the driver entered the exit ramp. Someone screamed from the back seat, "You are going the wrong way." He braked. The food slid. He grabbed. His tie and coat dipped into the catsup and baked beans. I grabbed for the coat and dragged the sleeve of my silk blouse through the gravy. We got onto the correct ramp and arrived, going the right way, at the theater, where we discovered I had forgotten the tickets. The usher remembered us from a previous play (of course he would) and let us in to sit in freshly varnished–and still damp–seats. None of us remembers if the play was good because during the first act my son decided to throw up in a friend's hat. We left our friends and went home. They called a cab.

EXAMPLE (narration essay):
NOTE: Student essay examples are above-average papers, but not necessarily "A" papers.

May 1

Ashley May

Prof. Achs

ENGL 1213

18 July 2005

Fish Story

I have spent the last five days with my father in Dallas. One day we paid a visit to Hillcrest Memorial Gardens. The trip to the cemetery is a time-honored tradition of ours. It is a special time of sharing between father and daughter. It also allows us to feed the fish.

The Hillcrest goldfish are famous. People from all over Dallas (and Oklahoma too!) stop at the cemetery to toss bread to the fish. The preferred brand is Mrs. Baird's, surely because there is a Baird's bread factory across the street from the Gardens. Since fish can smell too, I am sure the wonderful aroma of baking bread makes them hungry.

This last time we went to feed the fish, we came upon a man sitting on the bench next to the water. My father and I figured he was just sitting there for a moment or two to enjoy the view, so we decided to wait. Both of us took a seat in the lush grass several feet behind the man on the bench. As my father and I sat in the beautiful Dallas sunshine, I heard a sound. I turned and saw the man on the bench taking off his glasses and wiping his eyes. The sounds of sobbing drifted our way.

The man watched the fish, but he sorrowed. The sound of his sorrow chilled me to the bone. The man's grief was apparent, yet he was not afraid to let his feelings show. He had obviously lost a dear friend or relative and my young heart ached for him. After a few moments, he stood and walked away, casting a sheepish smile our way. I began to think about death and dying and sadness.

We went to feed the fish; I considered death and our customs of grief, tombstones, cremation, funerals, and saying good-bye. There, by the fish, I thought about pain and its inevitability. As the saying goes, "It's just a fact of life—and death."

EXAMPLE (narration essay):

NOTE: Student essay examples are above-average papers, but not necessarily "A" papers.

Nichols 1

Marti Nichols

Prof. Wye

ENGL 1113

31 Oct. 2005

Tyrell

He was a ten-year-old black boy who lived in the ghetto of Houston, Texas. I was a sixteen-year-old white girl from small town Oklahoma. At the time I did not realize how strange our friendship was; now it is one of my most cherished memories. From the first day I was there, Tyrell deemed himself my protector. I remember asking my mom why he felt as if he needed to protect me. It was then that I began to learn the extreme differences between the lifestyles of Tyrell the young black man and Marti the young white woman. The impact Tyrell had on my life not only helped me through my week's stay at Shriner's Hospital but has affected every aspect of my life.

From the different lifestyles Tyrell and I led, I learned how the color of skin can determine the outcome of life. Looking through his eyes and his experiences, I realized why he became my protector. At ten years of age he knew more about the outside world than I could ever dream about.

One day in the sunroom he told me about the drug deals that go on every day outside his home. He explained to me the pressure his neighborhood put him under. He wants to finish school; he even talked about college. Yet he talked with disappointment in his young voice. The drive-by shootings had just started, and Tyrell talked about the risk of just standing outside his front door. This amazed me. I always heard of those things, but now I was hearing them from one who lived them. He was equally amazed at how little I knew of his world.

In Shriner's the majority of the children were black. I might have had a hard time being accepted, but Tyrell made sure that I never experienced prejudice. The others there, including Tyrell, never saw their parents. He was there for treatment of a crushed leg. His estimated stay was about six months. When I arrived, Tyrell had not seen his mom or dad in over two months, in contrast to my mom, who stayed with me every day. Because my mom stayed with me, it caused some unreasonable jealousy until others got to know her and enjoy her as much as I did. Some even learned from her. Tyrell realized that Mom was a history teacher, and he had her explain all the famous black leaders in history to him.

Tyrell was my best friend that week. When I got home, I tried to tell my friends about him; but they could not appreciate him the way I could. They were not there to hear him talk about his hopes and dreams with disappointment, not eagerness. He gave me an education that week that I will carry with me for the rest of my life. Tyrell knew how lucky I was to be in my country-girl world. Yet he also wanted me to understand and be aware of the dangers in his world. I often wonder about Tyrell. He will be sixteen this year. I pray that the disappointment in his eyes has been replaced with the hope he so desperately needed.

DESCRIPTION DEVELOPMENT

Descriptive writing allows you to describe sensory experiences or to describe a person or people. Description emphasizes the senses–touch, taste, sight, smell, hearing.

EXAMPLE (description paragraph):

Morning is my favorite time of day. After the clock-radio comes on with a soothing tune, I can stretch luxuriously in the warm, cozy bed and decide just to lie there and coast for a few more minutes. In just a moment I will come more alive to the smell of fresh coffee brewing in the automatically-timed coffee pot and to the sound of bacon frying in the automatically-timed microwave oven. Then I know it is time to put one foot at a time into my soft, fuzzy slippers and one arm into my woolly robe and slouch to the bathroom to turn on the shower. The shower will fill the room with steam, and I will have to squeakily wipe off the mirror with a fluffy towel so I can peer into my own clean face. Breakfast is cooking; I am warm and clean. What more could I want?

EXAMPLE (description essay):

NOTE: Student essay examples are above-average papers, but not necessarily "A" papers.

Student 1

Sallie Student
Prof. Zea
ENGL 1113
16 Jan. 2005

Taking the Time to Grow

Out of all of life's tremendous challenges, there is not one that is as difficult to pass through unscathed as growing mentally, physically, and emotionally into an adult. The tattered paths of the quest for womanhood go from pigtails to perms, from nursery rhymes to rock and roll, and from total dependence to "total" freedom.

Studying the evolution of a female's hair, for example, can give much insight into the woman she will become. At age five, Miss Renee was given the ever-dreaded "Dorothy Hamil," a horrendous hairdo for which her mother, increasingly tired of combing the girl's hair, sinisterly placed a bowl on the child's head and proceeded to snip around the bowl. When the bowl was removed, and Miss Renee was turned to face the mirror, a shriek of horror filled the air as she saw that her once beautiful, luxuriously-long locks had been chopped to create an uneven, short-haired, crooked-bangs look that she knew would be the joke of her kindergarten class.

Miss Renee eventually learned to look herself in the mirror again, and secretly prayed all summer that her hair would grow back quickly, yet quietly enough that her mother would not notice and return with the dreaded bowl. This was Miss Renee's first lesson in confidence building. She lived through her shame and eventually convinced her mother to allow her to take care of her own hair.

Five years later, Miss Renee, then ten years old, visited the beauty parlor on many occasions with her mother. She smelled the very grown-up fragrances of hair coloring, perms, and the heat from hair dryers. She was ready, she told Mother, to enter the world from which no one returned unaltered--perm land.

Mother thought it was unrealistic to spend sixty dollars on a young girl's hair and decided to take the cheaper route--the home perm. Armed with Ogilve and two different sizes of curling rods, Mother believed she had seen her hairdresser roll curls enough times to have no problem doing it herself.

Three hours later, Miss Renee was bravely holding back the sobs choking her as the perm solution dripped into her eyes. Mother kept a close watch to make sure Miss Renee did not touch even one precariously-set rod. She rinsed. She set. She unrolled. She blew dry. The curls, which had looked startlingly Shirley Temple-ish wet, were now a frazzled mass of undefinable webbing. Miss Renee was devastated.

Miss Renee gained more confidence after the disastrous perm, and decided, two years later, after the last remnants of the bad perm had left her hair, that she would begin to save each cent until she could go to the beauty parlor and pay for a real perm herself. By the time she turned fifteen, she had finally gained control over her hair, learned how to apply make-up without looking as if she belonged on the stage, and had suffered enough hair hardships to make her strong and self-confident.

In addition to learning about herself and her freedoms and responsibilities as she learns about hair, a girl also learns about herself as her musical preference skips a beat from Mother Goose to Metallica. It is almost inevitable, much to the dread of some old-fashioned parents, that once a girl enters school, her tastes will change drastically. At the onset of kindergarten, Miss Renee was perfectly content to repeat a repertoire of "I'm a Little Teapot" and "The Wheels on the Bus." As she progressed through kindergarten and her first formative years of education, she was immersed in ditties of that nature, although often with altered words that taunted the teacher or the paste eater. Somewhere around ten years of age, however, the most important music became that which was transmitted through MTV. At this age Miss Renee danced and sang with the Top Ten and humorously rapped with M.C. Hammer.

Somewhere around fifteen, however, when Miss Renee was engulfed by the ominous cloud that seemingly blocks happy rays from hitting teenagers, she turned to heavy metal. She found solace in the depressing lyrics and release in the head-banging and slam-dancing. Her newly found hair-control allowed her to pouf the front and spike the rest and finally--she found her place in teenage hell.

This type of negativity did not last for very long, thankfully; and, although the music would always be a part of her, she realized that college and freedom loomed invitingly on the horizon.

Perhaps that is the best method of growth evaluation—the rough road between total dependence and total freedom. It was not until Miss Renee was off at college and no longer under her parent's roof that she began to feel independent and more like a mature woman. She realized that the grades she earned would remain with her forever. She realized that if she did not go to class she would only be damaging her own chances at success. And she realized that the pile of crumbled sour cream and onion potato chips would remain on her apartment floor until she bent down and cleaned them up herself. Miss Renee felt that it was time she spent alone in her own company that taught her the most about herself. She learned to be her own best friend and realized that, although having others around was great fun, and a great help, a woman can never truly be a good friend, a good employee, a good lover, or a good mother until she spends some quality time with herself.

Therefore, it seems that it was the combination of the passage through hair-hell, the rite of musical evolution, and living alone that opened the door and slowly allowed the tentacles of womanhood to wrap around her ankles, her wrists, and upward into Miss Renee's brain, implanting thoughts of nurturing a child while continuing to nurture herself--the true meaning of womanhood.

EXAMPLE DEVELOPMENT

In an example paragraph or essay, support comes from examples. The development may consist of a series of short examples as in the paragraph following, or it may consist of one long example. In either case, the topic sentence (or, in the case of an essay, the thesis statement) is illustrated and supported by the examples.

EXAMPLE (example paragraph):

My sister is a notorious story-teller. I do not mean that she lies; she never lies. She just makes a story out of everything that happens to her. When she goes to the supermarket and has a good experience at the checkout stand, she makes a story out of it. When she drives her car and meets a lunatic driver, she tells us all about it in a detailed story. She has favorite stories that she tells over and over–like the time my brother slept with the frogs and the time my father fell out of the window. And she tells about the time I got bucked off the tiny pony–when I was six feet tall and twenty-seven years old. We do not really mind. We even ask her to tell her stories!

EXAMPLE (example essay):

NOTE: Student essay examples are above-average papers, but not necessarily "A" papers.

Couch 1

Misty Couch

Prof. Ache

ENGL 1213

18 Feb. 2005

The Doll

In A Doll House, Torvald and Nora Helmer are a happily married couple—or are they? To society, Torvald and Nora appear happy together. However, Nora is actually unhappy. As Torvald tries to keep Nora his young, innocent doll, she does her best to escape her "doll house" to become a human being.

Torvald Helmer would like to keep Nora young and naïve forever. He tries to do this by calling her such names as his "little lark" and his "songbird." He keeps her sheltered from the "real world," just as her father had done. Torvald holds the attitude that the only thing that matters is what other people think. Even when he finds out that Nora forged her father's name to a loan, all he can think about is what other people might say and think. He is not concerned with Nora or with Nora's motivation or her feelings. He wants Nora to pretend that everything is normal and to remain naïve. Torvald talks negatively about Nora's father although, like her father, he continues to try to keep her locked away in her "doll house."

Nora Helmer has always had someone else to tell her what to think and how to act. Neither her father nor her husband bothered to teach her anything about the "real world." They sheltered her from the world to keep her "pure." Torvald wants Nora to be untaught so she will be innocent forever. Torvald had no idea that, by encouraging Nora's naiveté, she feels free to commit an action against the law. Perhaps if her father and Torvald had encouraged her to learn, she would not have committed a crime. Because she has committed a crime, because she has not learned, Nora feels she has to leave Torvald.

Nora leaves Torvald and their children to find out what being human is like. She feels she must go out and learn about getting a job, learn about taking care of herself—just as Kristine has done. She cannot stay sheltered in her "doll house" any longer. If she stayed, she would be fulfilling Torvald's desires for her naiveté, not fulfilling her own desires for completeness. In addition, she feels that a mother like herself should not raise children. She feels too much like a child herself. Knowing only her father's ways and Torvald's ways makes her corrupt and she fears she could corrupt her children.

Henrik Ibsen portrays Nora Helmer as a young and innocent doll who tries to get out of her dollhouse to become fully human. Her father and her husband have fostered her innocence and led her to crime; for her sake and for the sake of her children, Nora must leave the dollhouse.

DEFINITION DEVELOPMENT

A definition paragraph can be very much like an example paragraph. Support can be by one long example or by several short examples. The important distinction is that a definition paragraph defines a term. The definition may appear in the topic sentence in the form of a formal definition, or the topic sentence may simply introduce the term to be defined.

A formal definition has this form: The word to be defined is the general class to which the word belongs and the differentiating characteristics that make that word different from all the other members of that class. The formula reads

Word = general class + differentiating characteristics.

EXAMPLE (FORMAL DEFINITION):

A discophile is a collector of phonograph records.

↕ ↗ ↕ ↕

(word) (=)(general class)+(characteristics distinguishing the word from all other class members)

The topic sentence of a paragraph about a discophile may be the formal definition: *A discophile is a collector of phonograph records.* Then the paragraph would give examples of various discophiles and their habits.

The topic sentence may only introduce the term instead. For example, a topic sentence of the latter type may read like this one: *The term discophile can mean different things in different fields.* Then the paragraph might give examples of discophiles who collect records of radio shows or of one musical group or of one musical type or of one composer, etc.

EXAMPLE (definition paragraph):

One of the literary terms with which a reader should be familiar is that of conflict. Conflict means the strife between opposing forces in any work of literature. Usually conflicts fall into one of five major categories. One category is person against person, as in most of the "good guy/bad guy" stories, such as John Collier's "Witch's Money" in which the townspeople are pitted against the newcomer artist. Person against society, the Harlequin against the time-ordered culture in which he lives, appears in Harlan Ellison's "'Repent, Harlequin,' Said the Tick-Tock Man." In W. Somerset Maugham's "Appointment in Samarra," we see person against fate (or God) because the servant comes up against his fate in the form of death. Person against nature is the conflict in Jack London's "To Build a Fire" when the prospector has to fight the cold and the snow to survive. And person against self, the madman trying to convince himself he is not mad, shows up in Edgar Allen Poe's "The Tell-Tale Heart."

Definition development in an essay is also a kind of example development because support is by example, but definition development includes defining a term or terms. The definition may appear in the thesis statement or one or more of the topic sentences in the form of a formal definition, or the thesis statement may simply introduce the term to be defined.

EXAMPLE (definition essay):
NOTE: Student essay examples are above-average papers, but not necessarily "A" papers.

Howard 1

Damion Howard

Prof. Bea

ENGL 1113

31 Aug. 2005

A True Man

"What does it mean to me to be a man?" I have mixed feelings. I am sickened by the way a lot of men act. It seems to me there are a lot of requirements to be a true "man." I need a penis a foot long. I need to be strong enough to beat a fellow to death with my bare hands. I need to go out into the forest and hunt down little animals for sport, to prove that I can do it. I have to go berserk and hate whomever my country chooses for me to hate and to be willing to go to war with them. I need to have had sex with at least twenty women by the time I am twenty-one. I need to be able to drink a twelve-pack without getting a buzz. I need to drive a fancy car or a big mean truck to show off my masculinity. I need to keep my intelligent thoughts to myself. I should never cry; and, if I do, I should bash someone's face in to make it better. My spouse or girlfriend should be good-looking. I should never question the rituals of being a man, or I am "queer." I feel that most males have no idea what it means to be a true man.

My picture of a "true" man is of a humble one. A true man does not have to be big, strong, and handsome. I think it helps to not be these things. It makes a man have character if he has to deal with what he has. If a big strong man carries a piece of steel that is heavy, he has not had to put much effort into it. If a small man carries the same piece of steel, and it was difficult for him, but he does the same job, he has accomplished much. A handsome man who has women falling at his feet may not appreciate his good fortune. If a homely man finds a woman, he will be thankful; he is a better man because he has to cope and deal with his "hardship." When a man has earned what he has and has had to cope with problems, it makes him stronger; he has an advantage over a man who has luxuries. When a man is humble, he treats other people better than one who is arrogant. He will have more respect for and be more honest in his dealings with others. In the long run he will reap the rewards of his humble acts. Others will treat him with the respect and honesty he has treated them with. He will never be short of companions.

A true man should get along with his environment. If a man treats his environment with respect, he will get along better in it. When a man uses the land to make his living, he should respect it and take care of it and not abuse it. If a man has some excess oil, he should not pour it into the water that supports all life. He should care for the water as if it were an entity instead of polluting it. If all men respected their environment as if their life depended on it (it does), there would not be the problems we have now. A true man would treat the environment as if it were more important than the man himself.

A true man should be good to his family. He should be willing to sacrifice his life for theirs. A true man should treat his wife as an equal partner and communicate with her. A man should cherish his children. He should be willing to make time for them. He should teach them all that he possibly can, but let them know that he could be wrong and that they have their own minds and should use them.

A true man will be true to himself. He will follow when he feels it is right to do. He will lead when it seems right. He will stand alone when he feels it is right. A true man should always stand up for what he feels is right and back down when he is wrong, no matter what others think. A true man is always true to what he feels in his heart is right; if he is, he will have no regrets about his decisions.

PROCESS DEVELOPMENT

A process paragraph or essay tells how to do something. It is a series of explanatory steps telling the reader about how to successfully complete some task. You must be careful to remember the following specific guidelines.

1. **Remember the audience.**

2. Be sure to introduce the subject early in the paragraph, ideally in the first sentence. Do not rely on the title of the piece to tell the reader what your subject is. Specify the task in the piece itself.

3. Tell all the steps. Be sure not to skip anything because then the reader will not be able to replicate what you are describing.

4. Tell the steps in order. Nothing is more irritating than trying to follow instructions and finding that you should do a step earlier or later than you have done it, unless it is finding out that the step is missing entirely.

5. You may use the word *you*. This is the only time in formal writing that *you* is appropriate. It is possible to write a process paragraph or essay without using *you*. but using *you* is an option.

EXAMPLE (process paragraph, using second person):

You should know how to change a flat tire. Ordinarily you might just call a travel service, but what if you have a flat tire on a dark night on a deserted road and you have no cellular phone? What if there is no one else to whom to turn? You will have to change your own tire. First, make sure that the car will not roll. Set the emergency brake. Turn the wheel into the curb. If necessary, chock the wheels by putting a stone, brick, or other object behind the tire. Then, get everything you will need out of the trunk. Get the lug wrench, the jack, and the spare tire. Use the lug wrench to loosen the lug nuts on the flat tire. After the lug nuts are loosened slightly, place the jack in the location described in the owner's manual and raise the wheel off the ground. You may have to use the lug wrench as part of the jack handle on some makes of cars. After the wheel is raised, completely remove the nuts and then the wheel and tire assembly. Place the spare on the hub and tighten the lug nuts with the lug wrench as tightly as possible. (This will not be very tight because the tire will spin.) Lower the car. Tighten the lug nuts again with the lug wrench, taking care to tighten every other one until you have tightened each one. Pack the jack, the flat, and the lug wrench back in the car. Get the flat fixed as soon as possible.

EXAMPLE (process essay, not using second person):
NOTE: Student essay examples are above-average papers, but not necessarily "A" papers.

Kight 1

Rusty Kight

Prof. Sea

ENGL 1113

18 March 2005

Water Skiing

Ah, the allure of a hot, wet, and wild summer day at the nearby lake! What better way to spend this day than water-skiing? The season for water-skiing is just around the corner. Therefore, for all the beginners out there, a basic review of the sport is in order.

A skier must have proper equipment before hitting the lake. First of all, the skier must make sure that the boat has enough power or the skier will never get on top of the water. The boat should have forty horsepower or more. Next, the skier should make sure the rope is of top quality and made for water skiing. The skier should check the rope periodically for cuts from the boat's propeller or other sharp objects. An unsafe rope could be dangerous since it could part at an inconvenient moment. Last, of course, a skier needs a good pair of skis. Unless a pro, a skier will not have much fun skiing barefoot!

The most common cause of fear and apprehension for beginners is usually skiing itself, which is actually the easiest part. All the skier needs be concerned with is takeoff. The takeoff is easy if the skier keeps a few things in mind. While still sitting in the water, the skier must keep half of the ski length out of the water and upright. With the skis shoulder-width apart, the skier should point the skis at a forty-five-degree angle toward the boat. When the boat starts to take off, virtually every muscle in the skier's body should be locked and tense. For most people, those who make sure to have a comfortable stance by bending knees slightly to take the strain off the back, it is smooth skiing from then on.

As with most any activity, skiing can have setbacks. Injuries can occur. However, precautions can eliminate risks. First, the skier should make sure the boat driver is experienced in pulling a skier and has had absolutely no alcoholic beverages. Second, the skier should double-check all equipment; skimming on water at forty m.p.h. with faulty equipment could end in disaster. Last, but not least, the skier's body should be in a comfortable position; otherwise, a sport that involves so many muscles can lead to muscle strain and pulls.

Water-skiing is an enjoyable sport if done correctly. With proper precautions, the steamy summer day will be full of exhilaration. But the thing to remember is "Safety first!"

COMPARISON DEVELOPMENT (Including Contrast)

To contrast two items is to emphasize their differences. To compare two items is to delineate their similarities and their differences. Thus, when asked to write a comparison, it is always best to ask for clarification. Does the instructor want you to concentrate on similarities or to discuss both similarities and differences? Comparison generally means concentrating on both similarities and differences unless you are instructed otherwise.

You already know the three patterns of comparison intuitively; but, here it is in black and white. Generally, comparison paragraphs fall into one of these three categories. The categories depend on how the information is grouped. One type of grouping is by similarity and difference: all the similarities are grouped together and all the differences are grouped together. Which one comes first is up to the writer. Another type of grouping is by subject: one subject is discussed first and the second subject is then discussed and tied together with the first subject. The last kind of grouping is point by point. Each point is discussed in relation to each subject before the next point is approached.

No matter what grouping pattern is selected, a strong topic sentence is essential.

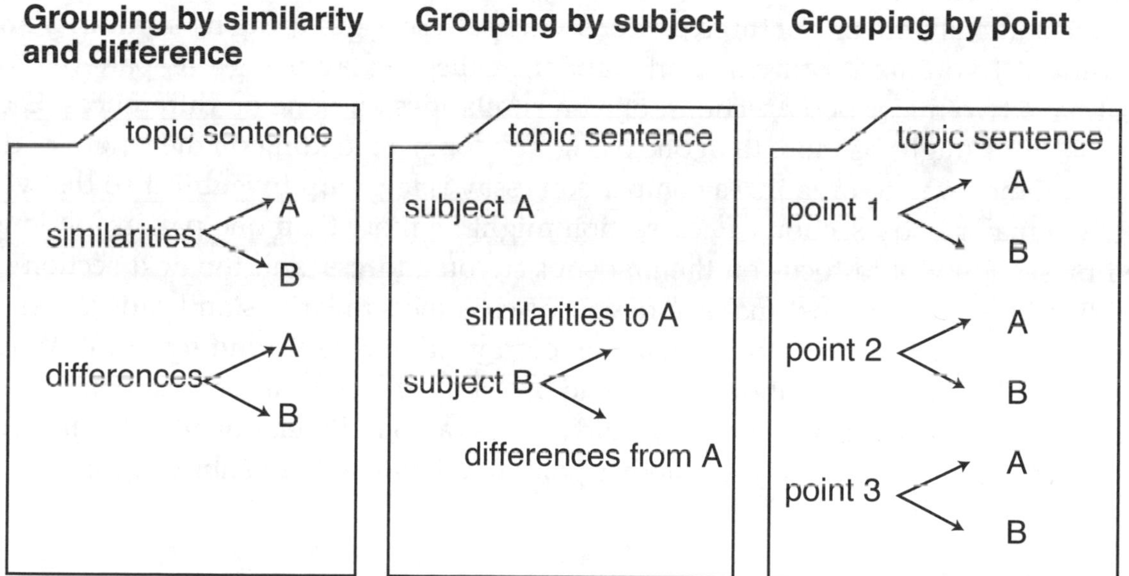

EXAMPLE (comparison paragraph grouped by point):

Even though they look alike, my two brothers are not alike. One is twenty-two; one is twenty-three, and both have brown eyes and salt-and-pepper hair, receding rapidly. Neither one could be called tall and elegant: they are more short and stocky. Everyone who sees them knows they are closely related. But they do not act closely related. My brother Bob is so calm and so even-tempered that the arrival of a maniac or a tiger in the backyard would bring a yawn and a quiet statement that he would take care of the situation. My brother Ted acts as if he sticks his finger in a battery charger every morning before breakfast. If the toast is a shade too brown or the paper is five minutes late or even if the world news from Zaire is not good, he begins to rant and stomp. Bob is generous; he has never known a stranger. He gives time, effort, and dollars to every worthy and unworthy cause. Ted is not like Bob. He never gives time and effort except in situations that will get him some social gain, and he only gives money when "everyone else" will know. Similar looks do not make similar actions.

Comparison development in an essay generally means concentrating on both similarities and differences unless you are specifically instructed otherwise. Comparison essays usually fall into one of three patterns. One pattern is **grouping by similarity and difference.** If you are writing a short standard college essay using this pattern, you might have two major body sections, one on similarities and one on differences. Each of the sections might be more than one paragraph long, depending on the length of the essay. Another way to organize a comparison essay is to **group by subject** so that you have two major body sections. Each section might be more than one paragraph long. The first section would focus on the first subject you address, and the next section on the other subject. You must make sure you discuss the similarities and differences of both subjects. The third type of comparison organization is **grouping by point**. When you use this kind of organization, you would probably group the information into three major body sections: the first section would address a point in relation to both subjects, the second section would address another point in relation to both subjects, etc.

EXAMPLE (comparison essay):
NOTE: Student essay examples are above-average papers, but not necessarily "A" papers.

Forler 1

Dianne Forler

Prof. Dee

ENGL 1113

11 May 2005

Politicians with Cause

With the election just a few days away, trepidations among politicians are high; campaign ads are filling the airways. Any vacant spot along the roadside which could possibly hold a candidate's sign on a stake gets one; and suddenly thirteen more stakes, each featuring another candidate, appear. The duties of campaigning become a blur, with one more hand to shake, one more baby to kiss, one more benefit dinner to attend--all in the name of politics. How does a person decide to pay such a price, to put family members through all the pressures of being in the public's eye and under close scrutiny of the media? What inner power enables a person to persevere through it all? Men and women who go into politics usually do so after carefully contemplating all the possibilities, taking into account all the sacrifices, and asking themselves lots of questions. The answers to these questions depend on the kind of politician asking them. Two kinds of politicians exist: those who enter a political race "just because" and those who enter for "just cause."

First, the background and environment of the man or woman who enters a political race can engage a "just because" politician in the act of becoming a politician. This man or woman has grown up around politicians. Being highly educated, having been graduated from "politically correct" schools, and feeling the influence of the home environment, this person becomes versed in the textbook fundamentals of economics, and, thus, able to discuss them at length. This person, thrilled with the idea of attending another benefit dinner "just because" such attendance affords the opportunity to be among those already in the limelight, asks "What if that were me?" Caught up in political affiliation, this person becomes involved with popular issues and, with speaking ability gained from lengthy discussions, becomes very popular among political circles. Special interest groups often call on this person to be a guest speaker at political functions. This enables the "just because" politician to become a key part of political activities, thus receiving attention from the media and adding yet more fuel to feed that inner ego. The ability to write off large expenses incurred for political reasons develops means to go places for pure enjoyment and self-interest, as well as for ambiguous political reasons. The aspirant's desire to be in the center of the limelight increases, and the statement, "Why, I could surely make a difference" begins to creep into conversation. While visibility has created a household name, this person has little or no experience applying any fundamental theories to the actual testing grounds of the work place and business world. Because of being able to "talk a good talk," the aspiring candidate gains supporters. Thus, this politician enters the race "just because" of all the attention received, building that ego higher still.

The other type of politician is concerned with how issues affect people, businesses, and service communities and enters a political race for "just cause." Being a proven leader in a business or other work environment, this person has real understanding of supply and demand economics, knowledge obtained by providing essential commodities or services to people or businesses. When a situation that affects the community becomes a major issue of legislature, or lack of legislation, this aspirant recognizes each solution's possible ramifications. As a concerned citizen, the aspiring candidate asks, "Is there enough information on this problem?" "Could I improve this situation?" The aspirant might then ask, "Could I really make a difference?" while thinking, "I know a possible formula for solving this problem." Other leaders recognize the aspirant as one they feel will apply expertise to the "cause." Thus, the "just cause" politician emerges and enters the race to accomplish the goal at hand. The "just cause" politician asks, "But what about my family? my other work? my community responsibilities?" and holds a discussion with family and colleagues, a discussion in which views and beliefs are expressed. Because the family and the colleagues share these views, they support the cause. It is with this kind of support and certainty that the "just cause" politician can endure the long road ahead.

All politicians think they have something to offer and, despite the dissimilarities in motivation, do contribute. Obviously, the "just cause" politician, if elected, will remain in office just long enough to ameliorate the "cause" and then will return to "the way life was." On the other hand, the "just because" politician will want to remain in office indefinitely, carefully climbing that political ladder, becoming the leader of special committees, and rising to even greater political heights. Not discounting their individual motives, they both have needs that are satisfied by the outcome of a successful political race and by subsequent political service. Who can say which one will be best for the "cause" and in the end get the job done? That question can be answered not with votes, but only with time.

NOTE: An organization plan page (see below) is not generally submitted with papers for regular academic classes. However, some writing classes, among them Composition I and II, may require that you submit not only an organization plan page, but all drafts as well.

Organization Plan Page

General Subject: Write an essay in which you classify politicians into categories or types.

Restricted Subject: "just because" and "just cause" politicians

Audience: classmates

Purpose: to inform my classmates about categories of politicians

Time:	two weeks
Length:	3-5 typed pages
Subject Elements:	"just because" politicians interested in self "just cause" politicians interested in issues and service
Title:	Politicians with Cause
Thesis Statement:	Two kinds of politicians exist: those who enter a political race "just because" and those who enter for "just cause."
Topic Sentence 1:	First, due to the background and environment of the man or woman who enters a political race, the process of becoming a politician permeates the core of a "just because" candidate.
Topic Sentence 2:	The other type of politician is concerned with how issues affect people, the business, and the respective communities in which he/she serves and enters the political arena for "just cause."

EXAMPLE (comparison essay):
NOTE: Student essay examples are above-average papers, but not necessarily "A" papers.

Howard 1

Dan Howard

Prof. Yee

ENGL 1213

2 Nov. 2005

A Comparison of News Coverage on Oklahoma Governor

David Walters' Plea Agreement

For over two years, a statewide grand jury investigated alleged campaign law violations by Oklahoma Governor David Walters, his campaign staff, and close friends. During this time the grand jury issued 20 indictments, one of those naming the governor. On Thursday, October 21, 1993, the story came to a climax when Walters appeared in Oklahoma County District Court and pleaded guilty to one misdemeanor ethics law violation. In return for that plea, the prosecutors dismissed eight related felony counts involving conspiracy and perjury that had been filed against him. An enormous amount of media coverage was devoted to the story. The priority given to the story, the amount of coverage it received, and the political slant that was applied to it depended on the news medium covering Governor Walters' plea agreement.

The priority given to the story by the news media set the stage for the focus of the future coverage. Shortly before the governor arrived at the courthouse on Thursday, Oct.

21, Channel Eight News of Tulsa interrupted regular programming to advise that a plea was expected soon. On Thursday, October 14, 1993, a week before the plea, the Daily Oklahoman printed a copyrighted story with headlines that read "Governor Secretly Indicted" (sec A: 1). These two reports indicated that this story was of the highest priority to these media. Channel Two News of Tulsa also reported on the story on Thursday, Oct. 21, but interrupted regular programming just once before its news broadcast at 10:00 p.m. Various other newspapers across the state, such as the Tulsa World and the Muskogee Phoenix, carried front page coverage of the story on the following day. However, they did not give the story the same degree of priority by printing any confidential information prior to the plea.

The amount of coverage the story received was extremely varied among the media throughout the state. The Wagoner Tribune, a small town newspaper, did not cover the story at all. The Muskogee Phoenix and the Tulsa World, for instance, printed front page reports covering approximately half of the entire page, which was about the average space devoted to the story by newspapers across the state. Channel Two News began its broadcasts with reports approximately four to five minutes in length for the first couple of days. However, Channel Eight News supplied approximately ten minutes of live coverage on the night of the plea, following with several days of five-minute coverage slots at the beginning of each broadcast. An enormous amount of coverage was undertaken by the Daily Oklahoman, with its peak of coverage encompassing the entire 20-page front section of its October 24, Sunday issue (sec A: 1-20).

The political slants applied to the story by the various media were easily identifiable. The Daily Oklahoman, considered to be a conservative paper, aggressively attacked the governor's plea deal and his actions during the campaign. The Oct. 24, 1993, Sunday editorial read,

> Of all the ludicrous things that have happened in Oklahoma, the sham that has ended statewide grand jury investigation into Gov. David Walters' campaign is the most outrageous.
>
> Prosecutors, in what had all the appearances of a backroom political sellout, simply let him off the hook.
>
> Only after adverse public reaction to his arrogance did Walters belatedly apologize to the public. (sec A:1)

That same issue also used four full pages of the front section to print the complete affidavit and indictment which contained sworn testimony concerning secret illegal conversations of the governor (sec A: 6-9). Nothing was printed in the Daily Oklahoman that could be construed as favorable towards the governor. The Tulsa World took a more liberal view in its Sunday edition on Oct. 24 by printing a color photograph of the governor smiling, with a quote below it stating, "Governor Walters felt much better Friday and even forced a smile as he met reporters at the state Capitol to discuss his guilty plea" (Ford, sec A: 1). The opinion section of the same issue was completely void of the issue and focused on angry citizens' complaints concerning the widening of Riverside Drive (1). On Oct. 25, 1993, the Oklahoma Observer attacked the governor with headlines that read "David Walters' Tribulations, Good Ol' Boy Politics," followed by a story bashing the governor for corruption (Troy 1). Channel Eight News of Tulsa was also aggressive in its anti-Walters coverage on Friday, Oct 22, 1993, with several reporters taking live interviews of citizens calling for the governor to resign. Channel Two News was fairly neutral during its broadcasts on Friday, Oct. 22, 1993, in avoiding excessive live interviews and programming interruptions, and in giving brief but informative reports on the story.

Many branches of the media can be found in Oklahoma and many different viewpoints can be found in their news reports. The United States Constitution protects the freedom that the press enjoys, and many believe that this is a fundamental part of the competition that is necessary for the public to get both sides of an issue from the media. Others are quick to lay blame on any certain medium for slanting the news too far. In either case, the stories, such as Governor Walters' plea deal, gain the press coverage that qualified editors deem necessary and they are usually slanted with some sort of political focus. All one must do to collect the full perspective on a major issue is monitor coverage from various points.

- **Note:** The Works Cited page is generally a separate page from the rest of the paper, and it is paginated as the next page in the series.

Works Cited

Channel Two News. KJRH, Tulsa. 21 Oct. 1993, 22 Oct. 1993.

Channel Eight News. KTUL, Tulsa. 21 Oct. 1993, 22 Oct. 1993.

Daily Oklahoman 24 Oct. 1993: A1-20.

"Editorial." Daily Oklahoman 24 Oct. 1993: A1.

Ford, John. "Walters Feels Better." Tulsa World 24 Oct. 1993: A1.

"Governor Secretly Indicted." Daily Oklahoman 14 Oct. 1993: A1.

Muskogee Phoenix 21 Oct. 1993.

Troy, Frosty. "David Walters' Tribulations, Good Ol' Boy Politics." Oklahoma Observer 25 Oct. 1993: 1.

Tulsa World 21 Oct. 1993.

Wagoner Tribune 21 Oct. 1993.

ANALOGY

One kind of comparison is the analogy. An analogy makes comparisons between things that are not usually considered similar. Analogy is usually used when the writer wants to reveal something with which most people are not familiar. The writer chooses something that people are familiar with to compare to his subject so that the subject becomes more real and believable to the reader. Familiarity with one part of the paragraph helps make the reader familiar with the other part as well.

EXAMPLE (analogy paragraph):

In the mornings our house is like an army field training camp. In an army camp before the sun is up, reveille sounds to wake up all the sleeping, still-tired soldiers. If a soldier does not arise immediately and assemble the correct clothing and field gear, the sergeant comes to his aid, to the chagrin of the soldier. The same thing is true at our house. Before the sun is up, reveille sounds. My father turns on the radio and the television at high volume. If a child or teen has trouble rising from the bed, my father will help, first by pulling the bed clothes from the bed and then by pulling on the toes of the errant child or teen. Toes are only delicately attached to the rest of the foot so fear of mutilation brings the miscreant promptly upright. Appropriate clothes are next on the agenda. If it is 35 degrees Fahrenheit outside, my father does not want to see shorts. Nor does he want to see tee-shirts. He wants to see fully-clothed bodies, with sweaters and scarves. Next is field gear. School bags must be ready by the door, full of the correct items. When at the car, no child, and especially no teen, dares to admit that some item like homework or lunch needs to be retrieved. It would be safer to admit there were no clothes under the coat. It might even be safer to be at those army field exercises.

EXAMPLE (analogy essay):
NOTE: Student essay examples are above-average papers, but not necessarily "A" papers.

Ziminsky 1

Heidi Ziminsky

Prof. Eff

ENGL 1113

10 Sep. 1992

A Cynical Look at Fairy Tales

The three fairy tales "Snow White," "Cinderella," and "The Princess and the Frog" have similar themes. These themes tell a girl that a man will save the day and take care of her. Once he does this, she will live "happily ever after." Although these concepts were idealistic when the tales were written, now, as the lights of the twenty-first century are flickering over the horizon, these stories seem even more far-fetched.

"Snow White" ends when Prince Charming gallops gallantly in on his handsome steed and plants the kiss of true love on Snow White's cool lips. Snow White is encased, supposedly dead, in a coffin made of glass and gold, so her new found friends--the dwarves--can behold her beauty, even in death. This in itself is extremely morbid. How long was she in that coffin? Not too long, apparently, considering her make-up was not flawed, nor her face decomposed beneath it. Prince Charminq and Snow White ride off to his castle and presumably "live happily ever after." (The wicked queen who caused the "death-sleep" has conveniently plummeted from a cliff, never to be heard from again.)

The average woman in 1992 (from here on, Ms. 1992) whose thin childhood skin is toughened by the years of sarcasm layered on like a prostitute's evening make-up and made more cynical by learning about her government and how it operates, can no longer look at "Snow White" from a child's perspective. It is quite possible (much to the horror of the above said government) that Ms. 1992 is a single parent, whose personal Prince Charming ran off with a stewardess or discovered he was a homosexual after sixteen years of marriage. While Ms. 1992 struggles to raise her two children, the childhood fantasy of fairy tales can no longer cut through walls of cynicism to which she has been exposed--walls built by the miserable realities of life in a world becoming more corrupt with every talk show's sniveling guests.

In "Cinderella," the heroine is swept off her feet by Prince Charming, too (or should I say Prince Charming II). Lucky Cinderella not only gets a lovely dress and a Fairy Godmother, she also has feet roughly ten times smaller than her wicked stepsisters, and apparently everyone else in town, too. Prince Charming places the glass slipper on her dainty foot and carries her off to "live happily ever after."

Once again, Ms. 1992 finds this difficult to swallow. She is sure that the only characters from this particular tale who could have survived into the twentieth century are the wicked stepsisters and the wicked stepmother, because only they have the perfect mixture of hard-nosed snobbery and brown-nosing humility to make it in modern society. Ms. 1992 also wonders if Snow White realizes that Cinderella is moving in on her turf, romancing Prince Charming and satisfying his foot fetish.

"The Princess and the Frog" has a different twist. The princess, who (once again) is sweet and gentle and kind, kisses an ugly, wart-covered, old toad. Then, presto-chango, the frog becomes a prince. Luckily this happens in a flash of pixy dust. The metamorphosis otherwise may have caused the poor lass's hair to gray and skin to wrinkle, which, in turn, would have sent Prince Charming running. It is certain that this Handsome Harry would not have settled for anything less than pure, innocent, young beauty—review how quickly he dumped the other two for a fresher specimen!

Ms. 1992 has kissed quite a few frogs in her time, although none of the green, four-legged variety. Not one became any more handsome after the kiss. She also cannot quite believe that a girl can possibly live "happily ever after" with him, knowing that her friends could conceivably call him "frog-breath."

But, alas, somewhere inside Ms. 1992's pessimistic exterior lies the little girl who believes in Fairy Godmothers and Prince Charmings. It is this inner child who wants to kiss a frog, or who dreams of a perfect, gentle, handsome stranger sweeping her off her feet. It is the similarities in these stories that make them fairy tales. And it is the fairy tale that affirms that, in the beauty and innocence of childhood, anything can happen.

DIVISION AND CLASSIFICATION DEVELOPMENT

Division divides things. Classification groups things. Division and classification divides things into groups. Usually a division and classification paragraph begins with a topic sentence identifying the subject to be discussed. The paragraph then continues by showing how the parts of that subject are related to each other.

To plan the division and classification paragraph, you must begin by dividing and grouping. Pick a subject. Write down all the "pieces" of the subject (divide) and then group all the similar pieces together (classify).

EXAMPLE (developing a division and classification paragraph):

- Suppose that the subject is media. List some forms of media with which you are familiar. Then decide what some of those media have in common and make those into a group. Continue until you have found groups for all the media. Then experiment with other types of groupings. In your paragraph choose only one type of grouping to discuss and use only those media that are most representative as examples.
- Write down types of media.

radio
television
 commercial
 public
 private
film
video
audio tape
compact disc
 audio
 video
audio/video

newspaper
 weekly
 daily
 monthly
 mainstream
 tabloid
magazine
 weekly
 monthly
 bi-monthly
 sporadically
journal

newsletter
books
 audio
 Braille
 hardback
 paperback
correspondence

- We could go on and on and on.

- Now find common groups for the types of media. They could be divided into visual, audible, and both. Another possible set is means of transmission and/or distribution. Another is frequency of appearance. Another is ownership. Yet another is audience. We could divide by a number of other criteria.
- Last, select the type of division and classification that you want to discuss and write the paragraph.
- **Division and Classification Paragraph**

Although media come in a variety of forms, they can be divided into two major categories. Those two categories are responsible and irresponsible, as shown by the language of the writers. The responsible category includes generally what are called "mainstream" publications, those that are read by a large number of different kinds of people. Mainstream publications would include Time, Newsweek, and New Republic. Even though each of those publications is of a different political slant, each generally takes responsibility for reporting accurately. Each one's penchant for responsible journalism is revealed in the language of the publication. Each one tends to use measured terms and avoid "loaded" words, words that elicit immediate emotional responses, like "femi-Nazi" and "jerk." On the other hand, the irresponsible category includes tabloid-style periodicals and television and radio shows, like The National Enquirer and some "talk" shows. These periodicals and shows are watched, read, or heard by specific audiences, occasionally audiences that are isolated from mainstream society. They tend to skirt the edge of journalistic ethics, rushing to get a story, if not the facts of the story. Their tendencies are revealed in the language they sometimes use, resorting to stereotyping and name-calling; they sometimes use words like "lesbo-feminist" and "cretin." This is not word usage that appeals to reasonable people who are looking for facts and not for "slams."

EXAMPLE (division and classification essay):
NOTE: See also comparison essay example "Politicians with Cause."
NOTE: Student essay examples are above-average papers, but not necessarily "A" papers.

Farrell 1

Andy Farrell

Prof. Ghi

ENGL 1213

10 Oct. 20--

Teenage Individualism

The beasts who are teenagers lurk in the shadows of every adult's past. The unavoidable changes brought on by puberty can lead to some, if not all, of the most embarrassing moments in life. The bulk of these moments occur during the period when teens begin to search for their own identity. In the period between the beginning and the end of this quest, teens look to outside sources to help them discover themselves. And so most of the humiliation, bumbling idiocy, and constant embarrassments that define teenage life are caused by one thing: the striving to find individuality—while still trying to be like everyone else.

Doggy Bone Day, Denim Shirt Day, Inside Out Day are just a few of the many obviously individualistic activities sponsored by the fine student council members of my high school. Unfortunately, this same student council is supposed to be training the leaders of tomorrow—and what do they promote? Mindless school spirit. While there probably is not much difference between student council and the national government (both simply seek to promote their school or country), it is not a good thing when our supposed leaders try only to force everyone into thoughtless conformity. Leaders should not be afraid to step in new directions that do not necessarily agree with the rigid codes of society. While school spirit probably does not do any lasting harm to individuality, it is still dangerous to put any kind of power to make people conform in the hands of teenagers, however harmless they may appear.

The place where individuality does not reside is in the junior high. Junior high—two most dreaded words of the English language. Nowhere on Earth, or probably the rest of the universe, is there a place that can strike as much fear into the hearts of the bravest women and men. There is not another single place where a miniscule pimple can ruin a life's reputation. Junior high is the strongest bastion of mindless conformity on the planet. It is the place in which teens begin their adolescent life, and in which many wish to end it. Not even in the military can people find such resistance to the idea of individuality. Teens are subject to the darkest side of human behavior when they begin the long trek down the frightening halls of junior high; if even a sock is worn wrong, isolation, ridicule, and complete banishment from life as it is known will occur.

Finally, the true test of a teen's individuality is the judgement of peers. Clothes, hair, even calculators can separate two people who had previously been friends for their entire lives. One of the most defining things about a teenager is dress. To most teens, their appearance is who they are since they do not have enough of a personality to hold a decent conversation. Fashions change from year to year, from grunge to retro to retro-grunge. Even grunge, a style that started as an individual statement, became incredibly conformed to the basic Doc Martens, old jeans, tee shirt, and flannel. Individualism has become so much in vogue that now the only true way to express individuality is to conform.

Individuality and conformity are true not only in fashions that teens wear, but in the music as well. "Alternative" music has become increasingly popular since the breakthrough of such bands as Nirvana and Pearl Jam. Much of what is now on the radio is "alternative" music. This music form has been around for some years now, but it has always been what its name implies—an alternative type of music. It is alternative no longer. The music industry saw what teens liked and began putting out more and more alternative hits. When something is called alternative, the implication is that it is an alternative to something else, but the music that once expressed teen individuality is now the mainstream, not the alternative!

Teenagers are basically evil monsters, but it is not their fault. The pressures of adolescence and puberty have much the same effect that heat and pressure have on carbon: they are compressed into hard lumps of blackened rock. The sad state of the student council in high schools, the horrifying junior high experience, and the conformity of fashion and music: all these are pressures to conform, to suppress identity and merge with the group. And so the struggle of teens everywhere lives on: the struggle to be one's own self while being sufficiently like everyone else to keep from getting lynched.

ANALYSIS/CAUSE AND EFFECT DEVELOPMENT

Analysis begins with a fact and goes backward from that fact to find out why it happened or forward to find out what will happen next. In other words analysis investigates cause and effect.

Causes and effects are not simple, and they are not isolated. Most causes go far back beyond the scope of history and most effects will go far beyond our lifetimes. The cause of an earthquake in Mexico City began eons ago with the first shift of a tectonic plate. The effect of someone's losing a newspaper in 1790 may be the development of a free, unlimited power source. But it would be a little hard to write a paragraph of this scope. So you must isolate. You must make cause and effect look more simple and discrete than it actually is.

EXAMPLE (cause and effect paragraph):

I did not do well in calculus for a number of reasons. First, as a freshman in college, I did not have the background for calculus. I had trigonometry in high school and made an A, but I did not learn it well. So I entered class inadequately prepared. Second, I had a graduate student for an instructor. He knew math, but he could not get it across to those of us who were struggling. Of course, my not doing well was not his fault because, third, I did not do the homework. It frustrated me to struggle with the problems so I just did not struggle. Fourth, I began to cut class. I had the class at 7:00 in the morning on the fifth floor of a building all the way across a cold, dark, windy campus from my dormitory which was warm and lighted. Fifth, I was having much too good a time doing other things to worry about a detail like five hours of engineering calculus. I passed, but barely: I still do not know how.

EXAMPLE (cause and effect/analysis essay):

NOTE: Student essay examples are above-average papers, but not necessarily "A" papers.

Rodriguez 1

Deborah Rodriguez

Prof. Ache

ENGL 1213

13 Nov. 2002

Women Meeting the Challenges of Life

Unbalanya Hill (A Group of Four Running Women) is a primitive drawing on the wall of a cave dwelling, depicting four aborigine women who appear to be running down a slight decline in the terrain. There is some indistinct object in front of the first woman of the group. The color used in the drawing is a clay brown earth tone. There is a subtle recognition of different shades of color in the rock upon which the drawing has been done. The women are unclothed, with their arms outstretched as they run.

The cave drawing, Unbalanya Hill (A Group of Four Running Women), was viewed and critiqued by a male college student and by me, a female college student. We each have very different perspectives concerning the interpretation of Unbalanya Hill.

Many men, as well as some women, share a belief that women, being physically weaker than most men, are in need of a man's protection from the harshness of the world and that women are incapable of taking care of themselves. This was the general assumption of the male members of our college classroom when the cave drawing Unbalanya Hill was viewed and discussed. Women in today's society as well as throughout the course of history, however, have proven that, when the situation requires them to be self-sufficient, they are able to meet this challenge.

Tommy Gage, a male college peer, views Unbalanya Hill as a representation of four women running away from something. He feels that the object in the drawing is a bow which is being held by the lead figure. It is Gage's assumption that in an aboriginal society the male would exclusively do all the hunting. He therefore concludes that the women are carrying the bow in self-defense and they are running away in terror from whatever unknown force may bring them harm. Gage thinks that the explanation for the women carrying the bow is that there is no male present in the group; if a man were in the drawing, the man would have the bow in his hand. It is Gage's belief that in today's society, most males continue to feel an obligation to protect women and that women are in need of the males' protection, including those women who do not feel the necessity for such protection.

When I viewed the cave drawing Unbalanya Hill, I felt that the drawing depicted something else entirely. To me the women do not appear to be running from something as though in fear; they appear to be running towards something in joy or freedom. The color of the rock above the heads of the group of women is in different shades, reminding me of the warm, bright sunlight as it filters down between the sparse leaves of spring growth. This sunlight reflects downward and warms their unclothed skin. These women appear to have no shame in their nakedness, only an unquenchable joy of life and freedom of emotions on such a perfect day. Their legs appear bent at the joints, almost as though they are dancing, not running. Their arms are lifted towards the heavens, the source of their warmth and joy. Perhaps they are running towards the streambed on this bright, sunlit day, anticipating the pleasure of the sensation of the cold, running water splashing on their sun-warmed bodies. The first woman carries an object. I want the object to represent freedom of new life or the joy of spring. Reality, however, leads me to believe that the object is a hunting bow. These women live in a world that is never free from harshness and unknown dangers. They must take along some object that will give them protection from the elements of their world when they leave the safety and protection of the cave. They do not take along a man to protect them on their excursion; instead, they take along the means to protect themselves.

When going back into recorded history, we see many examples of women taking care of their own needs without aid or assistance from a man. There are even some instances of women being looked upon for leadership and protection. Hebrew scripture (Judges 4-5) tells us the story of the judge Deborah, who summoned the tribes of Israel to military action against the Canaanites. Spurred into battle by Deborah, the Israelite forces sang praises to Yahweh that day for their triumphant victory. And, what would have become of the French people and armies during the Hundred Years' War had it not been for the unifying force and leadership of Joan of Arc? The pioneer women who helped settle this country could not always rely on a man's protection; they were frequently left alone with the children for days, weeks, or even months. These women learned to handle weapons for protection or for hunting, with as much ease and self-sufficiency as any male. They kept the homestead going with skill and confidence. In those countries which allow women full duties in military operations, women have proven themselves to be as capable to meet what is required of them as their male counterparts. It may be true that women are physically weaker than most men; however, this does not mean that women are any less capable of meeting situations which could put them in danger, or challenge them mentally.

Today's society seems to place an emphasis on a woman needing a male's presence, not only for her physical protection, but to meet the physical requirements of providing food, shelter and clothing for herself and/or her children. Women are led to believe that they are less capable physically and mentally to meet these needs than a man. Statistics from law enforcement and social agencies such as Domestic Violence Intervention Services show an alarming increase in numbers of women who are in abusive relationships. One of the more common reasons given for women remaining in this type of relationship is the belief that they would be unable to take care of themselves and/or their children without a male's presence in their lives. Yet it has been shown that women are physically and mentally just as capable as their male counterparts to meet this challenge. Opportunities and educational programs are available to teach these women to become independent and self-sufficient. Programs and self-help tools abound which can help a woman gain the self-confidence needed to know the joy and freedom of independence and self-satisfaction in the knowledge that they can meet any challenge on equal terms with their male counterparts.

Many individuals feel that in an ideal world there will always be a male present to handle challenging situations in which a woman may find herself. Today is not ideal. There will always be situations which arise in which women will be called upon to rely on their own skills and knowledge. A more complete concept of an ideal world would be one in which males and females each recognize the need for women to seek the same self-sufficiency as their male counterparts in preparation for whatever challenges life may bring.

- **Note**: The Works Cited page is generally a separate page from the rest of the paper, and it is paginated as the next page in the series.

Works Cited

Unbalanya Hill (A Group of Four Running Women). Australia. New York Graphic Society.

EXAMPLE (cause and effect/analysis essay):
NOTE: Student essay examples are above-average papers, but not necessarily "A" papers.

Gage 1

Tommy Gage

Prof. Eye

ENGL 1213

13 Nov. 2002

Unbalanya Hill: Four Women Running Without Men

For centuries males have been dominant in societies. Women are identified as a weaker sex and are not taken seriously. Men are usually looked on as protectors and providers. Taken by their separate roles, the sexes lead very different lives. Therefore, men and women have different views, leading them to interpret things different ways. The cave painting Unbalanya Hill was interpreted by a male and a female member of the classroom, and there are reasons the interpretations are different.

Unbalanya Hill is an aborigine cave painting of four women running. They are painted with "natural" colors, a soft clay brown for the bodies and a darker brown for the objects. The figures follow the fault or the flow of the rock on which they are painted. The rock on which the figures are painted is lighter than the surrounding rock, making the figures attract the eye. Left of the figures is an object in a darker segment of the rock. The figures of the women seem to be running toward the unknown object.

I interpreted the painting in two ways for one reason. My first reaction is that the women are running away from something in fear. When I first looked at the painting, I focused on the first figure. The woman is carrying an object that looks like a bow. If that is the case, then that alone indicates fear because of the taboos of aboriginal society. In most aboriginal societies, women were not allowed to touch the instruments of war or hunting, except during certain times. If their tribe were being attacked, the women would grab a weapon to either protect themselves or to attack the attackers. This leads me to my other interpretation: I also believe that the women could be running toward something in anger. As I have stated earlier, women were not allowed to touch weapons. They could touch them as a way of showing their spouses their unhappiness. An angered wife could go to her friends and/or relatives and ask for their help. If the friends or relatives agreed that the situation called for it, they would sneak up on the husband and steal his weapon for her. The spouse would then go to the unhappy wife and ask for the weapon back, apologizing for his treatment of her.

My classmate Deborah Rodriguez had a different way of perceiving the painting. She believes that the women are running toward something in the joy of freedom. She sees them as dancing and enjoying the sun beating down on their nakedness. She also interpreted the setting as a warm spring day. According to her the women's arms are flung up in praise for the warmth and their knees are bent in dance. The lead woman carries a bow to protect the women from the harshness and dangers of the world.

Rodriguez and I looked at the same painting and interpreted it in different ways: there are reasons for this. The first obvious one is the different backgrounds. I was reared to treat girls differently than boys. I was not to hit girls, was to hold doors for them, etc. I was also taught that if a male acted to deliberately harm a female, another male should step in to protect her. The word for this is chivalry. Rodriguez went through a divorce and is trying to cope with raising six children alone. She has overcome the difficulties that present themselves in that situation. Therefore, she sees women in a different way. She sees women "as capable of finding solutions to the problems of daily life without the input or assistance of a man" (Rodriguez). Rodriguez believes that if she can overcome problems and enjoy her life, every woman can. The other main reason for the difference in interpretation is that I feel men are generally pessimistic and women are generally optimistic.

Even though men and women have different roles in society that lead to different interpretations on just about everything, that does not mean that one or the other is wrong. Men should listen more to women, and women should do the same for men so the vital link we share will not be disrupted. I believed one thing when I began this essay. That belief was based on knowledge--knowledge of the aborigine cultures, but my friend Rodriguez and my girlfriend Stephanie keep reminding me of the emotional side to stories, pictures, and of life in general. For that, I am grateful.

- **Note**: The Works Cited page is generally a separate page from the rest of the paper, and it is paginated as the next page in the series.

Works Cited

Rodriguez, Deborah. "Evaluation of Unbalanya Hill." unpublished paper in Composition I, 13 Nov. 2002.

Unbalanya Hill (A Group of Four Running Women). Australia. New York Graphic Society.

ARGUMENTATION/PERSUASION DEVELOPMENT

Argument centers around controversy. In argumentation (also known as persuasion), you attempt to persuade the reader to your view. You offer evidence that your view is the reasonable one to hold. Collecting this evidence may involve doing research, as well as collecting case histories and analogies, so that you can support your point of view.

To write using argumentation development, first choose a controversial subject and take a position on it. Then, before beginning to write, ask yourself 1) if you want to convince the reader or only to raise his awareness of the issue, 2) if you want to promote action or to change attitudes and behavior, and 3) if you know enough about the subject to write knowledgeably or if you need to do research. Then decide 1) what your strongest point is, 2) what kind of appeal you will make (emotional or intellectual, covert or direct), and 3) what tone you will take. For example, you may decide that irony is better than a direct approach for your purposes.

EXAMPLE (argumentation/persuasion paragraph):

> Children with AIDS should be allowed to attend public schools. All children, handicapped, ailing, or ordinary, are entitled, by law and by social custom, to an education. Furthermore, these innocent victims need the support and care of the community, as represented by the school. But, what about risk of infection to the other children in the school? All medical and scientific evidence points to the fact that AIDS is not transmitted through casual contact. No verified cases of transmission to primary caregivers exist, even in those situations in which the caregiver must deal with body fluids. Only when those body fluids come in contact with an open sore or cut is contagion possible. And even that risk can be alleviated through the use of rubber gloves. Since the risk of infection to caretakers is slight and to classmates is none, the fear of contagion is not a valid reason to keep children with AIDS from the public schools. To refuse them this entitlement would be to imply that these children are not worthy of being part of society. Children with AIDS are not pariahs: they are victims. They deserve our consideration. Yes, children with AIDS should go to public school.

EXAMPLE (persuasion essay):
NOTE: Student essay examples are above-average papers, but not necessarily "A" papers.

Horsman 1

Melanie Horsman
Prof. Jay
ENGL 1113
30 April 1998

Take Action

The year before my daughter entered first grade, my son, a third-grader at the time, reported to me that his friend had seen a girl in their class being inappropriately touched by the gym teacher. My first concern was the truth of this situation and the effect of this knowledge on my son. This teacher was my son's gym teacher and shortly to become my daughter's gym teacher. I questioned my son thoroughly, then meditated on what action to take as a concerned parent. First, I thought, if this girl were my daughter, I would want this report taken seriously. Immediately, I reported the incident to the authorities. Amazingly, the investigator volunteered to me that this person had been under surveillance for over ten years. In fact this person was arrested in the past for molesting several young children, each time bonded out by his best friend, the principal. Unfortunately, perhaps because of the trauma of the molestation, the children were unable to testify. Meanwhile, the accused teacher contemptuously remarked to the authorities, "Prove it." For the protection of our children, school policy should require prospective teachers to be thoroughly investigated.

At this time, school policy does not require a national felony check before a school hires a teacher. Part of the reason for this is that national checks are expensive. Thus, systems are forced to use lesser measures. A statewide test is the only background check done on a teacher. This leaves a large loophole that allows criminals to get into our system. A sex offender can move to the state, work for a couple of years, acquire reference, and then turn in an application for hire.

We should hire the people who are reputable and not hire those who are not. A teacher is powerful. Teachers influence our children; they are our children's mentors. We should remember the strong impact that teachers have on our children. One teacher, recently, gave her life to protect a student during the Jonesboro, Arkansas, incident. Her husband, Carroll, stated that she was only "taking care of her children" (Hewitt 108). How can we insure that we hire the right people?

State Representative Mary Easley is now in the process of trying to get a bill passed to prevent felons in our schools. However, she commented that "People here [at the state legislative level] do not take the testimonies of children seriously" and that she "really can't understand why something to protect our children would be so difficult to work out" (Ford A1). As parents and as citizens, we must not sacrifice our children to the ignorance of indifference.

We must continue to work on three fronts, the political front, the legal front, and the legislative front. The laws are not satisfactory. We should not have to settle for this. We must work to change the law to require background checks on teachers. Oklahoma policy has to change for the sake of the children and their future. The only alternative is to let our children take their chances and hope they make it through another day at school unscathed.

- **Note**: The Works Cited page is generally a separate page from the rest of the paper, and it is paginated as the next page in the series.

Works Cited

Ford, Brian, and David Fallis. "House to Vote on Crime Bill." Tulsa World 16 Apr. 1998: A1.

Hewitt, Bill, et al. "Tragedy." People Weekly 49.14 (13 Apr. 1998): 102-08.

You may, of course, have more than one kind of development in an essay. Even if you do have more than one kind of development in the essay, you probably will only have one kind of development in each paragraph of the essay.

REVISION

Refer to the peer consultation sheets in the back of the *Guide to College Writing* for specific information on how to make suggestions on revisions for other people's papers.

Essay Organization: In general, make sure the organization of the essay is clear: the thesis statement is clearly stated as the last sentence in the introductory section, each topic sentence supports the thesis statement, each sentence in each paragraph supports the topic sentence of the paragraph, the paragraphs are arranged in logical sequence, etc.

Introductory Section: Check to see that the introduction catches the reader's attention, leads logically to the thesis statement, and shows the tone and style you will use in the essay.

Thesis Statement: Be sure the thesis is clear and specific and that it reveals the structure of the essay.

Body Paragraphs: Make sure that each paragraph is fully and completely developed and adheres to the principles of coherence and unity. Remove any information that does not support, develop, or illustrate the thesis.

Conclusion: Finally, check to see that the conclusion does not introduce material not covered in the essay but that it does develop logically from the thesis statement and body.

Editing: The last step in revision is checking for spelling, sentence structure, grammar and usage, and punctuation. If you have difficulty with any of these aspects, ask a friend, tutor, or someone else who you know is better at them than you to help you with them.

Revision is a major key to successful essay writing. Revise. Revise. Revise.

MANUSCRIPT PREPARATION

After you have revised and edited the paper, you need to prepare it for submission. No matter how well you learn to write, papers neatly prepared to hand in are always more impressive than sloppy ones: they show that you take pride in your work. Follow these simple guidelines for proper manuscript preparation. Submit only the best.

For **handwritten** papers,

1. Use regular notebook paper, 8 1/2 by 11 inches.
2. Never submit papers written on spiral notebook paper.
3. Write only on the front of the paper.
4. Use black or blue ink.
5. Skip lines at your instructor's request.
6. Leave the marked margins on both sides of the paper.
7. Leave a double line margin at the bottom.
8. The title should not be in quotation marks unless it was originally used by someone else. Center the title. Skip a line after the title and before you begin the text. The title is not part of the text; if you wish to make the title words part of your paper, use them in the text.
9. Indent the first line of each paragraph one-half inch.
10. Write legibly in upper and lower case letters.
11. Proofread and correct.
12. Staple papers together with one staple in the upper left-hand corner or fold all papers together, as the instructor requires. Do not dog-ear any papers.
13. Write your FULL name on each page in the upper right corner. Include the page number. Include class time and date on the first page. If papers are folded, write your FULL name, class time and date on the outside.

Organization

For **typed** papers,

1. Use regular typing paper, 8 1/2 by 11 inches. Do not use erasable bond or onionskin.
2. Double-space unless otherwise instructed.
3. Type only on one side of the paper.
4. Use letter-quality print, legible and dark. Use only typefaces such as Arial, Times New Roman, Helvetica, Courier, etc. Use type sizes of approximately 8-10 letters per inch.
5. For MLA format papers, use one-inch margins on all sides of the paper, unless you are to bind the paper. In that case, leave a margin of one and one-fourth inches on the left.
6. Indent paragraphs ½ inch.
7. The title should not be in quotation marks unless it was originally used by someone else. Center the title. The title is not part of the text; if you wish to make the title words part of your paper, use them in the text.
8. Staple papers together with one staple in the upper left-hand corner or fold all papers together, as the instructor requires. Do not dog-ear any papers.
9. Write your LAST name and the page number on each page in the upper right corner. Include FULL NAME, class time and date on the first page on the left side. If papers are folded, write your FULL name, class time and date on the outside.
10. Use Arabic numbers (with no periods or parentheses) in the upper right corner of the pages.
11. Do not justify the margins on both sides of the paper. Left justify only.
12. Proofread and correct all mistakes. If necessary, use black ink or even dark pencil.

EXAMPLE (MLA-FORMAT TYPED PAPER, FIRST PAGE):

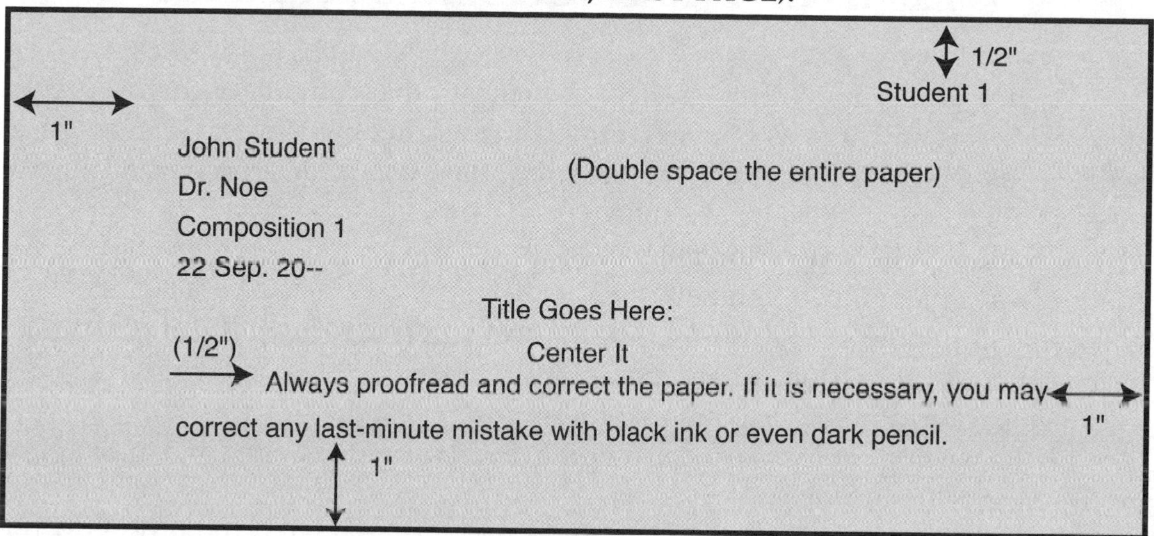

1/2"
Student 1
1"
John Student
Dr. Noe
Composition 1
22 Sep. 20--
(Double space the entire paper)
Title Goes Here:
Center It
(1/2")
Always proofread and correct the paper. If it is necessary, you may
correct any last-minute mistake with black ink or even dark pencil.
1"
1"

EXAMPLE (TYPED PAGE, NOT THE FIRST PAGE):

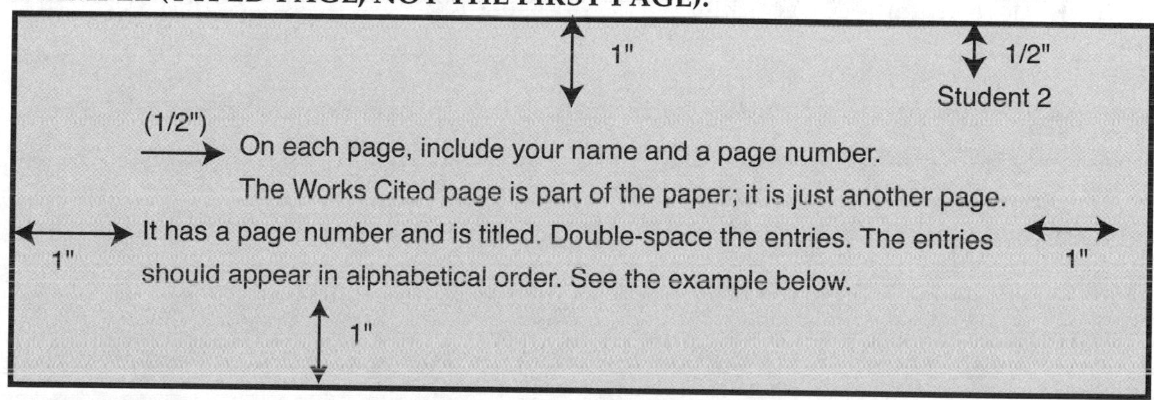

1"
1/2"
Student 2
(1/2")
On each page, include your name and a page number.
The Works Cited page is part of the paper; it is just another page.
It has a page number and is titled. Double-space the entries. The entries
should appear in alphabetical order. See the example below.
1"
1"
1"

EXAMPLE (RESEARCH PAPER, WORKS CITED PAGE):

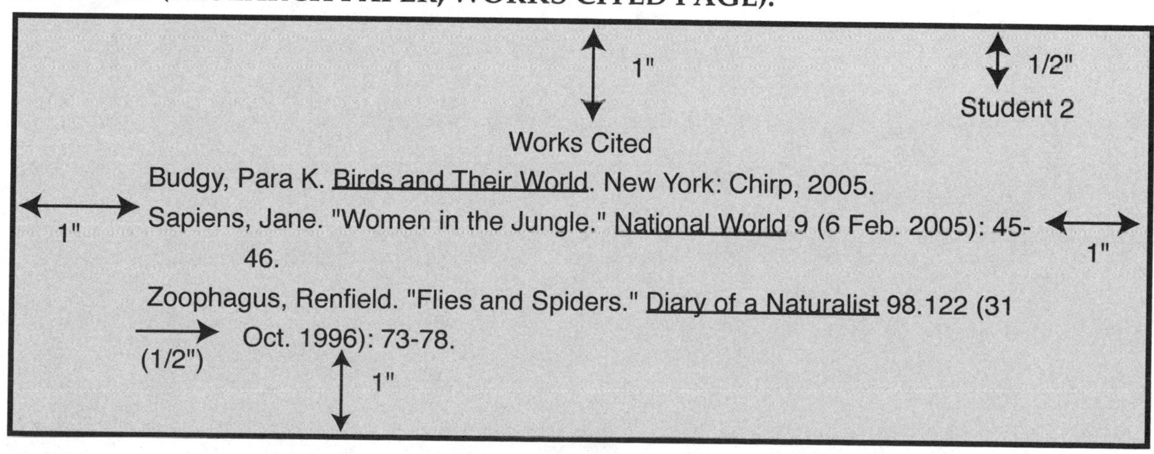

1"
1/2"
Student 2
Works Cited
Budgy, Para K. Birds and Their World. New York: Chirp, 2005.
Sapiens, Jane. "Women in the Jungle." National World 9 (6 Feb. 2005): 45-
46.
Zoophagus, Renfield. "Flies and Spiders." Diary of a Naturalist 98.122 (31
Oct. 1996): 73-78.
(1/2")
1"
1"
1"

WRITING: THE RECURSIVE PROCESS

Writing is a recursive process! Recursive means that you can return to a previous step or process at any time. We have discussed the writing process as if it takes place in discrete steps: first you plan; then you organize; then you write a first draft; then you revise, etc. As you probably already know, that is not actually the way writing works. You are always planning, organizing, and developing simultaneously. You are in a constant process of revision. At any point you can go back to a previous point and revise and repeat the step.

Writing is not step-by-step.
Writing is fits-and-starts.

So the writing process is not a straightforward one, it is more circular or spiral, a constant recurrence of steps.

How do you know when you are finished writing, then, if the process is not a straight one? You do not really finish writing because there is always something else you could do to the piece. You know you are finished with a piece when you run out of time!

Reading for Content and Reading for Writing

One of the things that you need to be aware of is how to read texts. "Text" in this instance does not mean textbook, but means any piece of writing. To begin with, we should think about how writing is usually structured. You will remember that, in earlier sections, we discussed that essays, or other pieces of academic or informational writing, generally have a statement of the main point the author wants to make, called the thesis statement. The thesis statement is generally supported by the remainder of the essay, which is contained in paragraphs. Each of the paragraphs generally has a topic sentence supported by the rest of the sentences in the paragraph. Basically, with the inclusion of an introductory section and a concluding section, this describes the structure of the majority of informational and academic writing.

With this in mind, we can take a piece of text and determine how that piece corresponds to the model we have described.

You can make the same determination when you are reading a textbook, when you are studying for a test, or when you are reading for information. Obviously the main idea of the information is of vital importance. And the major support for that information is also of importance. So, being able to pick out these points will help you understand what the author is trying to convey to you. In addition, being able to pick out these points will help you to learn the material.

Look at this piece of writing, a short essay that could be written in fifty minutes.

EXAMPLE (short essay, 50-minute essay):
NOTE: Student essay examples are above-average papers, but not necessarily "A" papers.

Ainperson 1

Cert Ainperson

Prof. Elle

ENGL 1113

10 May 2005

Models

If we look around, we can see models for planes, trains, and automobiles. Models introduce us to the miniature worlds of transportation, people, and imagination.

The most obvious miniature world is probably the world of tiny transportation. Even in a supermarket, children can find and lust for metal space shuttles and plastic dump trucks. They can drive and ride these through the air and over the mud or carpet and imagine that they are astronauts or garbage collectors, truckers or race car drivers, pizza deliverers or mechanics. In the majority of cases, the transport looks much like the original, but only the mind powers these miniature machines.

We can find another small world peopled by dolls and doll houses. In this world, furniture looks like furniture, even if the upholstery is hard and plastic. In this world, people can look like people and babies like Cabbage Patch dolls. Women can look like Barbie and men can style their hair like Ken.

These worlds are representations of the "real" world but there are other imaginary, miniature worlds. There are miniature universes that resemble and reflect reality and imagination almost equally. Out there, are worlds of trolls with emerald navels; of ponies with manes and tails longer than their bodies; of plastic potatoes with eyes, noses, and hats; of green slime and pink Slinkies.

Realistic or imaginary, these models become the world when they are played with. These miniatures, these models, allow children, and all the rest of us, to ride our dreams and shape our futures in the present, plastic and malleable.

Now that we have read the previous piece of writing, let us look at it and call it names! If we had to describe what kind of writing it was, we could call it a very short, descriptive essay. (See, we have already started to label it!) We could determine that, yes, it does fit the model by having a thesis statement: "Models introduce us to the miniature worlds of transportation, people, and imagination." That thesis is introduced by a comment about models in general, and supported by three points. Those points appear in the topic sentences of the paragraphs in the body of the piece. The first topic sentence discusses "tiny transportation," the second "people," and the third "imaginary worlds." Each of the topic sentences is supported by the remainder of the sentences in the paragraph. The piece concludes with a general statement giving us a judgment on where the author stands on models.

Now that we have decided on what basic information is conveyed in the text, we can decide whether the author uses that structure in an appropriate way. First, is the thesis statement descriptive of the information contained in the text? In this case, we could probably make the judgment that the thesis is FAIRLY focused. It does imply that the text will be about miniature worlds, which it is, although any thesis could probably be restated to make it clearer or more elegant.

Now we can decide whether the points revealed in the topic sentences support the main point made in the thesis. In this case the topic sentences tell us that at least three miniature world models exist: transportation, people, and imagination. Does this support the contention in the thesis statement? Yes. Very well? Probably not very well, but the essay is so short that something has to be left out. Does that mean the thesis should be more focused? Yes, it probably does.

Be a careful reader.

Next, is each paragraph complete? Does each paragraph contain enough information to support or illustrate the topic sentence? After re-reading the piece, we can say, yes, probably, each paragraph has sufficient examples to support the topic sentence. Of course, the paragraphs could all be longer and more complete, but that is a decision that the author has to make–what to put in and what to leave out.

Does the conclusion sufficiently end the piece? This conclusion not only ends the piece but leaves the mind of the reader thinking further on the same subject. If this is the intention of the author, and it seems to be, then the conclusion is successful.

In doing this analysis, or "engaging the text," we could proceed several ways. We might think through the structure as we have done here. We might outline the main points and then evaluate their effectiveness. (See **OUTLINES**.) We might annotate the text itself. This is a popular method. Annotating is sometimes known as highlighting and underlining, but it goes further than that! However, it works best if you read the piece first and then go BACK and underline and/or highlight. If we annotated the text, we would go back, after reading the text, and underline/highlight the main points. We would also make notes in the margins of the text as things occurred to us. We would make notes about whether we agreed or disagreed with what was said, with what connection we could make to other pieces we have read or other information we knew, with what we felt or thought when we read the passage.

Annotation of the text goes beyond a simple discovery of the structure of the text or the main points of the piece. It is actually an engagement of you and the text. You are actively involved with reading. Reading is not a passive activity. You have to filter what you read through your mind, assessing the relevance of what you read to you and your situation, deciding how the new information agrees or disagrees with what you already know or think you know, discovering how the new information fits into your own knowledge of the world and yourself. If you do not do this, you are not reading and engaged with the text. You are a couch potato and might as well be asleep! The information will not become YOURS without YOUR participation.

All of these possible ways to engage text work well, if a little differently. You need to find what works best for you.

Now, aside from learning the information in studying and for tests (and, of course, for your own personal satisfaction!), why would you want to follow any of these procedures? For one thing, you may be required to write pieces for classes or for your jobs that require this kind of analytic thinking. Summaries, reports, evaluations, précis, abstracts, reading cards, journal entries–all of these are names for writing that incorporates engaging text.

Think about what you read.

One of the reasons to "engage text" is to evaluate it. Evaluation may do any of a number of things. It may tell whether you liked or disliked the article and why, whether you thought it was good or not and why, whether you found the information interesting or not and why. It may tell what you thought about the work's topic, what you thought about the work's writing, how you assessed the effectiveness or the importance of the topic or the presentation, or how you could relate the work to others you have read–all of which must be supported by reasons why you made the evaluation you made–and many, many other possibilities.

The evaluation is the part of the report in which your opinion is vital. You are evaluating the work. In the evaluation you can tell how you feel about the article, the subject, the writing, and the relative value of each of these.

Or you can go beyond a personal reaction to a more analytic response. You can consider who the author is, who the publisher is, and what the date of publication is. This would enable you and your reader to determine if the selection were written by a reputable author, if the article were published by a reputable publisher, and whether the selection is dated or timely.

What difference might these things make? Well, what if you had read an article that asserted eating raw pork prevented trichinosis (which as you know, may be carried in raw pork)? And what if you found that the author was the owner of the largest pig farm in the world and had just been admitted to a psychiatric hospital? You might use this knowledge to decide if the article contained accurate information!

If you are going to make a more formal report, you might consider the length, organization, and style of the work. In that case you would have to decide if the work were too short for the amount of information, if it gave enough information, if the work were well-organized, if the work had a valid and well-supported thesis, and so on. You might want to comment on whether the work made sense. You might want to consider any or all of these things when you decide on what you want to comment in the reaction/evaluation part of the report.

As you read, you can tell if you like a work or not. In addition, you can make another determination. You can decide if it is good or bad. However, you have to realize that those are two different determinations. In other words, liking something does not necessarily mean it is good and not liking something does not necessarily mean it is not good. Deciding whether you like it is different from deciding whether the work has merit.

For example, many, many people like to read series fiction–like the Destroyer novels, or Harlequin Romances. Reading these is a lot like eating at McDonald's. You know exactly what you are getting. And so, if that is what you want, you like it. But that does not mean you cannot decide that some other works might be "better" in the sense of more artistic or more important, like Rachel Carson's *Silent Spring* or Oliver Sacks' *The Man Who Mistook His Wife for a Hat* or *Awakenings*.

Evaluate and assess what you read.

Making a decision about the quality of a work does not mean that there are things you should not like. It does mean that you should look at how you make the decisions about what you like and know that the decision about liking something does not mean the same as deciding about worth or importance.

An evaluation can also be a decision on whether the information or judgment is correct or incorrect, whether the information or judgment is applicable to your situation or that of another, or whether the information or judgment is right or wrong–in a moral, social, or political sense. Actually, you are making a judgment on a judgment!

It can be difficult or easy to make the evaluation. Sometimes it is obvious that what you have read is incorrect or irrelevant. For example, an article on beekeeping that suggests that you keep bees in the bathtub is hardly credible. In some circumstances, you may not be able so easily to distinguish between the possibilities. However, there are some steps that you can use to make this decision easier.

First, as a base, decide what the author actually says by finding the main idea and the major supporting ideas of the work. This is the basis of all evaluation and is also the basis for a summary.

Then decide what the author means by determining if the statements are fact or opinion, if the author might be biased in any way, and if you can relate the information to knowledge that you already have.

For example, in an article about food use, an author might say that eating ice cream leads to drowning. The article contains figures that show a relationship between the number of people drowned in a month and the number of gallons of ice cream consumed in that month. As one figure goes up, the other does too. As one goes down, the other does too.

Well, the argument looks as if it might make sense. But does it really? Are the statements fact or opinion? On the surface, the statements of the author seem to be fact. The numbers of people drowned and the numbers of gallons consumed are fact.

Is the author biased in any way? We find that the author has credentials and that the data in the article were gathered by two reputable organizations. The author does not own swimming areas or dairy farms. So the author is probably not biased in any sense that we can determine.

Then, can we relate the information to information we already have? Well, we know that ice cream consumption rises in the summer. This is borne out by the figures in this and in other articles. It makes sense that more people eat ice cream in warmer weather. We know that the number of people drowning rises in the summer because the number of people swimming increases in the summer. Such is delineated by figures in this and other articles. It makes sense that if more people swim, more people drown because the number of possibilities for drowning increase.

Does that mean that one causes the other? We also know that many things rise and fall cyclically that are not related to each other: hemlines and the stock market, the number of sparrows in fields and the number of aircraft. But they do not cause each other. They are not related as supply and demand are related. So we also can decide that the author has mistakenly determined that two things rising and falling cyclically have a cause and effect relationship. We will evaluate the article and conclude that the author is in error.

The more you bring to a work,
the more you receive from the work.

SUMMARIZING

A summary may be referred to as a précis or an abstract. (In technical writing, a distinction is made between these terms. If you are doing technical writing, you will need to know the distinction. In that case refer to a good technical writing text or manual or to the style sheet of the company initiating the report.)

The writer of a summary reduces material in an original work to its main points and key supporting details. A summary may consist of a word, a phrase, several sentences, or one or more paragraphs. Usually a summary is one or two paragraphs. This paragraph or paragraphs will include a statement of the main idea of the article (the thesis statement) and refer to the major points that support the main idea.

A report (which may also be called a review) usually contains two sections: a summary of the material and a statement of the report writer's reaction to the material. If you are the report writer, the reaction is your own evaluation of the article–whether you liked or disliked it and why, whether you thought it was good or not and why, and/or whether you found the information interesting and useful or not and why. (In technical writing, there are different types of reports. If you are doing technical writing, you will need to know the different kinds. Refer to a good technical writing text or manual or the style sheet of the company for which you prepare the report.)

To write a **SUMMARY** well, and relatively painlessly, follow the steps below:

1. Read the selection carefully, re-reading as much as necessary.
2. In your own words, write a summary of the selection.
   - A. At the top of the page, give the bibliographic information for the selection. Use the MLA format unless otherwise instructed. (See **DOCUMENTATION**.)
   - B. The first line of the summary section should repeat the name of the selection and the author.
   - C. The summary should convey your understanding of the main idea (thesis) of the selection and the major points used in developing this idea OR the major events in the short story or novel.
   - D. Usually confine the summary of an article to one paragraph. (See **PARAGRAPH DEVELOPMENT**.) This may seem brief, but a summary has one purpose—to summarize.
   - E. A summary should not exceed one-fourth of the length of the selection being summarized. Be skeptical of any summary which seems to require more than a page and a half.
   - F. Phrases or clauses quoted from the selection should be in quotation marks.
   - **G.** Do NOT include your opinion of the selection or your own knowledge of the subject in the summary paragraph. (This information belongs in the reaction paragraph of a **REPORT**–not in a summary.)

EXAMPLE (summary of an article/essay):

Trillin, Calvin. "It's Just Too Late." The Bedford Reader. 2nd ed. Ed. X. J. Kennedy and Dorothy M. Kennedy. New York: St. Martin's, 1985. 45-56.

Trillin's "It's Just Too Late" is an account of a sixteen-year-old girl's death. FaNee Cooper is the "perfect child" who, at thirteen, is discovered no longer perfect. She turns to alcohol and drugs and the people who use these substances. One night her father, wanting to take her from the company of one of her friends, chases her in a car. The car FaNee is riding in is wrecked. FaNee dies; the boy driving is convicted of involuntary manslaughter.

EXAMPLE (summary of an article/essay):

Etzioni, Amitai. "Parenting as an Industry." The McGraw-Hill Reader. 7th ed. Ed. Gilbert H. Muller. Boston: McGraw-Hill, 1997. 106-12.

In Amitai Etzioni's essay "Parenting as an Industry," Etzioni analyzes the woeful condition of parenting. He says the condition is a result of increased numbers of parents leaving "the nest" to seek careers outside the home. Etzioni believes the lack of quality and quantity time parents have to offer their children is resulting in insufficient bonding and education. In turn, these children will have difficulty growing into well-adjusted adults. In addition, Etzioni discusses the growing numbers of children being placed in child care centers and the failure of these centers to give children the quality care they require because of understaffing and poorly paid, unqualified personnel. Because of these conditions, the turn-over rate at child care centers is very high, making bonding between child and caregiver difficult. Etzioni expresses concern about whether parents should trust strangers to raise their children and form their personalities. Furthermore, Etzioni suggests that parents become more responsible in selecting child care and remain involved after placement. Etzioni recommends increased government supervision of centers and home facilities and financial assistance for parents struggling to afford quality care for their children. In conclusion, Etzioni asks the reader the following question: What is most important in our country—making more money in pursuit of the "American Dream" or striving to be effective nurturing parents to our children?

For an example of a **SHORT STORY SUMMARY**, see the **SUMMARY OF "YOUNG GOODMAN BROWN"** in the section on **WRITING IN RESPONSE TO LITERATURE**.

A specific kind of summary is the **rhetorical précis**. The emphasis in the rhetorical précis is on the rhetorical aspect of the work, written or spoken, that you are considering. Rhetorical study is the study of language use and communication. Thus, a rhetorical précis is designed to show the main points of the work, such as the name of the writer, the name and genre (or type) of the work, the manner of information delivery, the main and supporting points, and the relation between the writer and audience. The rhetorical précis consists of four sentences:

1. Sentence 1: The first sentence names the author, the genre (essay, novel, speech, etc.), the title (with the date of the work in parentheses) followed by a verb ("claims," "posits," "argues," etc.), followed by "that" and a phrase or clause in which you state the thesis of the work.
2. Sentence 2: The second sentence explains the manner in which the author supports the thesis. You do not do this by restating details but by explaining the rhetorical method which the author used to develop the support, such as narration, comparison, classification, etc.
3. Sentence 3: The third sentence states the purpose of the work. This may reflect the thesis but must include why the author has created the work. The third sentence contains a phrase or clause beginning "in order to," such as "The writer delineates his vision of the future in order to. . . ."
4. Sentence 4: The fourth sentence states the intended audience for the work and how the author positions him or herself in relation to that audience. (See the following example.)

EXAMPLE (rhetorical précis):

Gray 1

Laura Gray

Guide to College Writing

1 July 2005

Minsky, Marvin. "Will Robots Inherit the Earth?" The Writer's Presence: A Pool of Readings. Ed. Donald McQuade and Robert Atwan. Boston: Bedford/St. Martin, 2000. 460-70.

In his essay "Will Robots Inherit the Earth?" (1994), Marvin Minsky posits that the inevitable synthesis of human and machine offers an optimistic future for the human race, which will be "delivered from the limitations of biology" (461). Minsky supports his futuristic vision through scientific facts and statistics of Darwinian theory, biochemistry, genetics, and nanotechnology. His purpose is to convince his readers of the feasibility and desirability of machine/human augmentation in order to indict those who fail to embrace the inevitable merging of human and machine. Minsky establishes a problematic relationship with his audience through his dismissive tone that labels those who take issue with his particular world-view as "dangerous" (469).

REPORTS AND REVIEWS

To write a **REPORT OR REVIEW**, follow the previous steps for writing a summary. Follow Step 1; then follow Step 2 A-F. Then, instead of using the previous Step 2-G, include G from below:

G. DO include your opinion of the selection and your own knowledge of the subject in the reaction/evaluation paragraph.

When writing the reaction paragraph(s) of the report or review, you may consider the author, the publisher, and the date of publication: this would enable you and your reader to determine if the selection were written by a reputable author and published by a reputable company and whether the selection is dated or timely. (See **READING FOR WRITING AND READING FOR CONTENT**.) You might consider the length, organization, and style of the selection.

The reaction paragraph or paragraphs can be, and probably should be, analytical. (See **REPORTS AND REVIEWS: MAKING EVALUATIONS**.) Relate the information to your own thoughts and feelings and to your own knowledge of the subject. Decide if the information is useful or not, if you liked or disliked the subject and/or the author's style of writing, if you thought the selection was good or not. Do not stop with a simple statement like "I liked it." Tell why you liked or disliked it!

EXAMPLE (report on an article/essay):

> Trillin, Calvin. "It's Just Too Late." <u>The Bedford Reader</u>. 2nd ed. Ed. X.J. Kennedy and Dorothy M. Kennedy. New York: St. Martin's, 1985. 45-56.
>
> Trillin's "It's Just Too Late" is an account of a sixteen-year-old girl's death. FaNee Cooper is the "perfect child" who, at thirteen, is discovered no longer perfect. She turns to alcohol and drugs and the people who use these substances. One night her father, wanting to take her from the company of one of her friends, chases her in a car. The car FaNee is riding in is wrecked. FaNee dies; the boy driving is convicted of involuntary manslaughter.
>
> This essay was very distressing. I enjoyed reading it even though it made me feel uneasy. It shows how any child from any family in any community can go "bad." FaNee seems to be ordinary until she turns to drugs, but the essay shows that she is surrounded by hypocrisy and high expectations. Her parents turn against her because her mother discovers cigarettes in her drawer. The community and school reveal hypocritical standards: the "Ins" talk about not drinking, but there is no evidence that they actually do not. Against these expectations, false standards, and the knowledge she never can be "perfect," FaNee escapes to places and people of imperfections. Her escape leads ultimately to her death because she made wrong choices. Others, however, might feel guilt. Ironically, her father says he would chase her again, knowing his actions would cause her death. What kind of father is this?

EXAMPLE (rhetorical précis with reader response/rhetorical report):

Gray 1

Laura Gray

Guide to College Writing

15 July 2005

Minsky, Marvin. "Will Robots Inherit the Earth?" The Writer's Presence: A Pool of Readings. Ed. Donald McQuade and Robert Atwan. Boston: Bedford/St. Martin, 2000. 460-70.

In his essay "Will Robots Inherit the Earth?" (1994), Marvin Minsky posits that the inevitable synthesis of human and machine offers an optimistic future for the human race, which will be "delivered from the limitations of biology" (461). Minsky supports his futuristic vision through scientific facts and statistics of Darwinian theory, biochemistry, genetics, and nanotechnology. His purpose is to convince his readers of the feasibility and desirability of machine/human augmentation in order to indict those who fail to embrace the inevitable merging of human and machine. Minsky establishes a problematic relationship with his audience through his dismissive tone that labels those who take issue with his particular world-view as "dangerous" (469).

I found this essay both intriguing and problematic. Minsky sets an early tone of optimism for the future as he discusses science and technology as tools for improving human existence. He establishes ethos with his audience by presenting complex scientific information in easily readable prose. His rhetorical style is engaging and informative. Minsky's tone changes, however, as he addresses the possible criticisms of his particular world vision, and as he dismisses the deep spiritual and philosophical questions with a swift "I have no patience with such arguments" (467). Overall, I believe Minsky's argument fails because he refuses to adequately address the major concerns that his readers will likely have—what it means to our sense of humanity if we alter something considered fundamental to our makeup, the brain, through technological tinkering. Just because we can do something does not necessarily mean that we should.

MAKING EVALUATIONS

Sometimes you will be required to make evaluations of articles or books that are written to be persuasive or informative and that contain judgments of one kind or another. An evaluation is a decision on whether the selection is correct or incorrect, etc. (See **READING FOR WRITING AND READING FOR CONTENT**.)

To make rational evaluations of selections containing judgments, you might follow this process:

1. Summarize the main idea and supporting points.
2. Does the selection offer new information or a fresh approach or a new interpretation? What questions does the selection answer or fail to answer?
3. Determine if statements are facts, opinion, or both. Be sure to identify any authorial bias; i.e., an article on cars praising Fords, written by Ford Motor Company president, may well be biased. Does the author's opinion mar or enhance the selection? Does he/she plead for a special view? Is his/her plea based on fact or on prejudice?
4. Analyze the selection in terms of what you know. Have you experienced or researched the topic? Does your experience agree with the author? (It is not sufficient simply to agree or disagree. You must have some basis for agreement or disagreement.) Is the work credible?
5. Decide whether you will accept the work as accurate, reject it, or defer judgment on it until you have collected more information.

REVIEWS, CRITIQUES, AND EVALUATIONS

You may also be required to review artistic works. This kind of review is also called an evaluation or critique. In essence, you will be making your own judgment of the worth of the work; you will be critiquing the work.

Some reviews include bibliographic data and a summary. (See **SUMMARIES AND REPORTS.**) Some reviews, especially those for newspapers and for some classes, do not include either bibliographic data or a summary. Be sure to check with the person making the assignment to see what the requirements are. Then follow directions!

EXAMPLE (review of an art show, without bibliographic data or summary):

Terar 1

Deam Terar

Prof. Emme

ART 1223

15 May 2005

David Hockney: Still Images

The Gallery Space

David Hockney's latest collection of photographs and paintings illustrates the subtle and powerful changes in the artist's recent work. Hockney, now well into his sixties, has a renewed spirit and renewed energy; this is most evident in his mural The Things I've Done with a Camera. Here, Hockney's brushstrokes are bright and bold; colors appear to pop off the wall, leaving us a bit blinded by their intensity. It is as if Hockney has sliced his green from leaves, plucked red right off petals. The setting of this painting is his studio, yet the power of nature's hues stretches and twists across the canvas, over ten feet long and three feet high. An otherwise-innocent electrical cord, snaking its way from light to wall socket, glows with intense color, the electricity within slipping its way out. Tucked against the right edge of the mural sits a solid oak desk, its cocoa surface rich and milky. This same cocoa flows down to the desk's legs, firmly rooting it to the floor.

Hockney brings outside in, transforming interior to exterior with all of nature's unruly energy and brilliant pigments. This same energy is found in Hockney's work Still Life. In Still Life, Hockney's painting depicts a rather simple setting–oranges atop a cobalt sea, the table's legs peeking from beneath the cloth. The oranges assert solidity, their bruises inflicted upon each by the others, as they sink into the cloth. This same orange pigment splashes onto the surface of a goblet, slicing its way through the crystal.

A few paces to the left of Still Life hangs another painting, For Jeanne, illustrating the same fruits, as if they have simply bounced from one canvas to the next. Here Hockney plays with our curiosity to look back; he wants us to reconsider what we have just seen as we contemplate what lies ahead.

When we do look ahead, we discover many of the same images–oranges, tables, trees, in addition to the one image Hockney portrays most clearly–that of an artist in love with his paints, and with nature's beauty, once again.

EXAMPLE (book review, without bibliographic data or summary):

Danz 1

Macabre Danz
Prof. Enney
ENGL 2613
17 Mar. 2005

Stephen Dixon's Interstate: The Circuitous Path to Reality

A Book Review

Readers familiar with Stephen Dixon's sometimes quirky, often inventive fiction will feel quite comfortable with his latest novel, Interstate. Others not acquainted with any of Dixon's over three hundred published stories or the critically acclaimed novel Frog (National Book Award finalist and PEN/Faulkner Award finalist) may want to take a deep breath before cracking open this opus.

Dixon rarely tells a straightforward story. Instead, he allows his characters' thoughts and actions to hurriedly lead us this way and that, at times leaving readers the worse for wear. And in this novel of eight interrelated narratives, we find ourselves struggling to keep up with the main character Nathan Frey, who travels a circuitous path approaching two of contemporary America's realities: the sometimes maniacally-obsessive concern of parents for the safety and well being of their children and the tragic effects of random violence.

Frey, while driving his two daughters home from New York, comes face to face with a father's greatest fear: the death of a child, and as result, an inability to control an uncontrollable situation. And Dixon's candid approach allows Frey to stutter in his speech, stumble in his actions, and falter in his thoughts, thus rendering this father both hopeless and helpless. There are instances when Frey stands on the precipice of mental and physical collapse, times when his surviving (in one narration) daughter Margo appears more resilient than he, moments when Frey questions his every move and holds himself responsible for what's occurred: “But what I'm getting at is that if I'd acted sooner–got on the shoulder sooner, let's say–things would have been different. Much different. Maybe. Or maybe nothing I did would have changed things. . .” (126). Thus, what is most tragic is not the loss of Nathan's youngest daughter but the demise of Nathan himself.

Dixon not only illustrates the resulting pain of Margo's death (in one narration) but also Nathan's thoughts on the nature of violence and its perpetrators in the seventh of these narratives:

> What I'm really saying here, and say it well, already, is there's–is that there's a social malaise in this country–good, and good word too, malaise, came out spontaneously, though the “social” should go because it's such a cliché–and it seems to be spreading at its own speed through the–chuck the “at its own speed”: familiar, not needed, and what's it mean anyway? It's spreading, period, from here to there and nearly everywhere to the point where just about nowhere's safe. (217)

Ultimately, what one discovers when reading Interstate is that the doubts, digressions, fears, and fantasies of Dixon's characters capture the way we truly act, speak, and think. So, what some readers may consider as the rambling route to the “fiction” of this story ends up being the most direct path to its reality.

EXAMPLE (film review):

Sesmore 1

Blunt Sesmore

Prof. Ohe

ENGL 1213

15 June 2005

Nicholas Ray's Rebel Without a Cause

A Movie Review

Nicholas Ray's film Rebel Without a Cause is a provocative and timeless masterpiece featuring James Dean in his most memorable screen appearance. In Rebel, Dean plays Jim Stark, a troublemaker who is picked up by the police for being drunk and disorderly. While he waits at the police station for his parents, he notices Judy, played by Natalie Wood, a lonely girl who has been picked up for walking the streets after curfew. He also comes into contact with Plato (Sal Mineo), a disturbed rich kid who has been brought in for killing a litter of puppies.

The opening scene manages not only to link the three, but it also introduces the main theme of the film. This theme concerns the strained relationships between adults and teens. For instance, the real dilemma facing Jim is not that he's been ostracized by his peers; instead, it is his father's inability to take charge and be strong. So Jim, who is fighting his peers and his insecurities, also tries to fight his father's will to simply dissolve into the background. While Jim struggles with his own battles both inside and outside the home, Judy confronts difficult situations of her own. Judy and her parents also suffer through a strained relationship and this relationship acts as a catalyst for Judy's rebellious nature. Both situations are difficult for the respective families and the teens involved; however, Plato's situation is the most bleak. His parents are non-existent; he lacks any true communication with them and, as a result, he ends up grasping for the attention of both Jim and Judy.

In sensitive moments directed by Ray, we watch an insecure and afraid Plato look to Jim and Judy, not as peers, but as a young boy desperate for affection and approval. Ray handles such situations with grace and tact, careful not to overdo his direction. What he creates is the opportunity for the audience to empathize with these characters and their respective dilemmas. This is presented most effectively when Jim, Judy, and Plato retreat to an abandoned mansion. Here, the three become a family–Jim and Judy as parents to the child Plato. Ray lets us listen to their conversation yet does not let us intrude, does not allow us to spoil this intimate moment.

What does end up spoiling this intimate moment is the reality of their situation–their antagonists have arrived. As a result, the once-lonely, yet now seemingly-content Plato meets his death. In the film's final scene at the observatory, Ray illustrates two timeless images–a young James Dean and his famous red jacket, and teens trying to find their way in the world.

Works Cited

Rebel Without a Cause. Dir. Nicholas Ray. Perf. James Dean, Natalie Wood, and Sal Mineo. Warner, 1996.

EXAMPLE (film review):

Lusk 1

Winn Lusk

Prof. Peay

ENGL 2613

3 July 2005

Analysis of Rebel Without a Cause

I can understand why many consider Rebel Without a Cause a classic film. Although there are few special effects, the movie has an intensity that keeps my attention. Films created since the mid-seventies generally have added more and more special effects to keep the audience's attention. Rebel succeeds without special effects.

The movie does have minor flaws. One is the fact that the James Dean character, Jim Stark, is "drunk as a skunk" at the start of the movie; then after only four or five minutes he is totally sober. Devlin-McGregor Pharmaceuticals should market that cure because the company with such a panacea would make more money than the movie did! Another point of interest is the fact that the entire story happens in a period of about twenty-four hours. The start of the movie is in the late evening, just after curfew; and the end occurs in the early hours of the next morning. Too many events, too many emotional changes occur in that short time period. For example, Judy (Natalie Wood) purports to love, mourn, and love again all in less than a day.

One of the strengths of the film is thematic. The writers take three different teenagers and express three different problems that some teenagers have to deal with in life: a) a puissant father, b) an impotent father, c) a non-existent father. The puissant father refuses to show his love for his daughter, who desperately needs it to be expressed. The impotent father shows no "manliness," which embarrasses his son, who wants his father to be more assertive and not be pushed around by his wife and mother. The non-existent father is exactly that: non-existent. All this father does is send money for the support of his son. The mother is equally irresponsible because she leaves the care of her son in the hands of a nanny. This poor boy wants desperately to have a strong father figure in his life. He would have enjoyed some parental attention from his mother as well. All three of these problems exist for teenagers in every day life, at that time and in today's time, and not just in film.

Another theme is that of rebellion. Jim Stark is, as the title suggests, a "rebel without a cause." I believe that there is a "cause" for him to be a rebel: peer pressure! There is one moment in the film when Stark and Buzz, the leader of the tough gang, are about to have a contest to see which one is braver. As they prepare for the spectacular event, they have a small private conversation. Neither one really wants to have this contest, but they both know that they must. They are forced into this rash and dangerous decision by peer pressure. Teenagers have a strong need to feel accepted by their peers. Sometimes this need can cause them to rebel against the adults' society as they choose the teens' society.

This film takes several common but difficult problems that face teens in society and intertwines them into a smooth flowing picture. The artistry used in making Rebel Without a Cause may justify its reputation, but it is the universal thematic material that makes it a classic.

Works Cited

Rebel Without a Cause. Dir. NIcholas Ray. Perf. James Dean, Natalie Wood, and Sal Mineo. Warner, 1996.

ESSAY TESTS

Taking an essay test is an experience you will undoubtedly have in college, if you have not already. Taking an essay test may be frightening, as taking any kind of test can be, but it should not cause panic if you are familiar with the material to be covered.

Just follow these simple guidelines to a successful experience.

1. **Follow instructions**. Bring the designated supplies to the test: pen, paper, "blue book," anything else specified. Write your name in the designated position. Read the instructions first so you will know what instructions to follow. Remember that there are **two kinds of essay tests**: one in which you write a full, short essay of four or five paragraphs in answer to a question (see timed essays for examples) and one in which you write a paragraph or two in answer to a question. Note the instructions to see which kind of answer you should make.
2. **Read through the test.** This is both to make sure you know what the instructions are (see 1), and to reassure yourself that not everything sounds strange or new!
3. **Select the questions you will answer.** Often the test will list a number of questions from which you select. In that case, decide which questions you think you can best answer. Be sure you answer what the question is asking and not what you wish the question were asking.
4. **Jot down ideas**–either in the margin of the test paper or on a scrap of paper or in the back of the "blue book"–as they occur to you. As you select the questions you plan to answer, and as you think of things you might be able to use in your answer, write yourself a little note. Otherwise, you may forget that wonderful thought and not be able to recapture it as you answer. It is too late to recall it as you walk out the door. Make sure this does not happen to you–write it down as you think of something.
5. **Time yourself.** As you select the questions, decide how much time you can safely spend on any one answer. Allow ten minutes at both ends of the class for steps 1, 2, 3, 4, 6, and 11. That will leave you half an hour for answering questions if you are taking a fifty-minute exam. If you are answering five questions, you can only spend six minutes on each answer. (This calculation assumes all the questions are of equal weight and importance.) When you come to the end of the time you have allotted for the question, quit. You have programmed into your plan a cushion at the end in

which to fill in additional information if necessary. Remember: it is better to omit a couple of sentences in a few answers than to omit a complete answer, which is likely to happen if you do not plan your time.

6. **Look for direction words in the question**. Answer the question that is asked.

ANALYZE	means to **EXAMINE** closely, separating basic parts, steps or features, to look for cause and/or effect, to tell why or how.
ATTACK or **DEFEND**	means to take a position, for or against.
COMPARE	means to explain similarities, parallels and differences. Sometimes people mistakenly assume that to compare means only to tell the similarities (because **CONTRAST** means to stress the differences). When in doubt about the instructor's desires, ASK. It is too late to find out what the instructor wants after the test is returned with the answer marked wrong.
CONTRAST	means to stress the differences.
DEFINE	means to explain what something means or what it is. Begin with a basic definition and then use examples to clarify what you mean.
DISCUSS	means to explain, to analyze, to elaborate, even to debate. This is a general and fairly vague term so decide carefully which direction you are going to go and then stay with your plan.
ELABORATE	means to explain further, to develop a detailed explanation. Be careful to use both primary and secondary support. Make major points (primary support); include examples and details (secondary support).
EVALUATE	means to judge or to **ANALYZE** critically, discussing the pros and cons. Write a pro/con argument or a critical analysis. If writing a pro/con argument, be clear about which side you prefer even if you feel you need to spend time on both sides.
EXAMINE	means to **ANALYZE**.
EXPLAIN	means to clarify, interpret, explicate, summarize. The term explain covers all expository writing strategies. This is a general term so decide carefully which direction you are going to go and then stay with your plan. Do not write an argument (**ATTACK** OR **DEFEND**).
ILLUSTRATE	means to clarify. Begin with the basic generalization called for and then elaborate with a long example or with several short examples.

LIST means to write down a series of points. Use the 1, 2, 3 or the first, second, third approach.

OUTLINE means to discuss briefly, give a skeletal discussion, skip details.

7. **Plan your answer.** Plan your time, and plan your answer. Read the question and decide what points to cover before starting to write. You may want to jot down ideas or even do a simple outline. Do not just begin writing and trust to luck and your fairy godmother to make sure you hit all the important points before you run out of time or memory. If you just begin to write and write and write, you may find you have been writing the wrong things.
8. **Write neatly so the grader can read your answer**. No matter what you have heard or read, the grader must be able to read your paper. Otherwise, the grader is likely to assume you do not know the information at all and are trying to cover up by being messy. In addition, subconsciously the grader will be prejudiced in favor of your paper by neat, pleasing appearance. Fair? No, but make it work for you, not against you.
9. **Write a good answer**. Write in complete sentences. The more easily a grader can read your answer, the more likely it is that grader will be happy to read your answer. Be coherent and logical. Answer the question that is asked, not the one you wish had been asked.

   Believe it or not, graders can recognize blah-blah-blah.
10. **Write part of the question in the answer**. The grader should be able to tell what question you are answering by reading your answer. The grader should not have to refer to the question number, which you <u>must</u> include. For instance, as you are answering a question that says "What were the three major causes of Black Friday?" you should start your answer by saying "The three major causes of Black Friday were. . . ." This makes the grader happy. Probably more important, it solves the major problem for most people–starting out. You already have written part of what you are going to say. You are started on the answer and the worst is over.
11. **Determine the length of the answer by how long you have to answer it.** No other guideline can be applicable to the length of an essay question. Some questions could be answered in a short paragraph; some could take a book. But you do not have time to write a book. Judge how long the answer should be by how long you have to answer it. If you have two questions to answer, the answers should be 20 minutes long. If you have four questions to answer, the answers should be 10 minutes long.
12. **Re-read and revise but do not re-write**. After you have answered all the questions and run out of "answering time," you have the ten minutes you have allotted to go over your paper. Take this time to check your answers for various things. One of the things to check for is spelling and punctuation errors. Even if an instructor says that spelling and punctuation "do not count," you can be sure that they will influence the grader's reaction to your answer, even if only subconsciously. Check also for accuracy, for coherence, for logic, and for readability. This is also the time to go back and complete those questions you may not have completely finished. Do not take

the time to re-write the paper. You do not have time. If you have been neat and have planned, you will not need to re-write.

13. **Turn in the paper!**

EXAMPLE (essay question answer):

- The test you have been handed says,
  Answer both of the following questions:
    1. Discuss the irony in "Appointment in Samarra." Include in your discussion some comments on how the female figure of death functions as part of that irony.

    2. Discuss the two major images in "The Tell-Tale Heart." Include in your discussion how the images function as symbols.

- Your answer looks something like this:

1. "Appointment in Samarra" is an ironic short story. First, the servant thinks that Death has threatened him so he runs away from Baghdad to Samarra. But Death has only made a gesture of surprise since she has an appointment with the servant in Samarra. When the servant flees, he is running to his fate instead of away from it. This is an ironic aspect.

   Another ironic aspect is that Maugham has made Death female. In most stories, Death is seen as male. Usually, the female is considered the life-bringer, the fruitful. Usually, the male is seen as the force of destruction and death. Maugham has chosen to portray Death as female in an ironic reversal of the usual role for death. Since Death is female and since the servant is running to death at her hands, the story is ironic on two levels.

2. The two major images in "The Tell-Tale Heart" are the "evil eye" and the beating heart. The madman sees the eye of the old man as evil because it is filmy and clouded. He says he loves the old man but that the eye is evil and must be destroyed. The eye becomes the symbol for the madness of the killer and it becomes the symbol for the attitude of the killer as well. Since the killer says he loves the old man but is willing to kill him to kill the eye, the eye becomes the symbol for the madman's ability to divorce his fear of the eye from his "love" for the old man. He makes the old man into a bundle of parts and he wants to wipe out one of those parts. He makes the old man into an object by only looking at one aspect of him.

   The beating heart is a symbol for madness and for conscience. The heart is symbolic of the madman's conscience which will not let him rest until he confesses to the crime. The image of the heart beating more and more loudly under the floor becomes the symbol of the conscience crying out more and more loudly for the truth. The heart is also symbolic of the killer's madness since he imagines it beating long after the old man is dead.

EXAMPLE (essay question answer):

- The test you have been handed says,

  1. How has a film affected your life and/or your philosophy of life?

- Your answer looks something like this:

Renetta Harrison

Comp. II/Cinema

4 Sep. 1997

1. The film Schindler's List affected my life by making me more aware of discrimination, more knowledgeable on the history of the period of the film, and very angry. I am now much more against all forms of discrimination due to the film's depiction of the cruel treatment of the Jewish people during the Holocaust. I am appalled that anyone would treat others badly, not to mention kill them, based on religious preference. I am also more knowledgeable on the history of Hitler and the Holocaust because of the film. I can now actually hold an intelligent conversation with my "history buff" husband. That fact pleases us both. I feel it is very important for me to know about the events in history in order to help prevent recurrence. This movie also stirred my angry feelings toward those who continue to believe in a supreme race. This anger has made me stand more strongly for what I believe: racism is wrong. I feel Schindler's List brought me to a deeper understanding of what it will involve, including taking a stand and facing dangers, to defeat racism. Therefore, I believe Schindler's List definitely affected my life.

EXAMPLE (essay question answer):

- The test question says,

Choose one of the following terms. Define the term and illustrate the definition, using a work of literature that we have read in this class.

1. style 2. conflict 3. image 4. setting

- The answer says,

Margaret Dean

Introduction to Literature Mid-Term Test

1. Style is defined as a language usage technique that a writer uses to bring about a special effect. In the short story "Barbie-Q," Sandra Cisneros uses a specific style to mimic the language of a young girl talking about her dolls. She selects words that a young girl would know and use. She even chooses very specific accessories, such as "a sophisticated A-line coatdress with a Jackie Kennedy pillbox hat, white gloves, and heels included," precise words used to describe the details that a girl would want for her Barbie. The effect works because it gives the story a childish appeal. In another story by the same writer, "Eleven," she uses the same style to

depict the thoughts of a child turning eleven. The style adds attitude to the story because it is believable language. The narrator describes aging like a secret: "what they never tell you is that when you're eleven, you're also ten, and nine, and eight, and seven, and six, and five, and four, and three, and two, and one."

- Another answer says,

  Michelle Welch

  Introduction to Literature Mid-Term Test

  3. Image is a sensory experience in words, using descriptive vocabulary to produce a vivid mental picture. Coupled with imagination, language can create powerful scenes using the senses. Lawrence Ferlinghetti does this in the poem "Short Story on a Painting of Gustav Klimt." Even though the poem is based on an actual visual creation, it stands on its own because of the picture it generates. Ferlinghetti's use of the combinations "flowered bed," "tangerine lips," "languid claw," "Titian hair," and "jeweled tree" are highly efficient in stirring sensory images; one can actually see these things in the mind. Especially effective are the similes "one hand like the head of a dead swan" and "her eyes are closed like folded petals."

EXAMPLE (essay question answers):

- The test question says,

  1. Define one of the themes in *Much Ado About Nothing.*

- One answer says,

  Mike Mitchell

  1. The theme of a film is the central or controlling idea. Although the film Much Ado About Nothing has several themes, the predominate one is that reputation is desperately important. For example, Claudio is successful at displaying social grace; however, his strict adherence to social propriety enslaves him. Claudio abandons Hero at the wedding because he believes she is unfaithful. Leonardo is embarrassed as well because he thinks he matched Claudio with someone unchaste. Leonardo slaps his daughter, Hero, and she desires death when she is publicly humiliated. These events show the code of social values in the society.

- Another answer says,

  Debbie Stubblefield

  1. A theme of Much Ado About Nothing is that no matter what a person does to change things, the truth will always come out. Hero is vindicated in the end because the truth comes out that she was not the unchaste woman in the window. Also, the truth prevails because Don John, the villain, is punished in the end; evil and lies lose. And, the truth that Beatrice and Benedict love each other is also revealed in the end.

EXAMPLE (short essay in response to a prompt):

- The instructions follow:

You have fifty minutes to write this essay. Respond to one position in this statement: Students should/should not have to write research papers.

Foreman 1

Kevin Foreman

Composition II

Dr. Evans

10 Sep. 1998

Writing Research Papers

Many people do not like writing or, for that matter, spending endless hours in a library doing research, especially if that research is on a topic that is as dry as a cardboard box. But I believe writing a research paper should be a required activity in college for several reasons.

First of all, the valuable experience gained in using the library, such as experience with the computer system, the business index, the card catalog, or the Internet, gives individuals tools helpful in other parts of their daily lives. Many people are not exposed to computer systems such as a library can provide. If a person needed information he or she were not getting from a local car dealer, a library business index could provide valuable information for that person. An Internet connection might provide more information that will aid the customer.

Job-related situations may call for skills learned by doing a research paper. If a veterinarian needed up-to-date information on the treatment of exotic disease in a dog, he or she could use research skills to get information from books, periodicals, or the Internet. If a local newspaper reporter needed information on a celebrity visit to the community in order to write a feature, he or she could use the library skills to get quick and easy access to the needed information.

General exposure to the library is good for people. The necessity to write a research paper would give people great exposure to the library and its resources. They would then have the skills they needed to find information or just to check out a book for recreational reading.

Students should have to write research papers.

NOTE: The person writing this essay writes shorter and shorter paragraphs as the essay progresses. Obviously the person is running out of time. Planning ahead is vital. A one-sentence conclusion could be improved, as could the last body paragraph.

ELECTRONIC COMMUNICATION

E-mail is a communication device prevalent in the affluent twenty-first century. However, the most effective e-mail uses standard, professional "netiquette." Of course, any communication to a friend or relative can be written in the form and style preferred by the two of you. But any communication to a professor or for business purposes should follow the standard guidelines.

Follow simple rules for e-mail etiquette.

1. E-mail should be concise and clear. It should not be full of "pretties," such as colored backgrounds, pictures, and fancy font. Some servers cannot handle backgrounds and odd fonts, and, thus, your fancy communication might not reach the recipient.
2. In addition to avoiding unusual fonts, you should also avoid "smilies" or "emoticons," such as the smile :), etc. These symbols might be misinterpreted and do not look very professional or academic.
3. **Subject lines must be clear**. The recipient should know from the subject line exactly what the topic of the message is. **Do not use a subject line such as "Hello" or "Hi."** Such generic subject lines on e-mails are known to most recipients as clues that the e-mail may contain a virus.
4. The salutation may be formal, such as "Dear Professor Smith" or "Dear Dr. Beans," but you may begin the e-mail message without a salutation.
5. Be sure to **put your full name at the end of each message**. Your e-mail address and/or screen name are not usually sufficient identification for the recipient of your message. At any rate, it is only polite to identify yourself in the message.
6. Avoid using quotations (unless very short) or graphics at the end of the message.
7. The **main part of the message must be complete** enough so the recipient knows exactly what you are asking and/or answering and does not have to guess anything or try to reconstruct the previous communications.
8. The message should **use standard conventional grammar**, punctuation, capitalization, and spelling.
9. **Do not use all caps**, which is the electronic equivalent of shouting.
10. Remember that **e-mail is not private communication**: businesses, system administrators, etc., can and may access it.
11. Think about it before you send it. E-mail is so fast and efficient you may have the impulse to initiate a message or respond to one in the fire of emotion. This could be a mistake. Compose the e-mail; let it sit while you cool; consider it calmly; maybe you will want to re-compose the message. It might be wise.

THE RESEARCH PAPER

Writing a research paper is not as difficult as you may fear. If you follow some simple steps and allow yourself plenty of time, you should be successful in turning out a product of which you can be proud.

RESEARCH PAPER STEPS

Following are the steps in writing a research paper. The remainder of this section of the *Guide* is a full explanation of each step.

Simple steps make successful research writing.

1. Choose a limited topic. Remember the audience.
2. Collect a preliminary bibliography.
3. Make notes.
4. Plan the paper.
5. Write out a first draft, including necessary internal documentation and a Works Cited page.
6. Revise the draft. Type a second draft with internal documentation and a Works Cited page.
7. Correct, type, and assemble your final paper. Proofread!

STEP ONE: LIMITED TOPIC

Choose a topic and limit it so that your subject is not too broad or complex for the length of paper you are writing. Your instructor will probably give you a general subject–like Civil War generals. But in a single semester you cannot write on all the Civil War generals or even all about one Civil War general. So you must limit the subject to something you can handle within the time and space requirements–like General Pemberton's defense of Vicksburg.

STEP TWO: PRELIMINARY BIBLIOGRAPHY

After you select the topic, find out what resources are available. Research the topic by looking in the card catalog and in various indexes and bibliographies. (See **LIBRARY DISCOVERY**.) Keep track of the available resources by making "bib cards" index cards on which you keep bibliographic information for each source you find. Or use another method that works for you and keeps track of the information about sources.

Sources should be well-known magazines and/or newspapers, books and/or special references. **Do NOT use general encyclopedias**. General encyclopedias are useful to read for background information but should not be used as sources.

You may decide to search the Internet for sources, using search engines, which are programs that work with an Internet browser to locate information in the World-Wide Web. Search engines include www.altavista.digital.com, www.google.com, www.excite.com, www.lycos.com, www.metacrawler.com, www.yahoo.com, and www.netscape.com/escapes/search, among others. You might need to use more than one engine to search a subject.

Whether you find books, articles, or Internet sources, the bibliography cards (or alternate method) contain the bibliographic information you need to complete a Works Cited page. The Works Cited page contains an alphabetical list of the sources to which you have actually referred in your paper.

You may be more familiar with the term *bibliography* than with the term *Works Cited*. The bibliography is an alphabetical list of works to which you refer in your paper; it may also contain works that you researched, and that are relevant to the subject, but to which you did not actually refer in the text of your paper. A Works Cited page, not a bibliography page, is designated by the MLA (Modern Language Association) documentation style. An MLA Works Cited page includes **only** works to which you refer in the paper; MLA style is preferred by most faculty in the humanities. The APA (American Psychological Association) style requires a References page rather than a Works Cited page, but the principle is the same.

Bibliography information for the "bib cards" should be written in the format in which it will appear on the Works Cited page. (See **DOCUMENTATION**.) You may include other information that will not appear on the Works Cited page for your own convenience.

EXAMPLE (bibliography card):

You have found a magazine article by Gina Kolata called "Cannibalism: Fact or Fiction?" appearing in volume 17, number 12 of the Smithsonian magazine dated March 1987.

> Kolata, Gina. "Cannibalism: Fact or Fiction?" Smithsonian 17.12 (Mar. 1987): 150-71.

DOCUMENTATION

When gathering source information, be sure to collect all that is applicable.

For Books

1. Author(s)
2. Chapter or part of book
3. Title of the book
4. Editor, translator, or compiler
5. Edition
6. Number of volumes
7. Name of the series
8. Place, publisher, and date
9. Volume number of the book
10. Page numbers (when citing part of a book, such as citing a chapter on Plato in a book about the Greeks)

For Articles

1. Author(s)
2. Title of the article
3. Name of the periodical
4. Series number or name
5. Volume number
6. Issue number
7. Date of publication
8. Page numbers

Some of this information will not be relevant; however, if you have it all, you will not have to go back and look up anything again. You will need to examine some of the examples found in the section on **DOCUMENTATION**. These examples are not complete: there are other situations you may find in research. For a complete explanation of how to write entries, see the MLA or APA handbooks.

Remember that MLA style is not the only "style" which you can use to write a paper. You might use MLA style which requires footnotes. You might be using APA. You might be using another style entirely. The principles are the same; the differences are in format. When you are assigned a paper, you need to find out what format the instructor requires. If the instructor will not specify or says, "I don't care," then pick a style and be consistent.

DIFFERENCES IN DOCUMENTATION FORMS FOR MLA AND APA STYLES

TITLE OF SOURCE LISTING

MLA	Works Cited
APA	References

ENTRY FORMAT

MLA	indents the second and subsequent lines one-half inch
APA	indents the second and subsequent lines 5-7 spaces or ½ inch

AUTHOR'S NAME

MLA	includes first name and any middle initials
APA	uses only initials for first name and includes middle initials

ORDER OF AUTHOR'S NAMES (MORE THAN ONE AUTHOR)

MLA	reverses the order (last name, first name) for the first listed name; uses regular order (first name, last name) for subsequent names
APA	reverses the order (last name, first name initial) for all names

THE WORD AND FOR LISTING MORE THAN ONE AUTHOR

MLA	uses the word *and*
APA	uses the ampersand (&)

YEAR OF PUBLICATION

MLA	gives the year toward the end of the citation
APA	gives year in parentheses followed by a period, after author

CAPITALIZATION IN TITLES

MLA	capitalizes in accordance with capitalization rules
APA	capitalizes only the first word, a word after a colon, and proper nouns

QUOTATION MARKS FOR NAMES OF SHORT WORKS (ARTICLES, SHORT STORIES, ETC.)

MLA	uses quotation marks around the names of shorter works
APA	omits quotation marks around the names of shorter works

UNDERLINING AND ITALICS

MLA	uses underlining rather than italics to designate all items italicized in publications, such as titles of books, foreign terms, etc.
APA	uses italics for items italicized in print; does not use underlining as code for publication italics

PUBLISHER

MLA uses short forms if they are clear: Prentice for Prentice Hall, for example

APA uses the complete name but drops words such as Inc., Co., and Publishers

PUBLICATION MONTH ABBREVIATIONS

MLA abbreviates all months except May, June, July by using the first three letters followed by a period

APA does NOT abbreviate months

INCLUSIVE PAGE NUMBERS

Inclusive page numbers give the starting page number and the ending page number of a cited work, such as one article in a journal or one chapter in a book. Using inclusive page numbers signals that the cited work is on those pages and all pages in between. If that is not the case, use the style shown below for discontinuous pages.

MLA uses the full number through 99, then uses only the last two digits unless confusion would result: 101-09 is clear, but full numbers are needed for 897-910.

APA uses complete numbers

DISCONTINUOUS NUMBERS

MLA uses the starting page number followed by a plus sign (+): 44+

APA lists all pages, with discontinuous numbers set off by commas: 43-44, 47-49, 54-66, 76

- **NOTE:** In the following pages, you will find examples of both MLA and APA documentation. Be sure that you are using the correct format for the assignment you are given. Also remember you may have to look at more than one example in order to find the necessary information. For example, you might have to look at both "article in a magazine, signed" and "newspaper" to find how to do the entry you are working on.

SAMPLE MLA DOCUMENTATION EXAMPLES

BOOK with one author.

Dickens, Charles. Great Expectations. New York: Rinehart, 1948.

BOOK with two authors.

Biddle, Arthur W., and Kenneth M. Holland. Writer's Guide: Political Science. Lexington: Heath, 1987.

BOOK with three authors.

Frye, Northrup, Sheridan Baker, and George Perkins. The Harper Handbook to Literature. New York: Harper, 1985.

BOOK with more than three authors.
BOOK with an edition after the first.
BOOK with several volumes.
BOOK with several volumes, one of the volumes.

Blair, Walter, et al. The Literature of the United States. 3rd ed. Vol. 2. Glenview: Scott, Foresman, 1969. 3 vols.

BOOKS by the same author.
BOOKS with date of publication unknown.

Dickens, Charles. The Old Curiosity Shop. Garden City: International Collectors, 1953.

---. Oliver Twist. Garden City: International Collectors, 1953.

BOOK translated by another writer.
BOOK edited by another writer.
BOOK reprinted.

Gogol, Nicolai. Dead Souls. 1842. Trans. George Reavey. Ed. George Gibian. New York: Norton, 1971.

BOOK edited by another writer (citing material written by the editor).

Gibian, George, ed. Dead Souls. By Nicolai Gogol. 1842. Trans. George Reavey. New York: Norton, 1971.

REFERENCE BOOK/ENCYCLOPEDIA/DICTIONARY, entries in alphabetical order.
(Give entry author, if known.)

"Raze." Oxford American Dictionary. 16th ed. 1980.

ANTHOLOGY/REFERENCE BOOK with an editor (citing material written by editor).

Kennedy, X. J., and Dorothy M. Kennedy, ed. The Bedford Reader. 2nd ed. New York: St. Martin's, 1985.

ARTICLE (or SHORT STORY) reprinted in an anthology (citing the author).
ARTICLE appearing on more than one page, paginated in the hundreds.

Vidal, Gore. "Drugs." The Bedford Reader. 2nd ed. Ed. X. J. Kennedy and Dorothy M. Kennedy. New York: St. Martin's, 1985. 382-84.

TWO OR MORE ARTICLES reprinted in an anthology.

Baldwin, Gail. "The Hard Sell." Goshgarian 159-64.

Goshgarian, Gary, ed. The Contemporary Reader. 5th ed. New York: HarperCollins, 1996.

Persky, Bill. "Conan and Me." Goshgarian 259-61.

ARTICLE from a collection of reprinted articles.

Smythe, George. "Not in My Backyard—Nor Anyone Else's." In Social Issues Resources Series. Privacy. Vol. 3. Article 14. Boca Raton, FL: Social Issues Resources Series, 2002. 7-13.

ARTICLE in a magazine/journal, signed.
ARTICLE with part of the title in quotation marks.
ARTICLE in a magazine/journal with volume and issue number.
ARTICLE appearing on only one page.

- ***NOTE:*** *In citing dates, abbreviate the names of months except for May, June, and July.*

Wolkomir, Richard. "For the 'Tied Up' Businessman." Smithsonian 17.12 (Mar. 1987): 192.

ARTICLE in a magazine/journal with no volume number.
ARTICLE appearing on more than one page, inclusive pages.
ARTICLE from a magazine/journal published bi-monthly.

Fautin, Daphne Gail. "The Anemone Is Not Its Enemy." National Wildlife Oct.-Nov. 1987: 22-25.

ARTICLE unsigned.
ARTICLE appearing on more than one page, discontinuous pages.

"Saving Time." NewsMag 18 Apr. 1997: 70-76+.

ARTICLE, signed, in a daily NEWSPAPER.

McUsic, Teresa. "Stillwater Designer Followed Her Nose." Tulsa World 8 Mar. 1987, late ed.: G1.

EDITORIAL and LETTER in a daily NEWSPAPER.

"Campus Unrest." Editorial. University Times 14 May 1996: B6.

Davis, Marion. Letter. University Times 15 May 1996: B8.

BIBLE.

Today's English Version Good News Bible. New York: American Bible Society, 1976.

FILM.

Witness for the Prosecution. Dir. Billy Wilder. Perf. Tyrone Power, Marlene Dietrich, and Charles Laughton. MGM/United Artists, 1957.

TELEVISION PROGRAM.

"The Grizzly." National Geographic Special. PBS. KXON, Tulsa. 9 Mar. 1987.

RECORDING.

Holiday, Billie. "God Bless the Child." Rec. 9 May 1941. Billie Holiday: The Golden Years. Columbia, 1962.

INTERVIEW.

Martin, Dr. Richard. Personal interview. 5 Mar. 1993.

Docmanter, Eric. Interview. "In the Name of Unity." Spotright. UBS. KMIX, Cowinka. 31 Oct. 1996.

PAMPHLET with author credited.

- ***NOTE:*** *If no author is given, begin the entry with the title of the pamphlet.*

Drury, Matt. Ant Farms. Altus: Sheffield Press, 1987.

PAMPHLET or GOVERNMENT PUBLICATION.

United States. Dept. of Transportation. National Highway Traffic Safety Admin. Driver Licensing Laws Annotated 1980. Washington: GPO, 1980.

UNITED STATES CODE/FAMILIAR HISTORICAL DOCUMENTS.

These items are not listed on the works cited page; they are, however, cited parenthetically in the text.

PERFORMANCE.

• ***NOTE****: If, in your paper, you refer to one performer, author, etc., then you would begin the citation with that name, as in the following:*

Aldridge, Joyce Spivey, dir. Dracula. By Hamilton Dean and. . . .

• ***NOTE****: If referring to the performance as a whole, the entry would read as follows:*

Dracula. By Hamilton Dean and John Balderston. Based on Bram Stoker's Dracula. Dir. Joyce Spivey Aldridge. Rogers State College, Claremore. 23 Oct. 1987.

LECTURE.

Lurz, Diana. "The Goths and the Vandals." Humanities Image Forum. Rogers State University, Claremore. 16 June 1998.

LETTER/E-MAIL.

• ***NOTE****: If the letter is directly accessible, use the following format. If it is reprinted in another work, use the longer format below.*

Driver, Jeana. "1996 Senior Class." E-mail to E.R. Cagill. 27 May 1996.

CD-ROM, DISK, or MAGNETIC TAPE.

Recomp, Erica. "Computers and Film Focuses." Little University News 15 Aug. 1996: E6. University Newspapers On-disc. CD-ROM. New York: UPI-UP, Sep. 1996.

ON-LINE SOURCES.

• ***NOTE****: The format for on-line sources follows this model, using as much information as available:*

Author's last name, First name Middle initial. "Title of Short Piece or Document." ***Print Publication Data, using guidelines for print.*** *Site Title. Name of Editor. Version Number. Publication date or date of last revision. Name of Sponsoring Institution or Organization. Date of access <URL>.*

ON-LINE NEWSPAPER/PERIODICAL.

Recomp, Erica. "Computers and Film Focuses." Little University News 15 Aug. 1996: E6. Milling University. 1 Sept. 2002 <http://www.millingu.edu/univnews/>.

James, Wilfred. "Emark, the Published Text." English Eclectic 13.13 (8 July 1996). Milling University. 17 Aug. 1996 <http://www.millingu.edu>.

WEB SITE with credited author.

Driver, Jeana. Meteorology Pictures. 2001. Oklahoma School of Science and Mathematics. 1 May 2005 <http://www.ossm.edu>.

WEB SITE with no credited author.

The Romanov Conspiracy. 1 Jan. 2002. 16 Mar. 2004 <http://www.conspire.org/romanov>.

LIBRARY SUBSCRIPTION SERVICE.

Merrick, John. "GTO's and Other Hot Rods." Hot Rod Magazine Spring 2004: 61. Academic Search Premier. EBSCO. Rogers State University, Stratton Taylor Library. 4 May 2004 <http://www.epnet.com/>.

SAMPLE APA DOCUMENTATION EXAMPLES

BOOK with one author.

Dickens, C. (1948). *Great expectations*. New York: Rinehart.

BOOK with two authors.

Biddle, A. W., & Holland, K. M. (1987). *Writer's guide: Political science*. Lexington: Heath.

BOOK with three authors.

Frye, N., Baker, S., & Perkins, G. (1985). *The Harper handbook to literature*. New York: Harper.

BOOK with more than seven authors.
BOOK with an edition after the first.
BOOK with several volumes.
BOOK with several volumes, one of the volumes.

Blain, J., Blair, K., Davis, L., Walter, M., Smyne, H., Former, G., et al. (1996). *The life of Rexan*: Vol.2. *An anthology* (3rd ed.). (Vol. 2). Bloominton, IN: Exra University.

BOOKS by the same author.

Dickens, C. (1952a). *The old curiosity shop*. Garden Center: Collectors.

Dickens, C. (1952b). *Oliver Twist*. Garden Center: Collectors.

BOOK translated by another writer.

BOOK edited by another writer.

BOOK reprinted.

Gogol, N. (1971). *Dead souls* (G. Reavey, Trans.). G. Gibian (Ed.). New York: Norton. (Original work published 1842)

REFERENCE BOOK/ENCYCLOPEDIA/DICTIONARY.

The new dialect encyclopedia (2nd ed.). (2004). Marietta, OH: Maze.

ANTHOLOGY/REFERENCE BOOK with an editor.

Kennedy, X. J., & Kennedy, D. M. (Eds.). (1985). *The Bedford reader* (2nd ed.). New York: St. Martin's.

ARTICLE (or SHORT STORY) reprinted in an anthology.

ARTICLE appearing on more than one page, paginated in the hundreds.

Vidal, G. (1985). Drugs. In X. J. Kennedy & D. M. Kennedy (Eds.), *The Bedford reader* (2nd ed., pp. 382-384). New York: St. Martin's.

ARTICLE from a collection of reprinted articles.

Snark, M. (2002). More nasty stuff around than ever: Theory and practice. In H. H. Mandel (Series Ed.) & Q. E. Dee (Vol. Ed.), *Resources for a dying planet: Vol. 3. Dumping* (3rd ed., pp. 33-36). Nearl, FL: Wimple.

ARTICLE in a magazine/journal, signed.

ARTICLE with part of the title in quotation marks.

ARTICLE in a magazine/journal with volume and issue number.

ARTICLE appearing on only one page.

Wolkomir, R. (1987, March). For the "tied up" businessman. *Smithsonian 17*(12), 192.

ARTICLE in a magazine/journal with no volume number.
ARTICLE appearing on more than one page, inclusive pages.
ARTICLE from a magazine/journal published bi-monthly.

Fautin, D. G. (1987, October-November). The anemone is not its enemy. *National wildlife,* 22-25.

ARTICLE, unsigned, in a newspaper.
ARTICLE appearing on more than one page, discontinuous pages.

Saving time. (1997, April 18). *Newsmag,* pp. 70-76, 89, 91, 94.

ARTICLE, signed, in a daily NEWSPAPER.

McUsic, T. (1987, March 8). Stillwater designer followed her nose. *Tulsa world,* p. G1.

FILM.

Wilder, B. (Director). (1957). *Witness for the prosecution* [Motion picture]. United States: United Artists.

TELEVISION PROGRAM.

Cristobal, P. (Writer), & Forcer, F. (Director). (2002, May 11). Moving [Television series episode] In C. Sansobal (Producer), *Time of despair.* Los Angeles: Backyard.

PAMPHLET with corporate author credited.

Center for Abundant Life. (2004). *Living on yoga* (6th ed.) [Brochure]. Altus. OK: Sheffield Press.

GOVERNMENT PUBLICATION.

- ***NOTE:*** *When the authoring agency prints the publication, use the word "Author" in place of the publisher's name.*

United States Department of Transportation. (1980). *Driver licensing laws annotated 1980* (NHTSA Publication No. 55-5). Washington, DC: author.

ON-LINE SOURCES.

• ***NOTE:*** *The format for on-line sources follows this mode. Note that, if the source is originally a print source, you will not use the retrieval date or URL, but you will use the words "Electronic version" in brackets.*

Author's last name, First initial. Middle initial. (Publication date). Title of document [Electronic version]. <u>Title of complete work</u>. Retrieved Month day, year, from URL

ON-LINE NEWSPAPER/PERIODICAL BASED ON PRINT SOURCE.

Recomp, E. (1996, August 15). Computers and film focuses [Electronic version]. *Little university news* *17*, 17-25.

ON-LINE ONLY PERIODICAL.

Garth, B., & Remington, W.R. (2004, March 6). Referring to references. *Journal of on-line data*, *6*, 18- 32. Retrieved May 30, 2004, from http://source.data.stuff.htm

WEB SITES.

Meteorology pictures. (n.d.) Retrieved June 17, 2004, from http://www.ucco.edu/stud/met/99

LIBRARY SUBSCRIPTION SERVICE.

Merrick, J. (2004, Spring). GTO's and other hot rods. *Hot rod magazine*, 61. Retrieved May 4, 2004, from Academic Search Premier database.

Be picky about documentation details.
Those details are important.

STEP THREE: NOTES

After finding out what is available in the way of resources, investigate those resources for applicability and usefulness. Look at each of the resources and cull them. Some will not be especially useful, and you will discard these. Others will be relevant, and you will take notes on information to use in your paper.

ASSESSING SOURCES

You should always assess the value of the sources you find. If you follow the principles in "Reading for Content and Reading for Writing," you can decide if the text of sources you read is plausible. Assessing Internet sources is more difficult.

Generally you can expect that the sources available in data bases from the university library, such as FirstSearch and in InfoTrac, are credible. However, you may not be able to expect that other sources you find on the Internet are credible. Some people tend to think that whatever is in print or on television is true. Since you know that "everything" cannot be true, you will need to evaluate the sites you find.

Print periodicals and books have generally been through an editorial process in which at least one other, and sometimes an entire board of people, has agreed that the information to be printed is trustworthy. Even these sources may be slanted, depending on the editorial stance of the editor(s) and publishers. You have to determine how credible all sources are. For example, if the publication is printed by a company which owns a chemical processing plant and the article you see asserts that chemicals in the environment have never been proved to show harm, you might question the impartiality of the article.

Internet sources do not generally go through editorial process. Anyone can publish on the Internet, which means you need to spend even more effort determining the value of web pages. You need to be aware of the web address. A <.com> address, means a commercial site, posted by a commercial interest. If the address is an <.org> address, the site belongs to an organization. If the address is an <.edu> address, the site was posted under the aegis of an educational institution, either by the administration and/or faculty or by a student or students at that institution, which does not necessarily mean that the institution approves all of the site information.

When evaluating a site, look for the following items:

- **author** with his/her/their credentials and contact information: if you cannot attribute the information to a source, the information is not useful.
- **date(s)** the site was posted and/or updated: without a date, you cannot consider the site a resource.
- **clear citations:** an on-line source must be held to the same standards as a print source. If the site does not give references on which the writer based his/her conclusions, the site is not holding to the standards of scholarship.

Evaluate sources carefully.

- **language:** poor grammar and spelling are clues that the site is not posted by a careful, reputable scholar. In addition, you can sometimes distinguish "slanted" sites by language, which may call names or appeal to prejudices or convey stereotypes.
- **site associations:** a site belonging to a company, offering products for sale, or associated with a movement (political, social, or religious) may have an agenda. At the very least you should look carefully at the information for validity and confirm it with other, non-affiliated sites.
- **appearance:** if the site is so visually distracting that the information is difficult to perceive, this may not be an accident.
- **verifiability:** a site that takes a stance that is not taken by other reputable scholars may be questionable.

These points are only guides for you to use. Experience will lead you to your own conclusions. Ultimately it is your decision what sources to use in your work since you are responsible for what appears in your paper.

PLAGIARISM

Be sure that you avoid plagiarism. Plagiarism is unacknowledged use of someone else's words or ideas. To avoid plagiarism:

- NEVER copy word for word without quotation marks and without mentioning the author's name.
- NEVER copy key words or phrases without quotation marks and without mentioning the author's name.
- NEVER paraphrase, summarize, or otherwise borrow an idea that belongs to a specific author without mentioning that author's name.
- To be safe, introduce the quotation or paraphrase by using the source's name.
- ALWAYS document each and every quotation, paraphrase, or idea originating from a source other than yourself.
- ALWAYS put quotation marks around ALL quoted material.
- ALWAYS include a Works Cited/References entry for each source used in your paper.

You do not need to document items that are common knowledge. Common knowledge is knowledge that almost all fairly educated people at your level would know.

EXAMPLES (plagiarism and avoidance measures):

Chip Rogers
Guide to College Writing

Plagiarism Issues

What Is Plagiarism?
Generally, plagiarism is presenting as your own the work of someone else without properly acknowledging the source or sources; plagiarism is submitting material from a source without attributing the source. When ideas or information are common knowledge (and there is very little of this), you do not need to acknowledge sources.

Why Do We Need to Know About Using Sources?
Integrating the words and ideas of others into your own work is an important feature of academic expression.

How Can We Avoid Plagiarism?
But plagiarism occurs whenever we incorporate the intellectual property of others into our own work without proper acknowledgement of whose words, ideas, or other original material we are bringing into our work, either with quotation marks and direct mention of the source or through other means of clear and precise acknowledgement.

Plagiarism can, of course, be a purely intentional attempt at deceit, but whether or not there is conscious intent to deceive, plagiarism occurs any time you do not give proper acknowledgement of others' contributions to your work. Ignorance of the responsibility of acknowledging sources is not a legitimate defense against a charge of plagiarism, any more than not knowing the speed limit on a given road makes a person stopped for speeding less at fault. Since the consequences of being charged with plagiarism are serious, you must pay attention to the following definition of plagiarism to ensure your more precise understanding of what constitutes plagiarism, intentional or unintentional.

1. **It is plagiarism to copy another's words directly and present them as your own without quotation marks and direct indication of whose words you are copying. All significant phrases, clauses, and passages copied from another source require quotation marks and proper acknowledgement, down to the page number(s) of printed texts.***

   Source material from the "Notice" to Mark Twain's Adventures of Huckleberry Finn: "Persons attempting to find a motive in this narrative will be prosecuted; persons attempting to find a moral in it will be banished; persons attempting to find a plot in it will be shot."

Plagiarized: Surely it is an exaggeration to say that persons attempting to find a moral in Huckleberry Finn will be banished and persons attempting to find a plot in it will be shot.

Proper acknowledgement of source: Perhaps the author is exaggerating when he says that "persons attempting to find a moral" in his novel "will be banished" and "persons attempting to find a plot in it will be shot" (Twain 3).

Note that even brief clauses and phrases copied from source material require quotation marks. Also note that acknowledging the source without putting the quoted words in quotation marks is still plagiarism: put all quoted words in quotation marks.

2. **It is plagiarism to paraphrase another writer's work by altering some words but communicating the same essential point(s) made by the original author without proper acknowledgment. Though quotation marks are not needed with paraphrasing, you must still acknowledge the original source directly.**

Source material from Adolph Hitler by John Tolland: "Ignored by the West, the Soviet Union once more looked to Germany. Early in 1939 it accepted a Hitler overture to discuss a new trade treaty by inviting one of Ribbentrop's aides to Moscow; and a few days later Stalin gave credence to a sensational story in the London News Chronicle that he was signing a non-aggression pact with the Nazis" (721).

Plagiarized: When Western nations continued to shun the Soviet Union, the Russians drew closer to Germany, meeting with a senior Nazi official in Moscow to arrange a trade agreement in early 1939. Shortly after, Stalin admitted his intent to sign a pact of non-aggression with Germany.

Proper acknowledgement of source: In Adolph Hitler, John Tolland notes that when Western nations shuned the Soviet Union, the Russians drew closer to Germany, meeting with a senior Nazi official in Moscow to arrange a trade agreement in early 1939. Shortly after, Stalin admitted his intent to sign a non-aggression pact with Germany (721).

3. **Plagiarism includes presenting someone else's ideas or factual discoveries as your own. If you follow another person's general outline or approach to a topic, presenting another's original thinking or specific conclusions as your own, you must cite the source even if your work is in your own words entirely. When you present another's statistics, definitions, or statements of fact in your own work, you must also cite the source.**

Example 1: Say that you read Paul Goodman's "A Proposal to Abolish Grading," in which he claims that an emphasis on grades results in students' caring more about grades than learning subject matter, causing them to have a bad attitude when their grades are low and sometimes even leading them to cheating. In order to make these same essential points in your own work without plagiarizing—even if your development of these ideas differs markedly from Goodman's in examples and order of presentation—you must still acknowledge Goodman as the basis for your approach to the topic.

Plagiarized: Abolishing grades at the college level would allow students to focus on subject matter instead of grades, it would prevent students from getting a bad attitude towards a class when they receive low grades, and it would virtually eliminate the temptation to cheat or plagiarize.

Proper acknowledgement of source: As Paul Goodman argues in "A Proposal to Abolish Grading," doing away with grades would allow students to focus on subject matter instead of grades, it would prevent students from getting a bad attitude towards a class when they receive low grades, and it would virtually eliminate the temptation to cheat or plagiarize.

Example 2: If you found a source indicating that Americans consume more beer on Friday than on any other day of the week, to make this claim in your work you must cite the source to avoid plagiarism. If the source indicated that American beer-drinking on Fridays accounts for 21% of the whole week's total consumption, mentioning this statistic, or even approximating it, requires acknowledgement of the source.

Plagiarized: Americans consume more beer on Fridays than on any other day of the week.
Proper acknowledgement of source: Americans consume more beer on Fridays than on any other day of the week (Cox 31).

Plagiarized: Beer consumption on Fridays accounts for more than 20% of total U.S. consumption throughout the week.
Proper acknowledgement of source: Beer consumption on Fridays accounts for more than 20% of total U.S. consumption throughout the week (Cox 31).

4. Plagiarism includes allowing someone else to prepare work that you present as your own.

Allowing a friend, parent, tutor, or anyone else to compose any portion of work you present as your own is plagiarism. Note that plagiarism includes copying, downloading, or purchasing an essay or any other material in part or in whole via the Internet. Note also that plagiarism includes using online "translator programs" in foreign language classes.

5. **Plagiarism applies in other media besides traditional written texts, including, but not limited to, oral presentations, graphs, charts, diagrams, artwork, video and audio compositions, and other electronic media such as web pages, PowerPoint presentations, and postings to online discussions.**

Conclusion:

- If you are uncertain about any portion or aspect of this definition of plagiarism, ask your instructor to clarify or explain immediately. If at any point later in the semester you have questions about potential plagiarism issues, talk to your instructor about them before submitting the work in question.
- Students who plagiarize often feel pressured into submitting plagiarized work because they have either struggled with the assignment or waited until the last minute to get the work under way. You will always be better served discussing your situation with your instructor, however grim it seems, rather than submitting any work that is not entirely your own.

*The examples of proper acknowledgement of sources above follow the MLA (Modern Language Association) conventions for in-text parenthetical citation used in English classes and many other courses in the humanities. The parenthetical references point the reader to a list of "Works Cited" at the end of an essay. Other courses and disciplines may follow different conventions, such as footnotes, endnotes, or a variety of other methods of documentation (APA, Chicago Style, etc.).

Now that you know about plagiarism, you can feel free to add quotations to your notes. You may take notes on note cards or use another method of keeping notes. No matter what system you use, you will use the same principles: search out material and put the relevant material into a form that can be used in the paper.

There are four points to remember in making note cards:

1. When writing a paper requiring many notes, each note should have a heading that identifies the specific subject that the notes cover. Keep the notes arranged by topic.
2. These items should also appear in the heading:
   (1) the author's name (at least the last)
   (2) the title of the book or article (if you have multiple sources from an author)
   (3) the page number of the information.
   If you do not know who wrote the information and where it comes from, the information will be of no use to you when you write your paper.
3. In using direct quotations, find the sentences or phrases to best convey the idea you want to use and quote the author word for word. Delete irrelevant information by using the ellipsis (see **ELLIPSIS**).

4. Distinguish your notes from the author's words by using quotation marks around any quoted material.

Remember: There are three things that must be on each note–author, page, a way to distinguish noted from quoted.

EXAMPLE (note card):

Cravotta 20 Java on Internet

Java works as a virtual machine

"Java has security and authentication features, so users don't have to worry about letting strange programs into their computer from the Internet without testing them for viruses or other harmful processes. 'A thing called a verifier examines your program, and it does a certain amount of testing to see whether it plays by the rules,' says Gosling."

ANNOTATED BIBLIOGRAPHY

Sometimes you may need to include an annotated bibliography with your paper. An annotated bibliography is nothing more than a combination of notes and works cited entries. When you have determined exactly which sources you will use in your paper, you will create the equivalent of a works cited list and then add to it a summary of what each work is about.

EXAMPLE (annotated bibliography):

Lusk 1

Winn Lusk
Dr. Element
PHIL 1113
15 June 1996

Annotated Bibliography

Adams, Ansel. Ansel Adams: An Autobiography. Boston: Little, Brown, 1985. From this work, I developed the impression that Adams was a caring but complex person. He also happened to be a persistent person. When he became excited by an idea, he would pursue the notion until he acquired complete satisfaction.

Adams, Ansel. Ansel Adams: Letters and Images, 1916-1984. Boston: Little, Brown, 1988. This work deals with Adams's life from the age of fourteen. It contains some of his articles and letters about pure photography that caused controversy among photographers.

Alinder, James. Ansel Adams: Classic Images. Boston: Little, Brown, 1986. Many of Adams' photographs appear in Ansel Adams: Classic Images. The editors wrote story-lines and added them to the photos in order to help get across the emotions contained in the photos.

Ansel Adams: Photographer. Pacific Arts Video, 1994. This biography opens with scenery from Yosemite National Park. Adams narrates his biography and discusses what shaped his photographic profession. He discusses the beauty of nature and how he likes to preserve that image with photos. He even talks about conservation.

Newhall, Nancy. Ansel Adams I: The Eloquent Light. San Francisco: Sierra Club, 1963. Newhall puts together a brief history of Adams, complete with several photographs. Newhall collaborated with Adams for several books. Both are members of the Sierra Club and Newhall conveys the message of conservation. She shows how Adams's photography helped sway the public to more positive thinking about conservation.

STEP FOUR: PLAN AND OUTLINE

Now that you know what information is available and what you can use in your paper, plan your paper. Consider audience, purpose, logic, structure, and support. With all these things in mind, prepare a general outline to follow when writing your paper. (See **ORGANIZATION PLAN** and **OUTLINE.**) Structure your paper so that each point can be well developed and presented. The outline need not be too detailed. It is for you to use so that you stick to your subject and do not stray into unnecessary or ill-supported areas.

STEP FIVE: FIRST DRAFT

Collect and organize all your information. Compose a first draft of your paper, either writing neatly and legibly or typing. It is probably best to skip lines so that you will have space to revise. Be sure to include all the necessary internal documentation. (See **DOCUMENTATION.**)

USING QUOTATIONS IN THE PAPER

If you take care not to be guilty of plagiarism, you need not fear using quotations to support or to give examples about what you have said in your paper. Quotations are easy to handle if you use the following simple guidelines.

- If you are quoting, you must quote **EXACTLY**. That is what quoting means. The exact words of the author are reproduced in your paper (in quotation marks, of course).
- Quotations are incorporated into the text of the paper. You must introduce the quotation in some way with your own words. The quotation does not stand alone.

EXAMPLE (using quotations):

- The periodical which contains the information you need is *Carnegie Mellon Magazine*. In it you find the following passage written by Cravotta about Java programming language:
  Java has security and authentication features, so users don't have to worry about letting strange programs into their computer from the Internet without testing them for viruses or other harmful processes. "A thing called a verifier examines your program, and it does a certain amount of testing to see whether it plays by the rules," says Gosling.

- You decide to use part of this passage in your paper. You write the following in your own words and include a quotation:

One source says that Java, a programming language, "has security and authentication features, so users don't have to worry about letting strange programs into their computer from the Internet without testing them for viruses or other harmful processes. 'A thing called a verifier examines your program, and it does a certain amount of testing to see whether it plays by the rules,' says Gosling" (qtd. in Cravotta 20).

- **NOTE**: As you can see, the quotation is made part of what the paper is about. It does not function on its own without the support of your words to explain its relationship to what you have written elsewhere.

USING QUOTES IN THE PAPER: MLA INTERNAL DOCUMENTATION

You should know now that you must give credit every time you use words, phrases, sentences, or ideas from someone else. (See **PLAGIARISM**.) When using the MLA format, do one of the following things each time you borrow words, information, or ideas from someone else.

1. Cite in parentheses the information the reader needs in order to find the complete entry in the list of works cited.

   OR

2. Cite part of this information in the text and part in parentheses at the end of the passage. (It is possible to cite all the information in the text but it can be exceedingly awkward.)

EXAMPLE (MLA citations):

MLA Internal Documentation for Printed Material

- Suppose you were quoting from a book, A Handbook to Literature (third edition), written by C. Hugh Holman and published in 1972 in New York by Bobbs-Merrill Company, Inc. Information about Holman's book would appear on the Works Cited page in your paper like this:

Works Cited

Holman, C. Hugh. A Handbook to Literature. 3rd ed. New York: Bobbs-Merrill, 1972.

- If this were the only work by Holman listed on the Works Cited page, the only information you would need to include when citing it in your text would be the author's last name and the page number on which the quotation appears:

1. Author and page number cited in parentheses:
   One authority on literature has observed that a "characteristic quality of this Amerind language is its building of many ideas into one term" (Holman 18).
2. Author cited in text and page reference noted in parentheses:
   Holman has observed that a "characteristic quality of this Amerind language is its building of many ideas into one term" (18).

- What if more than one work by this author were listed on the Works Cited page? Then you would need to cite a full or an abbreviated title as well as the author's name and the page number in the text so that the reader would know to which work you were referring. With the addition of this information, the Works Cited page and the parenthetical reference would look like this:

Works Cited

Holman, C. Hugh. Dictionary of Literacy. New York: Kellman, 1987.

---. A Handbook to Literature. 3rd ed. New York: Bobbs-Merrill, 1972.

- Then the text of your paper would say,
  One authority on literature has observed that a "characteristic quality of this Amerind language is its building of many ideas into one term" (Holman, A Handbook 18).

  • OR

  Holman has observed that a "characteristic quality of this Amerind language is its building of many ideas into one term" (A Handbook 18).

Source Inside a Source

- If you have a source which quotes or cites another source, use the following format:
  Gosling maintains that Java checks websites for rule use (qtd. in Cravotta 20).

MLA Internal Documentation for Web Sites

- If you use an Internet source with no credited author or sub-pages, you would use the title of the web page. Web pages seldom have page numbers so you would not have a page number. The Works Cited and parenthetical reference would resemble the entry below. (Scholarly sources usually cite an author; if the page has no author, rethink your decision to use the source. There are exceptions: government and organization sites, such as the NIMH and Red Cross, do not usually credit authors, and they are acceptable and credible.)

Works Cited

The Romanov Conspiracy. 1 Jan. 2002. 16 Mar. 2004 <http://www.conspire.org/romanov>.

- Then the text of your paper would say,
  One site maintains that theories about the Romanov family continue today (Romanov).

Further examples of internal/parenthetical documentation of web pages follow:

Robin Pryor Murphy
Guide to College Writing

- In MLA, when using a website which does not have a credited author, place the name of the website in the phrase introducing the quoted, paraphrased, summarized, or mentioned material OR in the parentheses at the end of the sourced material.

  The title of the site is dogallergies.com. The title of the page is "Top Ten Foods to Avoid."

1. Web page cited in text:
In "Top Ten Foods to Avoid," John Smith, veterinarian, "suggests food with no corn products for dogs prone to allergies."

2. Web page cited in parentheses:
On a page about dog allergies, John Smith, a ten-year veterinarian, "suggests food with no corn products for dogs prone to allergies" ("Top Ten").

- When you summarize or paraphrase information from a website, you MUST refer to the website in the connecting phrase or parentheses. Failure to acknowledge the source of the material is considered plagiarism.

In addition, according to "Susceptible Breeds," Smith suggests watching a breed like the Dalmatian for excessive itching and a pink undertone to the skin.

NOTE: Use only the page in the introductory or connecting phrase or parentheses here, not the URL that would link to the exact page. Use the full URL on the Works Cited Page (see below) except when it is inconveniently long; in which case, use a truncated version.

- A Works Cited page for these two sources would look like this:

Works Cited

"Susceptible Breeds." Dogallergies.com. 12 Mar. 2005. 30 May 2005 <http://www.dogallergies.com/susceptiblebreeds/html>.

"Top Ten Foods to Avoid." Dogallergies.com. 12 Mar. 2005. 30 May 2005 <http://www.dogallergies.com/toptenfoods/html>.

- **NOTE**: On the Works Cited page above, the title of the subsidiary web page is in quotation marks, and the main website is underlined. The first date shown is the last day the website was updated. The next date is the date you accessed the website. The last part of the entry is the exact URL that will take the reader to the specific webpage used.

- **NOTE**: When citing material that was originally print and that is accessed from a database, remember two things:
  1. The URL in the Works Cited is the URL of the search page, as <http:/www.epnet.com>.
  2. The internal/parenthetical citations are identical to the citations you would use if you had accessed the work from a print source.

CITING LITERARY TEXTS

A knowledge of the methods in this section will enable you to document most types of sources, but there are also some special literary cases of which you should be aware.

When citing a literary work either in the text (internal documentation) or on the Works Cited page, follow the conventions for each genre. (See the *MLA Handbook* for details.)

- For poems use line numbers rather than page numbers
- For plays give act and scene rather than pages. Use Arabic numbers.

EXAMPLE (citing literary works, MLA format):

Paradise Lost begins with a call to the poet's Muse to "assert eternal providence, / And justify the ways of God to men" (Milton 1.25-26). Iago makes an ironic statement when he says, "He that filches from me my good name / Robs me of that which enriches not him / And makes me poor indeed" (Shakespeare, Othello 3.2.159-61).

- **NOTE**: The *1* following the author's name is the number of the book from which the quote comes, not an abbreviation for line. When quoting lines of poetry, insert a slash (/), with a space on each side, at the end of each line.

A paradox can be as simple as "the last shall be first, and the first last" (King James Bible, Matt. 10.16).

- **NOTE**: When you quote a religious work, give version (which should be underlined), book, chapter, and verse.

After writing your paper, use the bibliography information to compile a Works Cited page. (See **DOCUMENTATION** and **MANUSCRIPT PREPARATION**.) The entries on the Works Cited page should be double-spaced, as should the space between entries.

SPECIAL PUNCTUATION FOR QUOTATIONS BRACKETS AND ELLIPSIS

When you are quoting from a source, sometimes you need to use special punctuation to make the sentences read clearly or to clarify a point. One of these special punctuation marks is brackets. Brackets are punctuation that enclose information inserted within a quotation.

EXAMPLE (use of brackets in a quotation):

- Although it is not strictly necessary, you might have inserted the word downloaded in the passage to make the sentence easier to understand:

Java "has security and authentication features, so users don't have to worry about letting strange programs into their computer from the Internet without testing them for viruses or other harmful processes. 'A thing called a verifier examines your [downloaded] program, and it does a certain amount of testing to see whether it plays by the rules,' says Gosling" (Cravotta 20).

Brackets serve to help you when you run into a problem in exact quoting. The absolute rule is to quote **exactly** as it appears in the text. What if there is an error of some kind in the text? Can you fix it? No, you must quote exactly. Will the instructor assume it is your error or mistake and count off for this? Yes, probably. Is this Catch 22? No. The way to solve this problem is through a special use of brackets and of one Latin word, *sic*, which means "as it stands." Using *sic* means that you have quoted the text exactly "as it stands," since there is nothing else you can do, and you recognize the error or problem. Using *sic* lets the reader know that you found the error; you are no longer responsible.

EXAMPLE (use of brackets and *sic*):

- Suppose the text reads, "Columbus descovered America in 1492." You must quote this exactly; but, to avoid being charged with a spelling error, you do it this way:

According to G. Wrong, "Columbus descovered [sic] America in 1492" (72).

- Voilà!

Another special kind of punctuation is the ellipsis mark—punctuation that allows writers to eliminate inessential words or sentences. The ellipsis is a clue to the reader that the quote has been altered. For example, you might not need to quote transitional words, parenthetical expressions, repeated words, or sentences that amplify a previous statement. The ellipsis does not mean you can change the intent of the author in your writing. It does mean that you can smooth out your text or omit repetitious words that are unnecessary to what you are saying.

When you delete part of a quoted passage, use an ellipsis. The ellipsis is three spaced periods if you omit only part of a sentence. If you omit one sentence or more, use four periods (three for the ellipsis and one for terminal punctuation). (See **ELLIPSIS** in **PUNCTUATION**.)

If an author uses an ellipsis in his/her text, you must differentiate between the author's ellipsis and the one you are using to show a deletion by putting brackets around the ellipsis you add. Leave no space between the bracket and the initial and final period but do space before the second and third period. If the author does not use ellipses, you do not add brackets around the ellipsis you add.

EXAMPLE (use of ellipsis):

PART I

- Perhaps in your paper you might want to quote only part of the section in Carnegie Mellon Magazine. You might have the following as a passage in your text:

  Java, a programming language, "has security . . . so users don't have to worry about letting strange programs into their computer from the Internet. . . . 'A thing called a verifier examines your program, and it does a certain amount of testing. . .'" (Cravotta 20).

- The writer of the research paper has left out part of the quotation and shown that omission with the ellipsis. The part left out inside the sentence is shown with three spaced periods. The part left out at the end of the first sentence is shown with four spaced periods. Notice also that, since parenthetical documentation is included at the end of the second sentence, the omitted words are designated by three spaced periods and the parenthetical citation is followed immediately by the end period.
- The section the writer has quoted, which appears in quotation marks, also includes a sentence that Cravotta quoted. That sentence appears in single quotation marks.

PART II

- Perhaps you want to use part of the section above about ellipses in your paper. You might say,

  The ellipsis can be used to show omitted material. For example, "The writer of the research paper has left out part of the quotation and shown that omission with the ellipsis. . . . The part left out at the end of the sentence is shown. . . . Notice also that, since parenthetical documentation is included at the end of the second sentence, the omitted words are designated by three spaced periods. . ." (Dial-Driver 113).

- If you omit an entire sentence, use an initial period and three periods spaced before and after each period.
- You can see that the end of one sentence and the entirety of another are omitted in the example above.

As you can see from the examples, brackets and the ellipsis offer a convenient way to add or delete information within a quotation. Remember they should be used sparingly so that the flow of reading is not excessively interrupted. Instead of over-using these special forms, you can usually quote selectively and integrate short quotations into your own sentences.

SUMMARY AND PARAPHRASING

In addition to using quotations, you will also want to summarize some information and to paraphrase other information. (See **SUMMARIES**.) Remember that you must still document the source of that information. (See **PLAGIARISM.**)

To summarize, you must shorten and rewrite. To paraphrase, you rewrite in your own words but do not substantially shorten.

EXAMPLE (summary and paraphrase):

- A summary from the *Carnegie Mellon Magazine* about Java language might say,
  As Cravotta notes, Java is a programming language which has virus-check features (20).

- A paraphrase in your paper of that same passage might say,
  Cravotta states that Java is a programming language with safety features for users who will not have to be concerned about downloading programs from the Internet since Java will inspect them for viruses or other invasive computer problems. According to Java's creator, James Gosling, a feature of Java looks at the program and checks it for appropriate use of rules (20).

LONGER QUOTATIONS

Long quotations are defined as quotations of more than four typed lines in your paper. Long quotations are incorporated into your text; you use your words to connect them to what you are saying, but they are also set apart from that text in the way they appear on the page. MLA style specifies indenting long quotations one inch and double spacing. Because longer quotations are set apart from the text, they are not surrounded by quotation marks. Be sure that any long quotation is actually necessary. Use long quotations sparingly.

EXAMPLE (using a long quotation in the paper):

- Your paper includes information from the paragraph above and looks like this:

  Quotations of more than four typed lines are considered long quotations and are handled differently from quotations less than four typed lines long:

  > they are . . . set apart from that text in the way they appear on the page. MLA style specifies indenting long quotations one inch and double spacing. Because longer quotations are set apart from the text, they are not surrounded by quotation marks. Be sure that any long quotation is actually necessary. (Dial-Driver 114)

  A writer uses long quotations to support points and to elaborate on ideas but not to fill space or to save effort.

- Note that the final punctuation in this case comes after the quotation itself and not after the parenthetical citation.

APA CITATION

Of course, in APA style, as in all formats for documentation, you must give credit every time you use words, phrases, sentences, or ideas from someone else. (See **PLAGIARISM**.) When using the APA format, use one of the following types of citation each time you employ words, information, or ideas from someone else.

When you quote material, always include the page number with *p.* for one page or *pp.* for more than one page. If you do not mention the name of the author or the year in the sentence, include that information with the page number in the parenthetical reference immediately after the end of the quotation, even in mid-sentence. If your sentence includes the author's name, give the year of publication directly after the author's name, and the page number after the quotation. If your sentence includes both the author's name and the date of publication, then, as stated previously, only the page(s) appear after the quotation in the parenthetical citation.

For paraphrased or summarized material, APA style allows the writer to decide whether or not to give a page number, depending on whether or not the reader is likely to want to know the specific location of the information. As a student writer, you may be required to furnish the page number so the grader/reader can verify your source. Always check the requirements of the assignment with the person assigning it.

EXAMPLE (APA citations):

- **Direct quotation:**

  The language "has security and authentication features so users don't have to worry about letting strange programs into their computer from the Internet" (Cravotta, 1997, p. 20).

  • OR

  Cravotta (1997) says, "Java has security and authentication features so users don't have to worry about letting strange programs into their computer from the Internet" (p. 20).
- **Summary:**

  Java is a programming language which has features that check for viruses (Cravotta, 1997).
- **Paraphrase:**

  Java is a programming language with features for safety for users who will not have to be concerned about downloading programs from the Internet since Java will inspect them for viruses or other invasive computer problems. According to Java's creator, James Gosling, a feature of Java looks at the program and checks it for appropriate use of rules (Cravotta, 1997).

STEP SIX: REVISION

Revise and re-write the first draft. You might have other people read over the draft to check for mechanics and logic. (See **CHECKING THE PAPER**.) Type a second draft, double spaced.

You should type a draft? Yes, the reason to type the draft is to enable you to check the punctuation, spelling, internal documentation, and Works Cited entries accurately and easily. Of course, if you use a computer, you will save yourself some typing!

STEP SEVEN: FINAL DRAFT

Correct, type, and assemble your final paper. Be sure to proofread for errors. If you detect an error after you are ready to turn the paper in, correct it. Use black pen or even pencil, if necessary. Never leave an error. When assembling the paper to turn in, either staple the upper left corner with one staple or enclose the paper in a folder, according to your instructor's request.

HINTS FOR SUCCESS:

1. Of course, content, style, and appearance are important; but form is also very important, especially on the Works Cited page. Be sure that you follow the format described.
2. The paper should be typed.
3. The paper must meet superior criteria (including original style, quality content, good mechanics, and accurate format) to earn the maximum number of points.

4. One elementary mistake is too many. **Accuracy and proofreading are your responsibility**. The typist is not responsible for any mistakes–YOU ARE.

Research papers reveal what you know about research, what you know about a topic, and what you know about writing. Make your research paper show what you know!

CHECKING THE PAPER FOR YOURSELF OR FOR SOMEONE ELSE

Since the best papers usually are written in multiple drafts, the problem arises of how to review the paper before the next draft is written. Checking a paper for yourself is usually harder than checking one for someone else. This may seem odd, but you have written all the words in your own paper and they already seem familiar and right to you. Checking a paper for someone else can be easier because you are looking at it with fresh eyes. Checking either kind of paper can also be frustrating because you are not quite sure what to look for. The simple check list following can help you check someone else's paper; it can also help you check your own.

First check for contents.

1. Is there a thesis statement (or guiding idea) that you can easily find?
   Is there support for the thesis statement?
   Is there an introduction leading up to the thesis statement?
2. Does each body paragraph have a topic sentence?
   Is the thesis statement supported by the topic sentences?
   Does every sentence in the paragraph relate to the topic sentence?
   Do the quotations and other evidence from sources pertain to the topics in the paragraphs?
   Do the quotations and other evidence read as part of the text?
   Are the quotations tied into the text by the paper writer's own words?
3. Does the paper make sense?
   Is it convincing? Is it logical?
4. Does it end satisfactorily with some concluding remarks?
5. Is it enjoyable to read?

Last, check for mechanics.

1. Are the sentences well-structured?
2. Is the spelling correct?
   - Punctuation?
   - Agreement between subject and verb?
   - Pronoun and antecedent?
   - Capitalization?
   - Underlining?
   - Quotation marks?
   - Etc.?
3. Is the internal documentation correct?
   Is every statement drawn from a source documented?
   Is every quotation in quotation marks with parenthetical documentation following?
   Is every quotation adequately tied into the text?
   Is every quotation adequately introduced by the paper writer's own words?
   Are the mechanics of the documentation correct?
   - Parentheses?
   - Placement of quotation marks?
   - Placement of end marks, etc.?
4. Is the Works Cited page correct?
   Are all the works on the Works Cited page actually cited in the text?
   Are the mechanics of the documentation correct? (See **DOCUMENTATION**.)
5. Do the pages look as if the format (margins, etc.) corresponds to manuscript preparation form? (See **MANUSCRIPT PREPARATION**.)

REVIEWING RESEARCH PAPERS

Writing a research paper is difficult; it may be tedious; it can be extremely rewarding and revealing. Reviewing a research paper also can be extremely rewarding and revealing. The reader may discover a number of things about the writer, among them whether or not the writer can use coherent, logical prose about specific subject matter. The paper can show whether the writer has a good grasp of one aspect of the course. Another discovery may be whether the writer can in fact use the reference books required to function in the discipline. The reader may determine whether the writer can follow directions and function within a specified format consistently. Most important, the research paper reveals whether the writer has a grasp of the essentials of the course itself and of the college experience, namely how to accumulate knowledge.

The reviewer needs assess certain criteria for a research paper in any class:

1. Does the paper have a structure that is easily followed? In other words, does the writer tell the reader what the paper is going to tell about? Does the writer show a clear purpose for writing? Does the writer discuss the major subjects and divide them logically? Are the points sufficiently supported? Does the writer end with some kind of concluding remarks?

2. Is the paper coherent and logical? Can the reader follow the arguments without trouble? Does the paper make sense? Is it convincing? Is it interesting?

3. Are the sources used well? Do the quotations support what the writer has said or do they stand alone and have no clear relationship to what is being discussed? Are the sources reputable? Does the writer choose proper sources for the subject or are the major sources on the order of *National Enquirer* or even the *Desktop Encyclopedia*? Is the material quoted only enough to make the arguments convincing or has the writer quoted (or copied) large blocks of material (with or without giving credit)?

4. Are the mechanics of the prose (punctuation, spelling, sentence structure, etc.) good enough that the reader is not distracted by problems in these areas?

5. Are the mechanics of the paper, including documentation, acceptable? Does the writer consistently follow the guidelines of the required style of documentation? Does the writer give credit to the writers from whom he uses words, phrases, passages, or ideas?

A possible evaluation breakdown might include these factors:

Content		80%	
	Purpose and structure of argument (#1)		25%
	Coherence and logic (# 2)		30%
	Support of argument (#3)		25%
Mechanics		20%	
	Prose mechanics (#4)		10%
	Documentation mechanics (#5)	—	10%
		100%	100%

All of these factors are generally tied together, and a paper that is strong in content is probably also strong in mechanics.

WRITING IN RESPONSE TO LITERATURE

Before beginning a writing assignment of any kind, the most important step is to fully understand the expectations of the instructor. That means you must listen carefully to what is assigned. In the case of literary/artistic assignments, there are three words that you might hear: analysis, interpretation, and criticism. You must be able to distinguish between these words.

- **Analysis** of literature involves "taking the work apart" to see how it is made, to see how it "works," to discover what the parts are and what they do.
- **Interpretation** involves deciding what the work says.
- **Criticism** involves deciding how well the work says what it means to say and how well it is crafted. Criticism is not looking for the "bad stuff" in a piece of literature. Criticism in a literary or artistic sense means examination. Literary criticism is examining a work, section by section, aspect by aspect, very carefully, seeing how the work is put together and determining how well it is put together and how well it fulfills the function for which it is written. (See **EVALUATIONS**.)

Literary work begins with careful reading.

To analyze, interpret, or criticize, follow these general steps:

1. Read the story or poem or drama.
2. As you read, keep in mind questions of *who*, *what*, *when*, *where*, *how*, and *why*.
3. Remember the definitions of analysis, interpretation, and criticism. Decide what the parts of the work are and how they function. Decide what the author means and how you know that meaning. Decide how or why the author does what he/she does. Decide how well the author does what he/she means to do.

It will be necessary to cite evidence to prove your points. As you begin to search for a point from which to begin, you may consider a number of aspects. You may focus on the theme (or ethical insight), plot, character(s), point-of-view, setting, or language (sometimes called style). For example, you may choose to explain figurative language which will involve examples of metaphors, similes, alliteration, allusions, etc. Whatever you choose to focus on should be significant and should be interesting to you. Your focus will become the thesis of your paper.

4. Once you have identified a focus, read the work again, taking note of evidence you can cite in your essay.
5. Shape that evidence around your thesis and write a first draft.
6. Read your essay and revise it. Be sure that you have developed the thesis in the supporting paragraphs and used illustrations and evidence from the work.
7. Really good papers sometimes go through several revisions, so do not hesitate to revise until the paper pleases you and represents your very best efforts.

Writing in Response to Literature

Literary analysis, interpretation, and criticism are not simple summaries or the re-telling of a story. For examples of a summary, a report, and a four-section evaluation of the short story "Young Goodman Brown," see below. (See also **SUMMARIES AND REPORTS** for a summary and a report on a non-fiction literary work.)

EXAMPLE (summary of "Young Goodman Brown"):

Hawthorne, Nathaniel. "Young Goodman Brown." Imaginative Literature: Fiction, Drama, Poetry. 4th ed. Ed. Alton C. Morris, Biron Walker, and Philip Bradshaw. New York: HBJ, 1983. 3-24.

"Young Goodman Brown" by Nathaniel Hawthorne is the story of a young man recently married who leaves his wife to go on a journey into the forest. According to Young Faith, Young Goodman Brown's wife, this "night of all nights" is not a good time to be left alone; and Young Faith is near tears when she whispers softly and a bit sadly, "Dearest heart, prithee put off your journey until sunrise and sleep in your own bed tonight. . ." (Hawthorne 13). But Brown insists on making the journey. Brown's journey is filled with surprises, from seeing the staff bearing the likeness of a great black snake to finding Goody Cloyse, who had taught Brown his catechism, to discovering Faith's presence in the wood, and to spying the devil lurking behind the tree. The fiend-worshippers make one cry, "Welcome!" (Hawthorne 23), before Young Goodman Brown resists them with his shout, "Look up to Heaven, and resist the Wicked One" (Hawthorne 23). The narrator asks whether or not Brown has fallen asleep in the forest and only dreamed a wild dream of a witch-meeting. The question is not answered. Young Goodman Brown leads a dreary existence for the remainder of his life, and, "when he had lived long and been borne to his grave . . . they carved no hopeful verse on his tombstone, for his dying hour was gloom" (Hawthorne 24).

EXAMPLE (report on "Young Goodman Brown," including bibliographic data section and summary section):

Hawthorne, Nathaniel. "Young Goodman Brown." Imaginative Literature: Fiction, Drama, Poetry. 4th ed. Ed. Alton C. Morris, Biron Walker, and Philip Bradshaw. New York: HBJ, 1983. 3-24.

"Young Goodman Brown" by Nathaniel Hawthorne is the story of a young man recently married who leaves his wife to go on a journey into the forest. According to Young Faith, Young Goodman Brown's wife, this "night of all nights" is not a good time to be left alone; and Young Faith is near tears when she whispers softly and a bit sadly, "Dearest heart, prithee put off your journey until sunrise and sleep in your own bed tonight. . ." (Hawthorne 13). But Brown insists on making the journey. Brown's journey is filled with surprises, from seeing the staff bearing the likeness of a great black snake to finding Goody Cloyse, who had taught Brown his catechism, to discovering Faith's presence in the wood, and to spying the devil lurking behind the tree. The fiend-worshippers make one cry, "Welcome!" (23), before Young Goodman Brown resists them with his shout, "Look up to Heaven, and resist the Wicked One" (Hawthorne 23). The narrator asks whether or not Brown has fallen asleep in the forest and only dreamed a wild dream of a witch-meeting. The question is not answered. Young Goodman Brown leads a dreary existence for the remainder of his life, and, "when he had lived long and been borne to his grave . . . they carved no hopeful verse on his tombstone, for his dying hour was gloom" (Hawthorne 24).

I enjoyed "Young Goodman Brown" very much. It seems to be an allegory of sorts, and I appreciate reading stories that are multi-level. One level is the interesting story itself, with the relationship between Brown and Faith and the relationships between Brown and the villagers. Another level is the psychological one, with the development of Brown as a person who lives with a self-fulfilling prophecy. Another level is the religious allegory, with Brown allowing doubt to overcome faith. It could be, of course, that what Brown sees is not his own doubts but reality and that is the ambiguity in the story, an ambiguity that the author leaves deliberately since there can be no certainty in relationships, in psychology, or in religion. I think it is the ambiguity that appeals to me the most, leaving me to wonder exactly what Brown saw. As an optimist, I prefer to think that Brown sees only what he fears and that he is deceiving himself about his wife and his neighbors, that he brings his despair on himself. I prefer that scenario to the opposite one, that in fact everyone is evil and corrupt and Brown finally realizes the reality of the world. That thought is so depressing that I reject it!

EXAMPLE (four-section report on "Young Goodman Brown," including a bibliographic data section, a summary section, a reaction section, and an evaluation section):

Hawthorne, Nathaniel. "Young Goodman Brown." Imaginative Literature: Fiction, Drama, Poetry. 4th ed. Ed. Alton C. Morris, Biron Walker, and Philip Bradshaw. New York: HBJ, 1983. 3-24.

"Young Goodman Brown" by Nathaniel Hawthorne is the story of a young man recently married who leaves his wife to go on a journey into the forest. According to Young Faith, Young Goodman Brown's wife, this "night of all nights" is not a good time to be left alone; and Young Faith is near tears when she whispers softly and a bit sadly, "Dearest heart, prithee put off your journey until sunrise and sleep in your own bed tonight. . ." (Hawthorne 13). But Brown insists on making the journey. Brown's journey is filled with surprises, from seeing the staff bearing the likeness of a great black snake to finding Goody Cloyse, who had taught Brown his catechism, to discovering Faith's presence in the wood, and to spying the devil lurking behind the tree. The fiend-worshippers make one cry, "Welcome!" (Hawthorne 23), before Young Goodman Brown resists them with his shout, "Look up to Heaven, and resist the Wicked One" (Hawthorne 23). The narrator asks whether or not Brown has fallen asleep in the forest and only dreamed a wild dream of a witch-meeting. The question is not answered. Young Goodman Brown leads a dreary existence for the remainder of his life, and, "when he had lived long and been borne to his grave . . . they carved no hopeful verse on his tombstone, for his dying hour was gloom" (Hawthorne 24).

I enjoyed "Young Goodman Brown" very much. The story itself is interesting and the relationships between the characters are fascinating. Poor Faith tries to keep her husband from leaving her on a dangerous night. Her fears are borne out in Brown's subsequent attitude toward her and his suspicions of her and of all of his acquaintances. In addition to interesting characters, the author has supplied the reader with vivid imagery. The staff which is a living snake is a picture that will stay in my mind! The section which describes the "meeting" is also vivid, with Brown's fears about his neighbors come to life. Ultimately, I think it is the story's ambiguity that appeals to me the most, leaving me to wonder exactly what Brown saw. As an optimist, I prefer to think that Brown sees only what he fears and that he is deceiving himself about his wife and his neighbors, that he brings his despair on himself. I prefer that scenario to the opposite one, that in fact everyone is evil and corrupt and Brown finally realizes the reality of the world. That thought is so depressing that I reject it!

When I investigate "Young Goodman Brown" from a stance of evaluating significance of the plot, I find that the story functions on a number of levels. One level is the literal story itself, with the relationship between Brown and Faith and the relationships between Brown and the villagers. Faith tries to prevent Brown from taking his journey into despair but fails. That journey brings him to the belief that his world is peopled only with the corrupt and the fraudulent, leaving him to feel he faces evil alone and unprotected. Another level in the story is the psychological one, with the development of Brown as a person who lives with a self-fulfilling prophecy. When Brown determinedly sets out on a journey he need not make, he then decides that his neighbors and his wife are all evil. This causes him to further determine that his life is nothing but gloom. Each of those progressive steps into bleakness is made deliberately by Brown: he decides his reaction to each event, even choosing to accept the "meeting" as a reality and not as a dream. Another level is the religious allegory, with Brown allowing doubt to overcome faith. He refuses to keep his faith in the goodness of the world, instead preferring the gloom of despair. It could be, of course, that what Brown sees is not his own doubts but reality and that is the ambiguity in the story, an ambiguity that the author leaves deliberately since there can be no certainty in relationships, in psychology, or in religion.

Literary criticism goes much further than a summary. It incorporates only enough summary to make the thesis and support understandable to the reader.

Three elements actually comprise literary criticism: **analysis, interpretation, and criticism.**

ANALYSIS

Analysis is attention to elements of a literary or artistic work. For example, if you were analyzing "Young Goodman Brown," you would look at the structure, such as plot elements of inciting incident, conflict(s), climax, resolution, denouement, the characterization, the images, the symbols, the theme(s), the literary language, etc.

In class during a discussion or lecture about literature, you may find yourself saying, "I did not see that at all." Do not get discouraged. It takes practice to fully discover literature. You never learn all there is to know about it. You never come to the end of discovery. A person who has studied and taught literature for years will often be surprised by a new insight that a student offers. This same student (maybe you) will have said in other circumstances "I do not see where you got that."

You bring insight to each literary work.

The study of literature is the study of themes—ideas that are reflected in the literature, structure—how the work is put together, and of genre—the types of literature. **Genre** means type: a literary genre is a type of literary work. Generally, the literary genres are considered to be short story, poem, play (or drama), film, and also include the non-fiction genre, the essay.

To study any subject, you must be familiar with the specialized vocabulary which people use to discuss that subject. In the glossary is a list of very common literary terms. All of the terms are applicable to each genre of literature.

We can start our discussion of literary terms with **fiction**. Fiction can be based on fact, but it is not fact. If an author starts with an event and adds elements to the event that did not actually occur, the author is fictionalizing the event, no longer sticking to "just the facts, ma'am." If an author makes something up, he is creating pure fiction. If an author just tells what happens, as a newspaper reporter should report a news story, this is not fiction because the author is not "making up" anything.

One of the places fiction and non-fiction seem to get mixed up is in the "docu-drama," which is a romanticized or fictionalized television program based on an actual event. The writer takes an event and, to suit the desires of the media audience or to suit the needs of the network or production company, makes the event "larger than life" and more saleable. The "docu-drama" is supposed to be a combination of documentary and of dramatization of the subject to be documented, but usually the docu-drama is more drama (and much less fact) than documentary. Little, if anything, may be left of the "truth" when the normal docu-drama airs.

Now let us look at what happens in the work of fiction. What are the events in the short story? These are the things you undoubtedly notice first when reading or viewing anything. What happens, of course, is **plot**. And one of the things you should be aware of is whether the piece contains any **flashbacks**.

You can notice flashback most easily in a television "soap opera," now known as a daytime drama. If you watch a "soap," you may notice that characters and couples have their own theme music; that is, when the character or couple is on screen, the music accompaniment is distinctive, and distinctive to them.

When a plot line calls for a flashback, a character, usually a woman, accompanied by her character music, is on screen and says something like, "I remember when. . . ." and her voice fades off. The music changes and becomes slightly eerie or out-of-sync with her character. The edges of the picture blur, and there is a fade to black. When the scene clears and the music comes back up, another scene is on the screen, one that has already played days or weeks ago. The scene plays over, as it was originally filmed, with the original music and other sound. When the portion the director wants to re-play finishes, the music again changes, the screen becomes fuzzy and fades to black. The original scene returns with the character saying something like, "Yes, that was how it was. I remember." That was a flashback.

Another aspect of plot is the **climax**, the highest point in the plot. The climax is the point of greatest intensity in the events of the story. It is the culmination of all the conflict.

The climax often occurs with an **epiphany**, in which a character suddenly realizes something about him/herself, the situation, or others. The movie about the good guy and the bad guy may end with the good guy being forced to kill the bad guy at the climax. If the good guy realizes that he is now a bad guy because he too is now a killer, then this is the epiphany.

The **denouement** occurs after the climax. *M*A*S*H* is one of the television shows with a denouement. All the action in *M*A*S*H* occurs before the last set of internal commercials (the ones before the half-hour show break commercials). The climax is reached. The story is over. But the program continues. Between the last set of internal commercials and the credits, the program returns to the screen: Hawkeye and B.J. have a martini or somebody apologizes to Margaret or they all go to the club or someone tells a joke. These things are not necessary to the story line, although they are connected. What they do is leave the viewer with a good feeling, or at least a feeling of completion. This is the denouement.

Literary terms apply to fiction, films, television, etc.

The **conflict** in the story is what gives the story its action and spice. Conflict does not have to be Rambo shooting up the local terrorist camp. It may be very subtle. It may not even be external. The protagonist, or main character, may oppose, may be in conflict with, the antagonist, or second main character. These people may be just characters or they may represent something outside themselves, larger ideas. In the Superman comics, television programs and movies, Superman represents "truth, justice and the American way!" Usually the opposition, whether it be Lex Luthor or someone else, represents evil in one form or another, maybe "lies, injustice and unAmerican activities!"

Conflicts usually fall into one of five categories. One category, **person against person**, is a conflict in which two characters are in opposition. All the Rambo movies and the Rocky movies and the Superman movies and lots of other movies have this conflict. It is very easy to pick out. If someone hits someone else or blows him up or guns him down, the conflict is person against person.

Another category, **person against society**, is a conflict in which someone is in conflict with the society in which he or she lives, either with its mores and values or with its laws or with the representatives of those laws or mores—the people around him. This conflict can be seen in the film *Straight Time*, starring Dustin Hoffman as an ex-convict. The Hoffman character is on parole and comes into conflict with various segments of society and with each segment's expectations. His parole officer (a representative of the government and the law) expects him to stay away from all his old friends and companions; his old friends and companions (representatives of the fringe-criminal society) expect him to take up his old life at the point at which he left it; society as a whole expects him to get a job, support himself, and become a responsible citizen despite the fact he has no skills. So the Hoffman character comes into conflict with societal elements in various ways.

Person against God (alternately known as **person against fate**) is the conflict seen in the Oedipus plays by Sophocles, perhaps most easily in the first play of the cycle, *Oedipus the King*. In *Oedipus the King* (also known as *Oedipus Rex*), Oedipus' father is warned by Teiresias, the blind prophet, that his son will grow up to kill the father and marry the mother. To escape that fate, Oedipus' father has Oedipus exposed on the hillside. The king of a neighboring kingdom rescues the boy and brings him up as the king's own son. The boy does not know that he is adopted; and, when he hears a prophecy that he will kill his father and marry his mother, Oedipus runs away from the kind king. On his travels, Oedipus sees an old man at a crossroads who will not get out of the way. Oedipus, who is extremely arrogant, kills the old man and continues to a nearby kingdom, finding a beautiful queen who is widowed, marrying her, and becoming king. Plagues fall on the kingdom. Teiresias says that the plagues are caused by the fact that an evil man who has married his mother and killed his father lives in the kingdom; Oedipus vows to rid the kingdom of him. Oedipus discovers that the man is himself. Neither he nor his father is able to escape the fate prophesied for him.

Another conflict is a **person against nature**, seen in "To Build a Fire," the story by Jack London. In this short story, the main character, despite warnings from the "old-timers" in the "frozen North," takes his dog team, which he treats with cruelty, and begins a search for gold. Various adventures befall him, causing him to lose all his supplies except a few matches and all his dogs except one. He determines to light a fire and warm himself, feeling confident that he can endure the cold and survive. He drops matches or snow falls on the fire, etc., until he is left with one match. His hands are too cold to feel the match, and he knows that he will not succeed in lighting a fire with the match unless he can first warm his hands. He calls the dog to him, planning to kill the dog and warm his hands inside the body. The dog runs away. The story ends. In "To Build a Fire," a man has come in conflict with nature and lost.

The conflict of **person against self** is one of the conflicts in "Eveline," a short story in which a young woman must decide whether to stay with her abusive, but known, family or to accept a proposal of marriage and to enter a probably better, but unknown, situation. This conflict is largely internal, taking place inside a character. This kind of conflict is seldom seen to any large extent in a "bang, bang, shoot-'em-up" story.

A short story, novel or film, etc., may have more than one conflict. Usually a short story will contain one major conflict; and a novel, because it is so much longer, may contain several.

Aside from plot and aspects deriving from plot, literature has other aspects. The **setting** of the work is its time and place location. Sometimes the author leaves this deliberately vague. Sometimes the setting is very specific: Faulkner's "A Rose for Emily" is set in the South in the early 1900s or late 1800s.

An **image** in literature involves the reader in the imagining of a sensory experience, of sight, sound, taste, touch, or smell. One visual image in "The Tell-Tale Heart" by Edgar Allen Poe is the eye of the old man. The reader can "see" the eye in his/her imagination.

A **symbol** may also be an image, but it is more than an image. A symbol is something in the work that stands for something outside the work or that stands for something that is more than itself. A flag is a symbol. It is a piece of cloth, but it is a symbol of a country.

Santa Claus is a symbol.

A symbol may mean different things to different audiences. The flag of our country means more to us than does the flag of another country. A symbol also may change through time, meaning one thing to a child and another to an adult: Santa Claus is a good example of a symbol that changes with the age of the observer.

A symbol may also be an **allusion**, but not all allusions are symbols. An allusion is simply a reference to something outside the work, perhaps a political event or a person from another literary work. For example, a short story about a camping trip might allude to Huck Finn and his trip down the river with Jim. This is an allusion to characters in Mark Twain's *Huckleberry Finn*.

An **anomaly** may be an allusion or a symbol or it may be neither. An anomaly is something that does not seem to fit into the work, either in terms of plot or of setting or of theme, etc. A very simple example of something anomalous is a movie with Indians attacking the wagon train and wearing sneakers. This is not a significant anomaly; it is simply terrible movie-making. Most of the time anomalies are significant in a literary work and must be considered carefully. For example, in "Appointment in Samarra" a reader might consider the female figure of death to be anomalous since death is usually portrayed as a male figure. What point is Maugham trying to make when he presents death as female?

The **style** of the work is how the author has written or presented the work. Sometimes style also involves **tone**. The tone of the work can be serious, comic, ironic, etc. The style contributes to the tone, and to the overall effect of the work. Style is the way the work is presented. The author may use short sentences or long sentences; short journalistic-style paragraphs (Hemingway) or long, involved paragraphs (Faulkner); much description (Welty) or hardly any description at all (Asimov), etc.: all of these are aspects of style.

Another aspect of style is the decision of the writer on the **point of view** with which to write. The writer develops a **narrator**, a person telling the story. This person (called a **persona**) does not necessarily represent the writer and his or her feelings and views. The narrator tells the story from his (or her) point of view. The narrator may be the main character and tell the story in first person, saying "I was at the store to buy some milk. I saw a robber who pulled a gun on the storekeeper and then ran away. I was really scared." The narrator is the key figure. This point of view is known as first person central. You can see this point of view in "The Tell-Tale Heart."

The narrator could say, telling the same series of events, "I saw my friend John rob the store. He pulled a gun on the storekeeper and then ran away." John becomes more important than the narrator. This is **first person secondary point of view**.

Or the narrator with the **first person observer point of view** could say, "I saw a person in a store pull a gun and rob the storekeeper and then run away." The narrator, except for his presence as the narrator, stays out of the account.

In addition to first person points of view, there are several third person points of view. The writer still develops a narrator who tells the story but the narrator is not as personal as the narrator of a first person account.

In a **third person objective** account the narrator tells the story as if the story were seen by a movie camera. The narrator gives just the facts and does not offer any opinion nor does the narrator give the reader any idea of the thoughts or feelings of the characters involved. The reader does not know what any of the characters are like except through what they do and say.

The narrator's point of view establishes how you see the story.

In a **third person limited** account the narrator gives thoughts and feelings for a few of the characters but not for all. The reader gets to know something about a few of the characters by seeing how these characters feel without their expressing their feelings to other characters. The reader also finds out what these characters think by "hearing" what they think and not by watching only the actions and dialogue of the characters. "A Worn Path" is written in third person limited. The reader sees thoughts and feelings of only the main character, Phoenix, and not of any of the other characters.

In a **third person omniscient** narration, the narrator gives the thoughts and feeling for a majority of the characters, if not for all of them. Third person omniscient is the point of view in "The Open Boat"; the reader sees into the minds, sees the thoughts and feelings, of all the characters in the boat.

One of the most important aspects of a literary work is **theme**, what the work means or what it is trying to teach. This does not mean that the work preaches a moral, but that the work has one (or more) main idea(s) to present or to reveal. Finding the theme is part of interpretation; interpretation is based on the reader's decision on what the theme is. A theme is always stated in sentence form. You would not say, "The theme is love." You would say, "The theme is that love conquers all." One of the themes in "Appointment in Samarra" can be stated this way: "a person cannot run away from fate."

INTERPRETATION

Interpretation is deciding what the work–the film or short story or poem or play–is "all about," determining meaning. It is the weaving of all the elements into a coherent whole so that each part functions to illuminate all the other parts. Interpretation can function on more than one "level." The lowest "level" and the simplest interpretation is literal. In literal interpretation all the reader has to decide is what happened; **literal interpretation** is the equivalent of a plot summary.

Biographical interpretation is interpretation in light of the events of the author's life. It is looking at the work and trying to find what of the author is reflected in the work, aside from his or her imagination and craft. It is looking at the plays of Tennessee Williams and finding that at least one of the female characters in most of his plays is "flawed" in some way, usually psychologically, and making a connection between that fact and the fact that Williams had a dearly-loved sister who had mental problems.

Literature can be interpreted in terms of how it fits into a historical pattern or how it reveals a historical period (**historical interpretation**). Most of the novels of Charles Dickens can be interpreted historically since he reveals the culture and class problems and struggles of the times about which he writes. Literature can be interpreted in terms of how it fits into sociological or psychological theory or how it illuminates one of these theories (sociological and psychological interpretation). For example, the play *Oedipus Rex* can be interpreted in terms of the Oedipus complex, named by Sigmund Freud. Of course, since Freud named the complex for the play, this is rather circular.

Interpretation determines meanings.

Religious interpretation is interpretation of literature in terms of religious symbols and images. Langston Hughes' short story "On the Road" can be seen in terms of religious interpretation. The story abounds with religious symbols and images. The main character stands between two pillars and pulls a building down, reminiscent of Samson in the Bible. He is released from jail by a suddenly and mysteriously opened door, reminiscent of Peter. Of course, the fact that the main character converses with Christ is probably the key to religious interpretation of this story.

Each piece of literature can probably be interpreted in more than one way. For example, if you were interpreting "Young Goodman Brown," you might decide that the short story is about how a weak man's search for faith in a threatening world can lead him to despair, a religious interpretation and/or a psychological one. Or you might decide that the story reflects Hawthorne's society and its emphasis on faith, a **sociological interpretation**.

Just because someone else has not mentioned what you see does not mean that you cannot interpret the work in that way. However, this does not mean that you can read anything you want into a work. You must have internal evidence. Internal evidence is information in the work itself that serves as evidence to back up your interpretation. In other words, you cannot say that "The Tell-Tale Heart" is about Abraham Lincoln's dog's doctor because you can find no internal evidence to back up this far-fetched idea.

CRITICISM

Criticism is determining the worth of a work, deciding whether the work has artistic, social, or personal value. Remember that criticism is not negative: it is a balanced look, a precise look at the relative importance of the work. If you were criticizing "Young Goodman Brown," you might say it has social merit since it reflects one of the cultural tones of early America, or you might decide that it is of no worth to you personally because you are disinterested in people's relationships with each other and with God, or you might assert that the work is important artistically because it is well-crafted and engaging.

Criticism determines value.

EXAMPLE (literary analysis of "Young Goodman Brown"):

Amanda 1

George Amanda
Prof. Zeta
ENGL 1213
11 April 2005

Contrasting Symbols in "Young Goodman Brown"

"Young Goodman Brown," by Nathaniel Hawthorne, is the story of a man's encounter with evil. That encounter affects the rest of his life. Throughout the story of Young Goodman Brown's journey into the woods and his subsequent life are symbols that represent the contrasting forces present in his world. Investigating the symbolism of Faith and her pink ribbons, the man with the serpent staff, and the tombstone with no hopeful verse illustrates some of the conflict in the story and the life of Young Goodman Brown.

Young Goodman Brown's wife, Young Faith, with her flying pink ribbons, represents the good in Brown's life. Pink is a color of innocence and freshness, and it is innocence and freshness that Young Goodman Brown leaves behind in the person of his wife of three months. She has begged him not to leave her, on this night "of all nights" (Hawthorne 14). He turns from her and insists on making the journey into the forest. His turning away from her pleading represents his subsequent turning away from faith in the innocence, freshness, and goodness of humanity.

In addition, her name is an obvious symbol. Her name is Young Faith, and in fact the name represents that faith which is young and fragile. The faith that Young Goodman Brown turns away from at the beginning of the story is not only his own wife, it is his own faith. His own faith is so weak that he cannot hold to it. When tested, he resists by calling out, "Faith! Faith! . . . Look up to Heaven, and resist the Wicked One!" (Hawthorne 23); but his faith is so fragile that he cannot believe that Young Faith also resists. After Brown suspects he meets Faith in the forest at the witch meeting, Young Goodman Brown allows this to color his future relationship with his wife, causing him on various occasions to look "sternly and sadly into her face . . . without a greeting" and to shrink from her on "awaking suddenly at midnight" (Hawthorne 24).

After leaving Faith at home, Young Goodman Brown meets the stranger who has a staff, "which bore the likeness of a great black snake, so curiously wrought, that it might almost be seen to twist and wriggle itself like a living serpent. This, of course, must have been an ocular deception, assisted by the "uncertain light" (Hawthorne 15). This stranger with the deceptive staff represents the evil that Young Goodman Brown meets. More importantly, this stranger represents the uncertainty and deception that will plague Brown the rest of his life. The stranger takes Brown into the forest to meet all the people near whom he resides and whom he has trusted and loved. Brown is not strong enough to realize that not only his vision and the staff can be deceptive. Perhaps the whole episode is an illusion. Whether it is deception or not is immaterial because the stranger has succeeded in ruining Brown's life. The deception and "ocular deception" are the basis for Brown's ensuing actions.

The grave of Brown is headed by a tombstone, on which there is "no hopeful verse" for "his dying hour was gloom" (Hawthorne 24). This tombstone represents the conflict in Brown's life. After meeting the stranger and living through either the witch-meeting or the dream of the witch-meeting, Brown returns to his home. But he does not return joyfully. All of his relationships are soured by the memory of the night in the forest. His young faith is not strong enough to live as if the meeting had been a dream. He lives instead with doubt. Did it happen? It does not matter because doubt destroys him. The tombstone comes at the end of his life, but it very well could have been set at the moment he returned to the village and shrinks from its people "as if to avoid an anathema" (Hawthorne 24).

Brown has experienced an episode in which he allows himself to lose innocence and faith. He discovers that the world can be deceptive. But it is his choice, his actual reaction to that conflict between faith and doubt, in which doubt wins, that leads him to his gloomy death and gloomier life.

Works Cited

Hawthorne, Nathaniel. "Young Goodman Brown." Imaginative Literature: Fiction, Drama, Poetry. 4th ed. Ed. Alton C. Morris, Biron Walker, and Philip Bradshaw. New York: HBJ, 1983. 13-24.

Film Analysis

In your classes, you may have to deal with short stories, novel, plays, or poems. In addition, you may have to learn about films. Films affect your life if you go to the movies, rent videos, or watch television. Short stories, novels, and plays have been translated into film. Screenplays have become novels. Literature moves back and forth across the line to the visual art that is film. Films may begin with a story idea from literature, with a script, with a concept, and/or with a vision. Films are usually made in something like the following manner.

If a film begins with a concept, a scriptwriter writes a film **script**. The script is the skeleton that will become the production. The words will be interpreted by actors, director, editor, etc.

Although the **actors** are not the first people involved in making the film, the actors interpret the writer's concept and allow the translation of that concept to film. The skeleton that is the script begins to take form when the actors bring it to a kind of life. Just as no two people have exactly the same vision of a character in a short story, no two actors will interpret a part in exactly the same manner. The background and concept of the character, the actions and reactions of the character, the motivations of the character, the character itself will be interpreted differently by each actor having the role.

Remember all the remakes of the old movies? Or the remakes for TV of old movies? Did any remake ever duplicate the original? Were any characters for the remake just like characters in the original? Undoubtedly not. An actor will bring a personal view to a role and not even be able to (or want to) duplicate what was done before.

Probably the first person who will actually deal with the making of the film is the **producer**. The producer looks for financing and supervises the production, especially in terms of budget. In some cases, the producer also supervises the film in terms of concept, insuring that the concept of the film remains true to the original concept.

The **director** is also a supervisor. The director supervises the actual making of the film. In most cases the director is the person who has in mind the film as an entirety and directs the actors and camera personnel so that the concept in the director's mind becomes translated to the final product.

Some directors (and even some producers) become well-known for the personal stamp they put on films. These directors are known as auteurs. You can pick out who made the film from seeing what kind of film it is. Some of the directors who are easily distinguishable from other directors are Brian de Palma, Steven Spielberg, Alfred Hitchcock, Robert Altman, Quentin Tarantino, and Francis Ford Coppola, among others.

Either the **director** or a **camera director** or the director and the camera director decide on the camera shots and angles. How you see a scene will depend on how the camera sees a scene.

The camera becomes the eye of the viewer. You are manipulated by the action of the camera. You wander up the stairs in the *Psycho* house with the detective and are startled at the appearance of the knife in the hand of the murderer. Because you are frightened and fixed on the knife (and because the knife is what the camera lets you see), you do not see the face of the murderer.

What the camera sees at the beginning of *E.T.* is portions of people. You see feet in heavy boots, large hands holding swinging flashlights, key rings on belts, other large hands holding guns of various kinds. You do not see the whole person. The whole sequence of shots creates a moods. In this case the mood is ominous. We see the people in the sequence as objects, objects with frightening items. We know something not-too-good is going to happen.

The person in charge of **continuity** insures that each scene will flow smoothly and continuously one to another. In most cases, films are not made in sequence. That means that each scene is not shot as it would appear in the script and as it will appear in the final product. Instead the scenes are filmed in the most efficient manner.

Perhaps all the outdoor scenes in the rain are all filmed, then all the indoor scenes of the mansion, then all the outdoor scenes at the pool, and then all the indoor scenes in the restaurant. This is despite the fact that in order of time (and in the final order of the finished film) the scenes would run in this sequence: first an indoor scene in the mansion, then an outdoor scene at the pool, then an indoor scene in the mansion, then an indoor scene at the restaurant, then an outdoor scene in the rain, and then an indoor scene in the mansion, etc.

You can see that someone needs to keep track of how the actors have their hair combed and what clothes they are wearing in the restaurant, etc. Otherwise a male actor may appear in the restaurant in a gray suit and move outside to catch a cab in a green blazer and jeans. Keeping all this straight is up to continuity.

Lighting is important not just for visibility. Lighting creates a mood, enhancing the emotional quality of a scene. Lighting in the 1940s version of *Cat People* casts bars of light across the main female character in several scenes, foreshadowing and symbolizing her imprisonment in her plight and the leopard's imprisonment at the zoo.

Low light may create a feeling of impending doom or of fright. At the beginning of *E.T.* (and indeed through the bulk of the film), the lighting is subdued, leading the viewer to suspect that a relatively unpleasant event is coming.

Sound is also a critical part of a film. The soundtrack of a movie may be a work of art in its own right. The music enhances and reinforces the action and emotion portrayed on the screen and contributes to the effect of the film. Think about the sound in *Jaws*.

The editor on a film takes the final rolls of film and the soundtrack and combines all of the parts into a whole. Under the direction of the director and/or producer, the editor decides how long a shot will actually last, what will remain in the final product and what will be deleted.

Some techniques that an editor uses are **fade-in**, **fade-out**, **close-up**, **cut**, and **montage**. Fade-in and fade-out are rather obvious terms. In these techniques the film either fades out to black or fades in to the picture from black. Close-up is rather obvious as well. In close-up work the camera frames a subject so that you may see it closely.

Films can be analyzed, interpreted, and criticized.

Cutting and montage are more complicated, but not much more. **Montage** is the rapid juxtaposition of shots. One shot is quickly followed by another which is quickly followed by another, etc. Montage is a form of cutting. **Cutting** is switching from one scene to another. Cutting between several scenes is montage. Cutting between two scenes is just cutting.

Cutting also affects what you see in the film and how you react to it. Cutting can either allow the viewer to carry an emotion over from one scene to another if the scene is cut early enough or allow the viewer to fully enjoy a scene before reacting emotionally to the next scene.

In *E.T.* Spielberg allows many scenes to continue and does not cut at the point that many directors would. In the scene in which E.T. "dies," the camera continues to roll until every member of the audience is drained of emotional reaction to the "death."

This is a different cutting technique from that used by the editor in *An Officer and a Gentleman*. In the scene in which the main character helps his classmate over the wall, the joy of the audience at seeing this arrogant, self-centered, and self-contained man reach out to someone struggling (and to someone who has been struggling in several scenes in the film) is hardly experienced before the scene is cut and the next scene begins. The next scene is not a joyous one and the joy of the viewer is juxtaposed with his/her subsequent sadness. The cutting allows the viewer the almost simultaneous experience of the up and down of real life. And the spill-over from the first scene makes the second more palatable and acceptable as well as sadder.

A short story or novel can become a play.

A play can become a film.

Each genre adds some elements and loses others.

Other members of the film crew are important and include other sound and lighting experts, various camera personnel, production and director's assistants, "go-fors" of all kinds, etc.

The viewer is manipulated by film. Your emotions are involved and your response is motivated by what you see and how you see it. You should be aware of the techniques of film so that you are aware of how you are affected. Knowing techniques and effect does not subvert your enjoyment of a film. This knowledge allows you to enjoy and appreciate a film from a new perspective.

EXAMPLE (film analysis, literary analysis of a film):

NOTE: Student essay examples are above-average papers, but not necessarily "A" papers.

Hancock 1

Denita Hancock

Prof. Dial-Driver

ENGL 2613

23 Feb. 2000

Toy Conflicts in Toy Story 2

What do toys do when their owner is gone? Do they really just sit there lifeless? Most children wonder this at some time during their young lives. Toy Story 2 is an outstanding movie that makes toys come to life. An investigation into Toy Story 2 reveals conflicts that toys may have: rejection of owner, identity crises, and the possibility of leaving their present life to move on to a new life where they are more appreciated.

One of a toy's worst fears is that of being rejected or no longer wanted by its owner. Woody has been Andy's most beloved toy for several years and is looking forward to his most exciting summer yet with Andy at camp when tragedy strikes: "When Woody's arm accidentally is torn, Andy decides not to take him to camp, and Woody worries that his days might be numbered" (Caro 2). Todd McCarthy puts it this way, "Andy's mom adds the final sting with the comment, 'Toys don't last forever'" (83). These are the dreaded words every toy hates to hear. Woody feels very rejected by being left behind. Woody is again reminded of Andy's rejection later on in the movie. Stinky Pete, a member of a toy collection that Woody would complete, asks, "Do you really think that Andy is going to take you to college or on his honeymoon?" (Caro 3). Woody realizes that Andy will outgrow him someday, but does it have to be now? Andy is not the only one dealing with owner rejection in the movie. Jessie, another member of the rare toy collection, tells Woody "about her former owner, Emily, who tossed her under the bed and forgot her" (Ebert 2). Buzz sums it up best when he says, "You never forget kids, but they forget you" (Ebert 2).

Identity crisis is another conflict represented in Toy Story 2. Joe Morgenstern describes Buzz Lightyear as "a lantern-jawed space ranger, struggling with the realities of his existence--he's not really the intrepid galactic explorer he'd like to be but a plastic plaything manufactured in Taiwan" (W1). Not only is he a mere toy, but he also finds out (while trying to rescue Andy) that there are hundreds of him: "Buzz discovers that he is only one of many Buzzes, and must come to terms with existential questions about being mass-produced, one of the crowd" (Maslin E1). Even more devastating is the fact that he is the old model. There is now a "new and improved version of his likeness" (Caro 3). If this isn't enough to make a toy feel bad, Buzz is overcome by one of the new toys and stuck in his box, preventing him from helping with the rescue of Woody. Eventually Buzz escapes from the box to return to Andy's rescue mission, showing no signs of inferiority. Buzz handles his identity crises quite well and continues with his mission as a friend.

The biggest conflict is Toy Story 2 is the choice Woody must make in deciding whether to be rescued by his old friends to return to Andy or stay with his new friends and complete the collector's set which will be sent to Japan and placed in a museum forever. This decision is very difficult as Todd McCarthy says in his review, Woody "is torn between the 'blood' family of his old TV cohorts and his closest friends from Andy's house" (83). Woody is excited to know that he was once famous. He finds out that he starred in a TV show with his horse Bullseye, a cowgirl named Jessie, and a prospector named Stinky Pete. Jessie and Pete want Woody to stay with them to complete the collection so they can be sent to Japan. If Woody leaves to go back to Andy's house, "they'll be put back in storage" (Nichols E24). Jessie tries to persuade Woody by "tugging at Woody's heart . . . by pointing out that unlike Woody, who has enjoyed many years with a loving owner, she has endured a long purgatory in storage, bereft of any life worth living" (Nichols E24). Woody is in a terrible mess. Should he stay or go? "Besides, in the museum he'll be admired by many children for years, instead of living under the threat of being outgrown by Andy" (Vice 2). Lisa Schwarzbaum describes it by saying, "Woody weighs the safety of lying low with his new, untouchable teammates against the perils (and pleasures) of being loved and played with (but likely eventually discarded) by an imperfect little boy" (72). Just when Woody has made his decision to go to the museum, his group of old friends show up to rescue him. Buzz tries to persuade Woody to come home with several touching lines, such as, "It is better to be loved for the length of a childhood than admired forever behind glass in a museum" (Ebert 2); "You're not a collector's item, you're a toy" (Toy); and "Life's only worth living if you've been loved by a kid" (Toy). Woody refuses to go with his "old pals" and sends them on their way. It's only when he hears the song "You've Got a Friend In Me" that his heart is touched and he comes to his senses, knowing that he cannot forsake Andy. Woody comes up with the great idea of inviting Bullseye, Jessie, and Stinky Pete to come along with him to Andy's house. Everyone is thrilled except Stinky Pete who has never been out of his box to be loved by anyone. He tries to make trouble for the rescue team and eventually ends up in a backpack with a Barbie. Bullseye and Jessie are welcomed new toys at Andy's house, as expected. Andy closes with the thoughts, "It will be fun while it lasts, and besides, I will still have Buzz Lightyear to infinity and beyond!" (Toy).

Toy Story 2 may be about what toys do when no one is around, but it also can relate to real life situations in today's world. Many children deal with the same kind of conflicts that the toys do: owner (or parent) rejection, identity crisis (self-worth), and choices to stay with the old or join in with the new. It would be great if real life stories could end as happily as this story and everyone could have their own Buzz to be with "to infinity and beyond!"

Works Cited

Caro, Mark. "Toy Story 2." Metromix: A Chicago Entertainment and Restaurant Guide 17 Feb. 2000: 1-4. <http://metromix.com/movies/1,1419,M-Metromix-Movies-X!Article Detail-5855,00.html?search_area=Articles&channel=M2/17/00>.

Ebert, Roger. "Toy Story 2." Chicago Sun Times 17 Feb. 2000: 1-3. Ebert. <http://www.suntimes.com/ebert/ebert_reviews/1999/11/112404.html>.

Maslin, Janet. "Animated Sequel Finds New Level of Imagination." The New York Times 24 Nov. 1999, late ed.: E1.

McCarthy, Todd. "Toy Story 2." Variety 377.2 (22 Nov. 1999): 83.

Morgenstern, Joe. "What? A Good Sequel? A Brilliant 'Toy Story 2' Proves it Can Happen." Wall Street Journal 26 Nov. 1999: W1.

Nichols, Peter M. "The Terrors of Toyland: Collectors." The New York Times 26 Nov. 1999, late ed.: E24.

Schwarzbaum, Lisa. "Second That Emotion: A Rare Sequel That Lives Up to Its Predecessor, the Blissful Toy Story 2 Makes You Feel as Giddy as When You First Thrilled to the Adventures of Woody and Buzz." Entertainment Weekly 515 (3 Dec. 1999): 72.

Toy Story 2. Pixar/Disney, 1999.

Vice, Jeff. "'Toy Story 2' Among the Disney Studios' Best Films Ever." Desertnews 24 Nov. 1999: 1-2. 17 Feb. 2000 <http://www.desnews.com/dn/view/0,249,135007050,00.html?>.

POETRY ANALYSIS

Many people say they hate poetry. Some people panic when asked to read or analyze a poem. Others say they do not understand it so they don't like it. If you look at the subject in one way, much as you would look at music, you might realize that you do not have to understand poetry to enjoy it, just as you do not have to understand what a contralto voice sings or what harmonic relationships are in order to appreciate a song or a tune. It is enough that the sound and the feeling are appealing and satisfying.

But it does add to the appreciation and understanding of the meaning of the poem to analyze, interpret, and criticize the poem (called by some people "picking it to death"). Analysis, etc., is not difficult. It is something you have to learn how to do. With practice it comes more easily, until you can do it without thinking about it or breaking the process down into steps. Until you reach that point, you might consciously follow the steps of the following process.

Poetry can be analyzed and understood. Answer the questions to begin the process.

1. What is your immediate emotional reaction to the poem?
   Does it make you feel depressed? Does it make you feel happy or uplifted?
   Does it make you feel sad? (No, *bored* is not a valid answer to this question.)

2. What is the title?
   What is the significance of the title? The title of a poem will frequently be related to the theme or at least give a starting point which the first line of the poem will take for granted.
   Does the title specify a locale for the poem?
   Does the title specify a person? Is the poem addressed to this person? Is the poem about this person?
   Does the title specify an incident or action about which the poem is written?
   Does the title specify a dominant purpose for the poem?
   Does the title allude to some incident or event in literature, life, the Bible, or a myth which the poem assumes as its starting point?

3. What is the form of the poem?
   Is there regular rhyme pattern? What is it?
   Is there regular rhythm pattern? What is it?
   Does the poem have a recognizable verse form? What is it? Is the form significant to the purpose or theme of the poem?
   Is each line a single thought unit or does the thought continue to the next line or lines?
   Is each stanza a separate thought unit or do some of the thoughts continue to the next stanza or stanzas? Why do you think this is so?
   Is the poem arranged on the page in any manner that does not look usual to you?
   Why do you think this is so? Are the words arranged or used in unusual ways? Are the stanzas used or arranged in unusual ways? Why?

4. Determine the context of the poem.
   Who is the speaker of the poem? Convention assumes that almost all poems will have a speaker. Some speakers will simply function as an organizing point of view. Other speakers are clearly someone other than the poet himself. This kind of speaker is called a persona and may be as multi-faceted as a character in a play or short story.
   Is the speaker male or female, young or old? Does the speaker have a name? What are the speaker's characteristics? Does he or she have a well-defined identity or is she or he only a focus or narrator?
   How does the speaker feel about the events, incidents, people or objects described in the poem? Does the speaker express any feelings in the poem? Do the attitude and emotion of the speaker coincide with the way a "reasonable person" might be expected to feel?
   Who is spoken to? Is the person whom the speaker addresses different from the reader?
   What kind of person is the one addressed? What significance might this have?
   Where is the speaker? Why is the speaker at that place?

5. Summarize the events of the poem.
   What happens? Tell the events or emotions of the poem in your own words. Do this line by line. This is called **explication** and will help you understand what is actually happening in the poem.

6. Discover the mechanics of the poem.
   What kind of imagery does the speaker use in his description? Do these images have anything in common? Do they cluster around a dominant impression?
   What kinds of words does the poem contain? What is the diction of the poem? Are slang words used? Is the language formal or informal; is it standard or a dialect? What do the word choices reveal about the situation and the speaker?

Are there allusions to events or works outside the poem? Do the allusions serve to broaden the significance of the poem, to universalize the experience, or to give you added insight?

Are there anomalies in the lines? Do the anomalies serve to give you a new view of what is said or meant?

What words or ideas are repeated? Anything repeated is worth investigation because it must be of significance. A poem is a kind of shorthand; and, if the poet feels something is worth repeating, then it must be important.

What are the symbols in the poem? What is their significance? What do they mean? How do they function?

7. What is the theme of the poem?

What is the poet trying to say to the reader? It is customary to consider all the things you have discovered about the poem–all the characteristics, all the effects, all the minor meanings–and develop an expression of the theme of the poem.

Once the theme is discovered and stated, the purpose of the analysis is to demonstrate that the theme is appropriate and that the statement of theme can be supported by references from the poem itself. Any statement of theme must have this support. A poem may have many themes. You may discover a theme that a classmate overlooks and vice versa. But a poem (or a short story or a novel or a play or a movie) does not mean whatever you want it to. You cannot say that a poem about the discovery of the alphabet is about Abraham Lincoln's doctor. The statement of the theme must be defensible with internal evidence from the poem and all the parts of the poem must fit into this statement.

8. Evaluate your reaction to the poem.

Your response to the poem is a factor that must be taken into account. Did you like or dislike the poem? On what do you base this reaction? Did the reaction change as you came to understand the poem better?

EXAMPLE (analysis of poetry):

NOTE: Student essay examples are above-average papers, but not necessarily "A" papers.

Gay 1

Rick Gay

Prof. Sesso

ENGL 1213

15 April 2005

Carnal Poetry

Poetry could be described as "painting with words." It is man's attempt to give linguistic form to thoughts and emotions. While a short story or novel may use pages to build a scene, poetry strives to create vivid imagery with only a minimum of language, achieved by any number of ingenious methods. The styles of poetry are as myriad as the number of poets themselves. For example, some poets are reasonably straightforward about their subject. But, others teasingly offer only brief glimpses of profundity while demurely concealing their velvet message. Still others use symbolism and metaphor to obscure the message with an equivocal haze. Although any subject can be treated in a variety of poetic styles, every technique endeavors to push the reader toward a climactic epiphany.

Sharon Olds's "Sex Without Love," for instance, Is an example of literal poetry which purports to be about the same subject as the symbolic "she being Brand" of E. E. Cummings. These verses both extol the joys of sex, but each uses widely varied means to achieve their ends. Although Cummings' work is ostensibly about a new car, it actually details a youthful sexual romp, perhaps taking place in the back seat of a car (Cummings 1-38). Olds' poem, on the other hand, is more open and obvious about its subject, even incorporating it into the title so that its meaning is unmistakable (Olds 1-24). While these two poems are about the same subject, their poetic techniques are of a decidedly contrasting nature.

The style and tone of these two works contrast. Cummings uses a light and almost comedic tone to accent his already bizarre style of poetry. This forces the reader to look beyond the words themselves in their given form and dig for a more abstruse meaning. Moreover, Cummings' use of extended metaphor creates an ambiguous framework, showing how one scene or setting can elicit a message entirely apart from its interpretation. When the car is viewed as being symbolic of a women, all the poem's descriptive language consequently takes on sexual connotations. Like "she being Brand," many poems draw their power from the vagary of double meanings. Conversely, some poems find strength in a decidedly singular approach.

Olds's "Sex Without Love" presents itself with a serious tone and a literal style, utilizing metaphor to impart its message. The words display their meaning with an open directness that is designed to allure the reader. The poem begins by asking how a person can have sex without love: "How do they do it, the ones who make love / without love?" (Olds 1-2), seemingly presenting a moralistic admonishment on promiscuity. However, this message becomes diluted as the reader reaches the mid-section of the poem in which the physicality of sex seems to be celebrated but asks how lovers can "come to the / still waters" (Olds 9-10). The movement continues as the narrator's metaphor compares sex to exercise, a solitary pursuit: the lover knows "they are alone / with the road surface" (Olds 18-19), and the partner is "just factors" (Olds 21), like cold and wind. Then, by the end, the "single body alone in the universe" (Olds 23) is brandished by the lover as the center of importance, but still ironically "alone."

Both Olds's and Cummings's verses use a traditional technique, the metaphor, to reach the climax of the poem. However, Cummings's extended metaphor delves into some curious avenues with its unusual use of a car as metaphor for a woman and a ride in the car as a metaphor for sexual activity. Cummings first lines, "She being Brand / -new;and you / know consequently a / little stiff" (1-4), begin the extended metaphor. He continues the metaphor as the driver continues the trip, turning the "corner of Divinity / avenue" (21), and finishing as the trip ends with the car "tremB / -ling / to a:dead. / stand- / ;Still)" (34-38). In the end, both methods, simple and extended metaphors, achieve their desired goal, but the degree of satisfaction depends on individual tastes.

Although the traditional style of poetry may be the most socially accessible, it does not sate the appetite of all who indulge. Some hunger for darker and more bizarre poetic practices. While mainstream society continues to prefer a more missionary approach, double meanings and unusual wording hold an undeniable allure for a certain segment. This extreme style is not for the faint at heart. Poetry virgins would be well advised to begin their experimentation with a subject that is easy to grasp and has limited moral characteristics. Once this conquest is made, the reader can move on to a more intimate affair with an enjoyable subject. But the intense satisfaction that poetry offers can only be fully experienced when the reader becomes completely immersed in the subject. As one moves beyond the surface, into deeper areas, the readings should slowly build and build toward Cummings. One should always save the best for last.

Works Cited

Cummings, E. E. "She Being Brand." The Compact Bedford Introduction to Literature. 4th ed. Ed. Michael Meyer. Boston: Bedford, 1997. 484.

Olds, Sharon. "Sex Without Love." The Compact Bedford Introduction to Literature. 4th ed. Ed. Michael Meyer. Boston: Bedford, 1997. 485.

GLOSSARY: LITERARY TERMS

In the following glossary, examples appear in parentheses. Questions to help you determine the function of the term in a specific literary work appear in brackets.

ALLITERATION: repetition of consonants, especially at the beginning of words or of stressed syllables.
(Example: The tiny tot told a tall tale.)

ALLUSION: a reference to something outside the work itself–to the Bible, to another literary work, to an event, to a common myth, etc.
(Example: He strove as Samson to overcome his foes.)

ANALYSIS: the discovery of a work, determining what the parts of a work are, what purposes the parts serve, or how a specific aspect of the work functions in relation to the work as a whole.

ANOMALY: a deviation from the expected.
(Example: Using "shroud" in a poem about birth is anomalous.)

ASSONANCE: repetition of identical or related vowel sounds, especially in stressed syllables. The word sound, not the spelling, is pertinent.
(Example: How now brown cow?)

CACOPHONY: use of harsh and unmusical sounds, discordancy.
(Example: The jangled monkey jerked.)

CHARACTERIZATION: the representation of a person/being.
[Who are the characters? What are their characteristics: mental, physical, behavioral, verbal? How do they see themselves? How do others see them? How do they react to others? How do others react to them? How do they think or reveal thought? Are they fully developed (**ROUND**) or stereotyped (**FLAT**)?]

CLIMAX: the turning point of the plot, the outcome of the struggle.
[When does it occur and what does it reveal? Is there an **EPIPHANY**?]

CONFLICT: the opposition of forces in the fiction.
[Who is the main character (**PROTAGONIST**)? Who is the character who opposes the protagonist (**ANTAGONIST**)? Are the forces in opposition just characters or do they represent larger ideas? What is the type of conflict: **PERSON AGAINST PERSON, PERSON AGAINST SOCIETY, PERSON AGAINST GOD/FATE, PERSON AGAINST NATURE, PERSON AGAINST SELF** (internal conflict)?]

CONSONANCE: repetition of consonant pattern, with changes in intervening vowels.
(Example: A diller, a dollar, a duller scholar.)

CRITICISM: determination of artistic quality and value of a work.

DENOUEMENT: the falling of the action after the climax of the fiction; the "untying of the knot" in which unsolved complications are resolved.

EPIPHANY: moment at which a character perceives truth about self or others.
[When does it occur? What truth is perceived?]

ESSAY: work of non-fiction, usually meant to be read in one sitting.

EUPHONY: a pleasant, melodious effect.
(Example: "The tolling and the rolling of the bells." –Poe)

EXPLICATION: explaining the work, line by line or paragraph by paragraph, etc., in words other than the original.
(Example: The line by Dylan Thomas says, "Twenty-four years remind the tears of my eyes," and you, the reader, explicate the line by saying, "The speaker is twenty-four sad years old.")

FICTION: literary work portraying imaginary events and characters.
[What is the name of the work? Who is the author? When was it written?]

FIRST PERSON CENTRAL: See **POINT OF VIEW.**
FIRST PERSON OBSERVER: See **POINT OF VIEW.**
FIRST PERSON SECONDARY: See **POINT OF VIEW.**

FLASHBACK: a technique by which past events are told by the narrator as if the events were happening in the present. [When does the flashback begin? When does it end? What function does it serve in the work? Why is a flashback used instead of straight narration of events of the past?]

HYPERBOLE: extravagant exaggeration used either for serious or comic effect.
(Example: He ate enough breakfast to feed an elephant.)

IMAGE: a sensory experience in words.
[What are the overriding images and what senses do they involve?]

INITIATION: a type of story in which a person moves from one stage of life development to another.
[At what stage in life does the character begin? At what stage in life does the character end? What causes the character to change or grow? Is the initiation actualized or a failure?]

INTERPRETATION: analysis which involves discerning what the work is about.
[Possible interpretations include **LITERAL**, **BIOGRAPHICAL**, **HISTORICAL**, **SOCIOLOGICAL**, **PSYCHOLOGICAL**, and **RELIGIOUS**. How do the symbols in the work function in each interpretation?]

METAPHOR: a word which in ordinary use signifies one kind of thing, quality or action that is applied to another without express indication of the relationship between them.
(Examples: His name is mud. Her brother is a pain in the neck. Life is a song.)

METER: rhythm pattern in poetry.
[What kind of meter exists in the poem? Each rhythm unit, which consists of accented and unaccented syllables, is called a **foot**, which is the poetic equivalence to a measure of music. The standard feet are **iambic** (unaccented, then accented syllable, as — /), **trochaic** (/ —), **anapestic** (— — /), **dactylic** (/ — —), **spondaic** (/ /), and **pyrrhic** (— —). A one-foot line is called **monometer**, two feet is **dimeter**,

three **trimeter**, four **tetrameter**, five **pentameter**, six **hexameter**, seven **heptameter**, etc.]

ONOMATOPOEIA: use of words whose sounds seem to resemble the sounds they describe.
(Examples: hiss, buzz, rustle, bang.)

OXYMORON: a paradoxical statement combining two terms that in ordinary usage are contraries.
(Examples: bitter joy, pleasing pain)

PARADOX: a statement that seems absurd and self-contradictory but which turns out to have a tenable and coherent meaning.
(Examples: "He who is last will be first." "He who would save his life must lose it." –Bible)

PERSONIFICATION: a figure of speech in which either an inanimate object or an abstract concept is described as being endowed with human attributes, powers or feelings.
(Example: Justice is blind.)

PLOT: action; what happens, the sequence of events.
[Is the action told in perfect, chronological order? Is it told in **FLASHBACKS**? Is it told in the present or past tense?]

POINT OF VIEW: the position from which the fiction is told by the narrator.
[Is it told in first person (I or we)? If so, is the narrator a major character (**FIRST PERSON CENTRAL**) or a minor character (**FIRST PERSON SECONDARY**) character? Or does the narrator just tell what he sees (**FIRST PERSON OBSERVER**)? Is the story told in the third person (he or they)? If so, does the narrator seem to know everything (**THIRD PERSON OMNISCIENT**) or just certain character's thoughts (**THIRD PERSON LIMITED**) or only the actions taking place, almost as a movie camera would function (**THIRD PERSON OBJECTIVE**)? How does the point of view color the story? Is the narrator reliable?]

RHYME (also RIME): similar or identical sounds in accented syllables.
[What is the rhyme scheme of the poem? Rhyme schemes are determined by putting a letter at the

end of each line of the poem, the same letter for rhyming words, and are designated by those letters, as *aabba* or *abcabc*, etc. Rhyme may be end rhymes as discussed previously or internal rhyme, rhyme which occurs within a line of poetry, as "In mist or cloud, on mast or shroud" –Coleridge, "The Ancient Mariner"]

SETTING: the environment of the fiction, its time and space location.
[When did the story take place? Where did it take place?]

SIMILE: a comparison between two essentially different items, expressly indicated by the terms *like* or *as*.
(Example: A pretty girl is like a lovely tune.)

STYLE: the use of language in the fiction to achieve desired effect.
[What kinds of words, phrases, sentences, and paragraphs does the author use?]

SYMBOL: something concrete in the work which suggests something abstract outside the work or recalls something else concrete in the work; an item in the work meaning more than its physical entity.
[What could be the symbols in the work? What do they mean?]

THEME: central or dominating idea of the work.
[What does the work mean? What is it trying to teach or reveal? **NOTE**: Specific themes are always stated in a clause or a sentence. For example, a writer might make this statement: One theme of *Much Ado about Nothing* is that truth will prevail.]

THIRD PERSON LIMITED: See **POINT OF VIEW.**
THIRD PERSON OBJECTIVE: See **POINT OF VIEW.**
THIRD PERSON OMNISCIENT: See **POINT OF VIEW.**

TONE: the attitude of the writer to the subject.
[Is the story or poem serious, comic, tragic, ironic, etc.?]

JOB INTERVIEWS

Sooner or later you will face a job interview. An interview is the formal name for the exchange of information and impressions between you and a potential employer. So an interview is not simple conversation. It is serious business. It is not, however, the most difficult thing you will face in life and you should not feel that it is. Preparation is the key to feeling confident (or at least not feeling petrified). For additional guidance and information, see an instructor in the business department or go to a career planning counselor. Following is a short list of interview tips:

1. Find out the time and place of the interview. Go alone.

2. Find out about the company. Some of the things you might need to know are the name and address, field or industry, kinds of clients or customers, location(s), growth, and prospects.

3. Be on time for the interview.

4. Dress properly, neatly and cleanly. Do some research, if possible, to determine the type of dress favored by those employed by the company and dress accordingly. Otherwise, wear subdued or neutral colors (navy blue, tan, gray, black) in business-type apparel. Look like you could start immediately. Never wear jeans, shorts, tee-shirts, athletic shoes or other athletic gear, or sandals.

5. Greet the interviewer, preferably by name, as you enter the office.

6. Be enthusiastic. Talk positively and concisely.

7. Be poised. Be confident (but not arrogant). Be direct, not evasive. Maintain eye contact with the interviewer. Avoid irritating mannerisms. Do not smoke or chew gum.

8. Have some goals, preferably that do not include being a millionaire by the time you are twenty-five. Have clearly defined objectives and career plans. Interviewers look for people with a purpose.

9. Be interested in the company. Show you are willing to learn about the company, but avoid seeming to shop for the best deal.

10. Know your qualifications. Carrying a résumé and a transcript is a good idea. Know you can do the job. Know also you may have to start at the bottom and work up: conceit, arrogance, and unrealistic expectations will cause an interviewer to look elsewhere.

11. Do not stay too long. Once the interviewer has indicated the interview is over, leave quietly, courteously, and quickly.

12. Immediately after an interview, send a short, type-written letter to the interviewer, thanking the interviewer for the opportunity and experience of the interview. This will bring your name to the interviewer's mind and reinforce the interview.

BUSINESS LETTERS

Sometimes you will need to write a business letter for one reason or another. No matter what the reason, the basic format is the same. Whether you write to complain that you found a spider in your cracker or whether you write to inquire if the computer part you need is stocked by that company, a business letter follows the same basic format. Only the body of the letter–what you want to say–differs.

Remember that all the things you learned in English class (spelling, grammar, format, etc.) are just as important in writing a business letter. The only thing you have to represent you to that consumer complaint department or manager (or prospective employer or senator or city official, etc.) is what you have typed in your letter. Make it impressive by making it correct and accurate.

Also remember these things:

1. Get to the point fast.

2. Use formal English. Keep the language simple. Do not try to impress with long, difficult words.

3. Consider the reader. Treat him or her with courtesy and respect. Be concise. Be clear.

4. Keep it neat. Keep it correct.

Be sure to use an envelope of the correct size for the letter. Usually a business-sized envelope looks neater and more professional than an envelope of smaller size.

Also be sure to fold the letter or document neatly for insertion. Usually the correct procedure is to fold the bottom of the letter (or document) up a scant one-third of its length and fold the top of the letter (or document) down over the first fold a scant one-third of its length.

One of the kinds of business letters you may be most interested in is the letter of inquiry about a job opening or possible position. This letter of inquiry is also called a job application letter. (See **EXAMPLE (job application letter)**.)

EXAMPLE (business letters–block format):

Your Street Address
Your City, State and ZIP Code
Date

Name of the person you are writing to
Title of this person
Company name
Company address (include ZIP)

Salutation: **(Be sure to address a specific person if possible.)**

Body of letter

(Use proper spacing–one line between the return address and the "to" address, one line between the "to" address and the salutation, one line between the salutation and the body, one line between the body and the close, three lines between the close and the typed signature block. If the letter is short, center the letter on the page.)

Sincerely yours,

< You must sign the letter in this block>

Your name

The US Postal Service recommends an envelope format that allows machine reading, using block letters and no punctuation.

EXAMPLE (business envelope):

JOE GRADUATE
1600 SUCCESS RD
CLAREMORE OK 74017

MR HOWARD H DRUCK
PERSONNEL DIRECTOR
CALCUTEX INDUSTRIES INC
1800 FINANCIAL BLVD
SUCCESS CITY OK 72233

EXAMPLE (job application business letter–block format):

1600 Success Rd.
Claremore, OK 74017
April 17, 2005

Mr. Howard H. Druck
Personnel Director
Calcutex Industries, Inc.
1800 Financial Blvd.
Success City, OK 72233

Dear Mr. Druck:

The Tulsa Daily World recently reported that Calcutex Industries is building a new data processing center just north of Tulsa. I would like to apply for a position as an entry-level programmer at the center.

I am a recent graduate of Rogers State University in Claremore with a Bachelor of Science degree in Information Technology. In addition to taking required courses, I have served as a computer consultant at the college's computer center, where I helped train novice computer users. Since I understand Calcutex Industries produces both in-house and customer documentation, my technical writing skills (as described in the enclosed résumé) may be particularly useful.

I will be happy to furnish any additional information you may need. I will contact your office Wednesday, April 24, 2005, to arrange for an interview. Please feel free to contact me (AC 918 555-1200) if there is a convenient time prior to that date.

Sincerely yours,

Joe Graduate

Joe Graduate

ENCL: résumé

RÉSUMÉS

With the job application letter you will want to enclose a résumé. To begin compiling a résumé, take a self-inventory. Find the facts: gather information about education, interests, professional memberships, civic activities, volunteer activities, employment–include title(s), dates, company names, complete company addresses, and responsibilities. Decide what your three most notable attributes are. Are you loyal, dependable, conscientious, reliable, energetic, intelligent, trainable, and/or adaptable? Then write what you want from a career in less than twenty-five words. For example, you might want to "secure a position as office assistant with management possibilities."

The effective résumé reflects favorably on you and stimulates interest in you because it draws attention to your special abilities and reflects your qualifications. It attracts the eye with a professional appearance and is concise enough to be read quickly. It is completely accurate in spelling and grammar.

The effective résumé

- does not include information that works against you,
- does not list every job you have had if the marginal jobs are not relevant,
- does not include hobbies unless they are directly related,
- does not include salary history,
- does not include references,
- does not lie.

The effective résumé uses effective words. Try to use positive words, words that show action. Use words such as *trained, coordinated, saved, supervised, demonstrated, led, innovated, conducted, installed, produced, initiated,* etc.

The effective résumé is tailored to the job you want to get. You will not slavishly follow a format if it is not appropriate to you or to the position you are seeking. The effective résumé sells you–the best way possible. It may emphasize education, or perhaps experience, or maybe skills, etc. No matter what is emphasized, the purpose is the same, to show you at your best, to get you the job.

EXAMPLE (résumés):

GREGORY D. ABLEMAN
7809 Potter St.
Altmore, OK 77999
(918) 555-6548

JOB OBJECTIVE

Secure a position as automotive company representative and diagnostician to dealerships. Willing and eager to travel.

EDUCATION

B. A. in Liberal Arts
Rogers State University
May 2005

EMPLOYMENT HISTORY

Management	Service Manager: Managed the service department of an area Olds/Buick/GMC dealer. Supervised mechanics. Scheduled. Initiated policies, dealt with customers. Trained under-qualified new employees. Improved relations with General Motors Corp. in warranty work. Fegs Motor Co., Altmore, OK 1/99-8/03
	Self-Employed. Ableman Auto, Altmore, OK 8/03-Present
Technical	MMM Transmission and Motor Co., Tryn, OK 9/92-1/99 Sears Automotive Center, Yarkan, AK 5/92-8/92 Hull Oldsmobile and Fiat, San Diego, CA 2/92-8/92
Sales	Self-employed. Engine part sales, Gregory, OK 1/90-1/92

OTHER TRAINING

Diesel Mechanics Certificate — Oklahoma State Tech

REFERENCES FURNISHED ON REQUEST

GREGORY D. ABLEMAN
7809 Potter St.
Altmore, OK 77999
(918) 555-6548

JOB OBJECTIVE Secure a position as general manager in automotive dealership with several lines of automobiles.

EDUCATION

B. A. in Liberal Arts
Rogers State University
May 2005

Diesel Mechanics
Certificate
Oklahoma State Tech 1990

EMPLOYMENT

MANAGEMENT:

Self-Employed: Ableman Auto, Altmore, OK. Diagnose/repair all makes. 8/03-Present

Service Manager: Managed the service department of an area Olds/Buick/GMC dealer. Dealt directly with customers. Scheduled jobs, trained and managed personnel. Initiated policies. Fegs Motor Company, Altmore, OK 1/99-8/03

TECHNICAL:

MMM Transmission and Motor Co., Tryn, OK. Mechanic/Assistant: Repaired and rebuilt transmissions. Handled office, customers, money for owner in his absence. 9/92-1/99

Sears Automotive Center, Yarkan, AK. Mechanic: General and air conditioner repair. 2/92-8/92

Hull Oldsmobile/Fiat, San Diego, CA. Mechanic: Repair, trouble shooting, diagnosis. 1/90-1/92

SALES:

Self-employed: Engine part sales, Gregory, OK. Sold, ordered, recorded, delivered products. 1/90-5/92

REFERENCES FURNISHED ON REQUEST

Now that you have the job, you must write to accept it. Please note that in an acceptance letter it is important to state the job title and salary you are accepting. Specify the date on which you will report to work, and do not forget to state your pleasure at joining the company.

EXAMPLE (letter of acceptance–block format):

1600 Success Road
Claremore, OK 74017
April 30, 2005

Mr. Howard H. Druck
Personnel Director
Calcutex Industries, Inc.
1800 Financial Blvd.
Success City, OK 72233

Dear Mr. Druck:

I am pleased to accept your offer of a position as a trainee in the Programming Department at a salary of $1200.00 per month.

Since finals end on May 8, I plan to leave Claremore on Tuesday, May 12. I should be able to locate suitable living accommodations within a few days and be ready to report for work on the following Monday, May 18. Please let me know if this date is satisfactory to you. I may be reached at (918) 555-7890 for the next few weeks.

I look forward to a rewarding future with Calcutex.

Sincerely,

Joe Graduate

Joe Graduate

Many times we are called upon to write a letter of recommendation. What to say (and how to say it) often poses a real problem.

EXAMPLE (letter of recommendation–block format):

2001 Success Road
Claremore, OK 74017
April 20, 2005

Mr. Howard H. Druck
Personnel Director
Calcutex Industries, Inc.
1800 Financial Blvd.
Success City, OK 72233

Dear Mr. Druck:

As her employer and former professor, I am happy to have the opportunity to recommend Susan Scholar to you. I have known Ms. Scholar for the last two years, first as a student in two of my classes and, for the last year, as a work-study assistant.

I have found Susan to be an excellent student, with a 3.95 grade point average. On the basis of her GPA and her pleasant and responsible attitude, Susan was offered and assumed unusual responsibility in the Composition Writing Lab. She has kept accurate and complete reports concerning students working in the lab. Her reports are well-written, meeting my requirements and more. She is courteous, helpful, pleasant, dependable, and very conscientious.

I strongly recommend Susan for her ability to work independently, to write clearly, and to organize her time efficiently. Please let me know if I can be of any further service.

Sincerely yours,

Ella Efficient

Ella Efficient
Professor of English

EE: jp

MEMORANDA

Memoranda, or memos, are useful in inter-office communications. Generally, the rules for memos are the same as those for letters, etc. Keep it short. Make it clear. Use correct mechanics–grammar, punctuation, spelling, etc.

Memo form is very simple. The heading consists of four categories: *to*, *from*, *subject*, and *date*. After the body of the memo, which will contain the information to be transmitted, there may appear a typist's notation like *EH/dm*. This notation means the memo was written by Evelyn Horton and typed by Dan Martin. The next section (headed Dist.) is the distribution section and lists those people who will receive a copy of the memo in addition to the writer and the person to whom the memo is written.

EXAMPLE (memorandum):

TO: Dr. John North

FROM: Dr. Evelyn Horton

DATE: Aug. 15, 2005

SUBJECT: Slides for Aug. 25 Meeting

The plans for the Aug. 25, 2005, meeting are completed. Your department is in charge of furnishing the 50 slides showing distinctions between species of gram-negative and gram-positive bacteria. Slides should be labeled by number and accompanied by a list with corresponding numbers and description of those slides.

If you could have those to the presenter, Dr. H. Cummings, or me by Aug. 20, it would facilitate practice of the presentation. I would appreciate your attendance at practice on Aug. 24 at 4:00 p.m. in the Assembly Room. We need your comments on how the presentation can be improved.

Please let me know how you want your acknowledgment to appear on the program. The program will be useful to the participants, and they will all appreciate knowing who helped make this such a success.

EH/dm

Dist: Dr. H. Whitebird
Dr. G. Adams
Mr. N. Carracolough

LAB REPORTS

A class in one of the sciences will usually involve a laboratory, and that means laboratory reports. No, writing a lab report is not hard. Simply follow the instructions for the demonstration or the experiment, collect the data, and write up the results that you have found, using the report form required by the class. One suggested form follows.

EXAMPLE (lab report):

LABORATORY REPORT

NAME____________________ PARTNER'S NAME____________________

EXPERIMENT TITLE____________________________ DATE______

PURPOSE: State what you are trying to do, find, verify, examine, measure, etc.

METHOD:
a. Sketch the apparatus or circuit diagram.
b. Briefly describe what you did.

DATA: Record your observations and measurements (format may vary depending on data collected).

CALCULATIONS: Show all mathematical computations necessary to obtain your results.

GRAPHS: All graphs will be plotted on separate sheets of graph paper.

CONCLUSION: Make a statement, similar to the purpose, of what you found. References to calculations and graphs are appropriate here.

SOURCES OF ERROR: List measuring devices and techniques used to get your data that would cause the measurements to be less than 100% accurate.
Also include calculations of percent error and/or difference.

GRAPHS

Many times in a science lab you will be required to make a graph as part of the demonstration of the collection of the data. Graphs are not complicated. Remember that you want the scale of the graph to be the largest possible that will fit the graph paper and that everything should be clearly and completely labeled.

EXAMPLE (graph form):

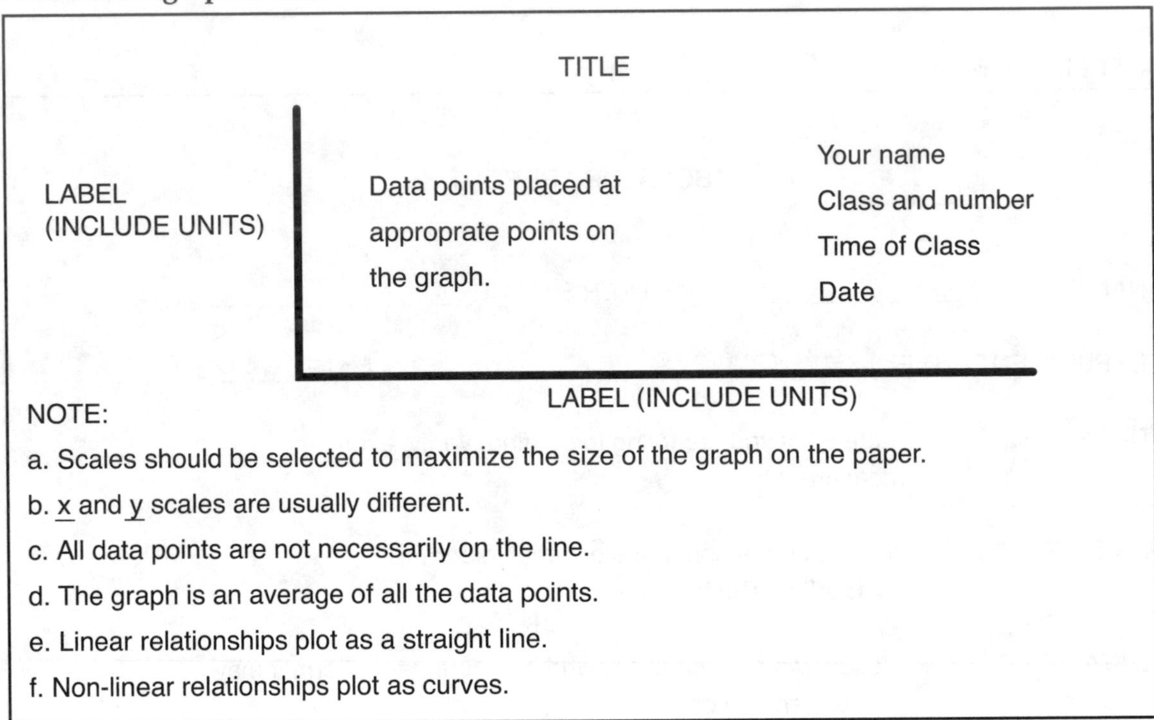

NOTE:

a. Scales should be selected to maximize the size of the graph on the paper.

b. x and y scales are usually different.

c. All data points are not necessarily on the line.

d. The graph is an average of all the data points.

e. Linear relationships plot as a straight line.

f. Non-linear relationships plot as curves.

EXAMPLE (graph):

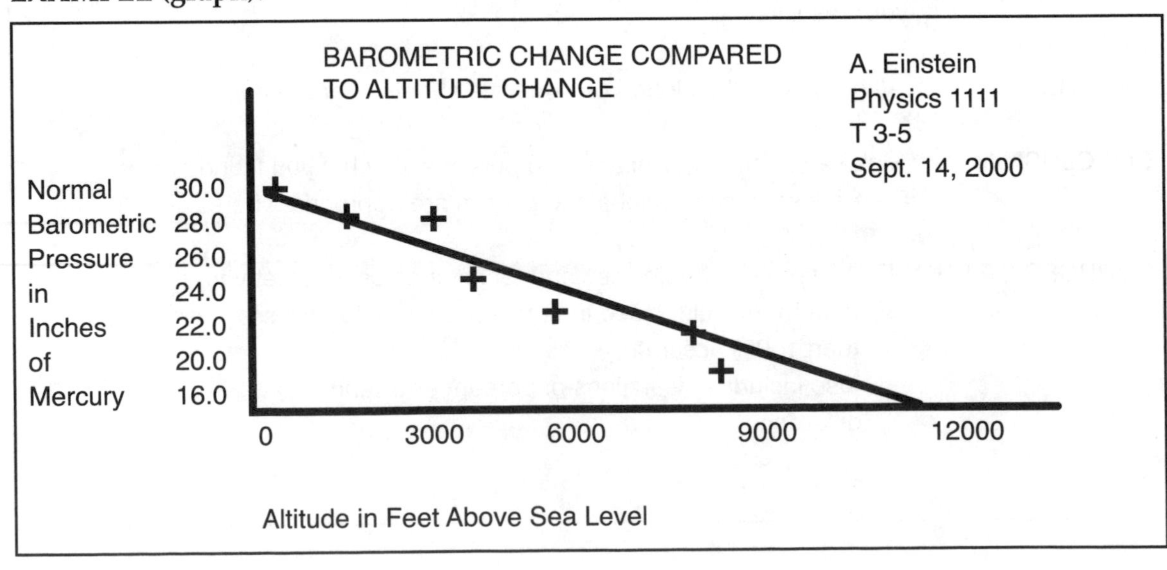

LIBRARY DISCOVERY

A library may look like an imposing edifice on the outside (and to some it looks imposing on the inside too), but in fact a library is a treasure chest, a cornucopia of intellectual delights. And you do not have to be an "intellectual" to use one. The library is available to all with only a few skills needed to open the treasure chest and to taste the fruits in the cornucopia.

The first skill needed is the courage to open the door. Once you have passed that point, everything else is easier. Look around and investigate the landscape. How is the library arranged? What furniture is where? Where are the fattest books? Where do the newspapers rustle and the magazines crackle? Where do the globes spin? Where do the microfilm and microfiche machines fill the air with their distinctive acrid odor? Where do the computer stations connect to the electronic world?

After you become familiar with the library's physical plant, you should investigate the resources. A casual glance shows you that the library has many, many books. How do you, overwhelmed by the sheer volume of volumes, choose which book to pick off the shelf? You can, of course, just browse around and pick up books at random until you find one that interests you. But this is probably most effective when you just want to read for pleasure. And even then it is most effective when you want to read fiction for pleasure. What if you want to find a book on a specific subject, or with a particular title, or by a certain author? Go to the card catalog!

CARD CATALOG

Some libraries have card catalogs that are made up of cards. Most libraries have computer or on-line catalogues. In this case, the works available in book form in the library appear on a computer screen. Either on-line or in print, books are catalogued by author, title, and subject. No matter which of the three you know, you can find information about a book and discover the other information you need to locate the book.

Remember, when looking up the title, that the title is alphabetized by the first word of the title that is not *a*, *an*, or *the* (unless the article is an integral part of the title). After you find a listing for a book, then you have to understand how to find the book. You must understand the call number based on the Dewey Decimal System number or the Library of Congress number.

One way to catalog books is the Library of Congress system, which classifies all books, fiction and nonfiction. Each book is assigned a letter corresponding to a subject category–like *P* for *Language and Literature*. Subject categories can be subdivided by adding another letter. Then each book receives an individual number. A book of Nineteenth Century American literature might have the Library of Congress call number *PS 3319*. The Library of Congress categories are

A General Works
B Philosophy, Religion, Psychology
C History, Auxiliary Sciences
D History (General), History of Europe
E History: American
F History: American
G Geography, Recreation, Anthropology
H Social Sciences
J Political Science
K Law
L Education
M Music, Books on Music
N Fine Art
Q Science
R Medicine
S Agriculture
T Technology
U Military Science
V Naval Science
Z Bibliography, Library Science, Information Resources

Another way to catalog books is by the Dewey Decimal system, a ten-category system based on subject. Novels and short stories are labeled fiction and found in a separate, alphabetized section. The Dewey Decimal categories are

000-099	Generalities: Facts and Information, including encyclopedias, bibliographies, periodicals, facts, world records, journalism, handbooks, etc.
100-199	Philosophy and Psychology, including philosophy, psychology, conduct, supernatural, etc.
200-299	Religion, including religion, mythology, theology, etc.
300-399	Social Sciences, including sociology, political science, law, economics, occupations, communications, education, etc.
400-499	Language, including dictionaries, grammar, writing, language (including foreign language) study, etc.
500-599	Natural Sciences and Mathematics, or Pure Science, including mathematics, astronomy, physics, chemistry, earth and life sciences, botany, zoology, etc.
600-699	Technology (Applied Sciences), including engineering, home economics, medicine, agriculture, aviation, invention, manufacturing, building, etc.
700-799	The Arts, including architecture, art, photography, music, recreational and performing arts, sports, etc.
800-899	Literature and Rhetoric, including poems, short stories, plays, literature of America and the world (as well as untranslated literature of other languages), etc. Does not include novels or short stories, which are found on the fiction shelves.
900-999	Geography and History, including geography, history, biography, travel, etc.

Each category is further divided. Science, for example, has the following categories:
500-509 General Science,
510-519 Mathematics,
520-529 Astronomy,
530-539 Physics, etc.

And then these categories are sub-divided:
511 Arithmetic,
512 Algebra,
513 Geometry,
514 Trigonometry, etc.

The categories are then further divided into sub-categories shown by numbers behind the decimal point. A letter at the end of the number or on the second line of the number designates the first letter of the last name of the author. This combination of numbers is the Dewey Decimal system call number.

EXAMPLE (finding a book source on a topic):

- **Dewey Decimal System**

A book titled *Technology and the Changing Family* is about family and is catalogued in the Dewey Decimal system in the Social Science category. The author's name is Ogburn. The book has the number 301.42 as the first line of the Dewey Decimal system call number and OG2 as the second.

A book titled *Open Marriage* by O'Neill is also on the subject of family and is catalogued in the Social Science category. The Dewey Decimal System call number is 301.42 on the first line and ON2 on the second.

A book on television and feminism is edited by Rory Dicker and Alison Piepmeier and titled *Catching a Wave: Reclaiming Feminism for the 21st Century*. The Dewey Decimal system call number is 305.42, followed by C284.

- **Library of Congress System**

A book on television and morality is written by Gregory Stevenson and titled *Televised Morality: The Case of Buffy the Vampire Slayer*. The Library of Congress call number is PN1992.77.B84, followed by S74 2003.

A book on television and feminism is edited by Rory Dicker and Alison Piepmeier and titled *Catching a Wave: Reclaiming Feminism for the 21st Century*. The Library of Congress call number is HQ1426, followed by C284 2003.

- **All Systems:** To find the books, look along the shelves (also called stacks) to find the correct area for the call number for which you are looking. This is not hard since the books are shelved in numerical order.

What if you cannot find what you want in the card catalog? If it is simply a matter of not finding the exact subject heading for which you are looking, then perhaps you can choose to look under another word that is close in meaning to the one with which you started. Or you may have to go to a broader category.

EXAMPLE (finding a book source on a topic):

- If you have been looking for information on the Iditarod Dog Sled Race and you know it takes place on the Iditarod Trail in Alaska, you would probably start looking for all the easy choices, like *Iditarod* and *dog sled*, and you may even go to *racing* and *Alaska*. Under racing there is nothing about racing dogs, and under Alaska is information on population and geography. What now? Go to a broader category. Look under *dogs*. Surely there is some relevant information you can use in one of the books about dogs. But that may not be enough.

- You may have to ask a librarian to use the *Library of Congress Subject Headings*. This index will give you lists of alternative choices of words under which to look.

If a source is just not available in the library, you may want to investigate inter-library loan. Most libraries can obtain books and other material from other libraries. All you have to know is the name and author of what you want. But that is just what you were looking for! What now? To discover the names of authors and of works, find one of the specialized indexes. (See **SPECIAL HELPS** and **ARTICLES FROM MAGAZINES AND NEWSPAPERS: INDEXES**.) Or you might go to a computer data base. (See **COMPUTER AND INTERNET SOURCES**.)

ARTICLES FROM MAGAZINES AND NEWSPAPERS: INDEXES

What if what you want to find is not a book? What if you want to find a current or topical item that has not had time to become the subject of a book? Or what if you just want the latest information? Then you would go to the magazine and newspaper indexes, many of which are available in databases of various kinds and some of which are still available in hard copy in small libraries. Two of the most popular indexes are the *Reader's Guide to Periodical Literature* and the *New York Times Index*.

In the *Reader's Guide,* articles from more than 175 magazines are indexed alphabetically by author and subject. A complete explanation of how to read each abbreviation and entry is found in the front of the *Reader's Guide.*

EXAMPLE (using the Reader's Guide to Periodical Literature):

- The *Reader's Guide* entry reads like this:
  NAIL guns
  Electric nail gun for the home handyman. R. Capotosto. il Mech Illus 76:64-5 Mr '80
- The subject you have found is *nail guns.* The article listed will be about nail guns. The title of the article is "Electric Nail Gun for the Home Handyman." The article is illustrated and appears in the *Mechanics Illustrated* issue of March 1980 in volume 76 on pages 64 and 65.
- The bibliographic data, according to the *MLA Handbook,* would be written like this:

Capotosto, R. "Electric Nail Gun for the Home Handyman." Mechanics Illustrated 76 (Mar. 1980): 64-65.

- In APA style, the bibliographic data would be written like this:

Capotosto, R. (1980, March). Electric nail gun for the home handyman. *Mechanics illustrated, 76,* pp. 64-65.

The library will probably not have all the magazines indexed in the *Reader's Guide.* You may check the availability of magazines by looking for a list of periodicals or by asking a librarian. (Remember that the inter-library loan service applies to articles as well as books.)

Some magazines are on the periodical display shelves. Earlier issues may be bound and found on the bound periodical shelves. Or they may be available on microfiche or on microfilm.

The New York Times Index indexes *The New York Times* newspaper. A complete explanation of how to read an entry is contained in the front of each index volume. The *New York Times Index,* with abstracts and with full-text articles, is also available on CD-ROM and through electronic databases.

EXAMPLE (reading the *New York Times Index* entries):

- An entry from the *New York Times Index* for July 16-31, 1987, might look like this:

  Aged. See also
  Age, Chronological
  Medicare
  Medicine and Health, Jl 22,23,26
  Nursing Homes . . .
  Organization in Greenwich Village called Village Visiting Neighbors has 'Shop and Escort' service, arranging for volunteers to help area's elderly residents with their shopping and other errands (M), Jl 24,II,4:2

- The heading is "Aged." Other headings under which you might look for information on this topic are "Age, Chronological," etc. Under the alternate heading "Medicine and Health," the index lists specific date references, those for July 22, 23, and 26. Therefore, under "Medicine and Health," you would look for the entries for those specific dates to find references to aging.

- The reference you have found under "Aged" is to the Village Visiting Neighbors. You do not know either the title (because newspapers do not have "titles") or the headline (because this information is not given). You do have a short synopsis of the article itself and it gives you the gist (and only the gist) of what has appeared in print. To see the whole article and to find the headline, you will have to go to the newspaper as it appears on microfilm. To find the article on microfilm, you will look up the microfilm roll for the paper printed on July 24, 1987. The article (of medium length) will appear in section B, page 4, column 2.

- The bibliographic data, according to the *MLA Handbook*, would be written like this:

"Help for Elderly New in Village." New York Times 24 Jul. 1987: B4.

- In APA style, the bibliographic data would be written this:

Help for elderly new in village. (1987, July 24). *New York times*, p. B84.

Aside from the *Reader's Guide* and the *New York Times Index*, there are other specialized indexes to periodicals for certain years and for specific subject areas. Two major on-line indexes, the Infotrak Search Bank and First Search (see **COMPUTER AND INTERNET SOURCES**), are usually available.

NON-PRINT

What if you are looking for non-print sources? Many libraries have audio tapes, audio books, video cassettes, and compact discs listed alphabetically in the catalog.

SPECIAL HELPS

Where do you look for special help? You may, of course, look in an encyclopedia for information. It is not customary, or advisable, to use a general encyclopedia in doing research at the college level. After all, the authors and editors of the encyclopedia would then be doing the research for you. But it is both feasible and advisable to go to a general encyclopedia for easily accessible background information on a subject in which you are interested. Some special encyclopedias, encyclopedias on specific subject areas, are listed in the appropriate subject sections.

Never forget the wealth of information available in the simple dictionary (some of which are not so simple). The largest dictionaries are those called unabridged dictionaries, which are full dictionaries, not abridged (cut down) versions.

Some dictionaries are specialized dictionaries, such as *Funk and Wagnall's Standard Handbook of Synonyms, Antonyms, and Prepositions.*

Some general reference books such as yearbooks and almanacs can be helpful. These books are useful sources for factual information on dates, lists, events, etc. These include the *World Almanac* and *Book of Facts.*

If you need information on geography (which can include information on economics, agriculture, biology, ecology, political divisions, and weather in addition to the locations of mountain ranges and rivers), look for an atlas. Atlases are divided into two general categories–historical and general.

General atlases give information on geographic data of the year published, such as economic, political, agricultural, and other data. Some general atlases include the *Oxford Atlas of the World, Times Atlas of the World,* and *Macmillan World Atlas.*

Historical atlases show the world of different eras: for example, *The Times Atlas of the Second World War.*

Business indexes contain various kinds of information. One of these indexes may tell you company names, product lines, major personnel (by name and position), addresses, subsidiaries, parent companies, net worth, capital, etc. Try *Thomas Register* or *Standard and Poor's Register of Corporation Directors and Executives.*

If you need information on a person in history, literature, or politics, look in one of the biographical references, which include information about contemporary or past notables. These references include *Current Biography* (outstanding personalities of our time), the *Dictionary of American Biography* (distinguished Americans no longer living), the *Dictionary of National Biography* (distinguished English people no longer living), the *New Century Cyclopedia of Names* (more than 100,000 proper names, including persons, places, events, literary works and characters, works of art, mythological and legendary persons and places), *Webster's Biographical Dictionary* (biographies of famous people through the ages), *Who's Who* (distinguished living British and Commonwealth persons–includes parents, schooling, spouse, children, accomplishments, etc.), *Who Was Who* (distinguished dead British and Commonwealth persons), *Who's Who in America* (distinguished living Americans), *Dictionary of Scientific Biography, Notable Twentieth-Century Scientists, New Grove Dictionary of Music and Musicians,* and *Notable American Women 1607-1950.*

Biographical references solely about authors are also available: *Contemporary Authors, European Authors 1000-1900* by Kunitz and Colby, *World Authors* by Wakeman, *American Authors 1600-1900* by Kunitz and Haycraft, *British Authors Before 1800* by Kunitz and Haycraft, *American Writers* by Unger, *Twentieth Century Authors* by Kunitz and Haycraft, *Dictionary of Literary Biography, Magill's Cyclopedia of World Authors,* and *Dictionary of American Biography.*

Other literary reference books include some specialized works: *Bartlett's Familiar Quotations* (lists of famous authors and their quotations; lists of quotations and their sources); *Granger's Index to Poetry* (lists of titles, authors, first lines of poems, titles of books containing poems); *Home Book of Quotations, Classical and Modern; Untermeyer's Modern British Poetry; Encyclopedia of Poetry and Poetics.*

Other specialized reference books include information from specific subject areas.

COMPUTER AND INTERNET SOURCES

What if you want even more information than you are finding? You might want to investigate some of the major databases and/or the Internet. Library computers are connected to the Internet; you can search an enormous volume of material for the subject in which you are interested. In addition to web sites, etc., libraries have access to electronic databases. Those databases have either article abstracts or full-text articles or both. Some databases include unpublished material, doctoral dissertations, and conference presentations, in addition to journal articles. Databases can be a valuable source for anyone doing extensive research on a subject.

Two major databases include Infotrak Search Bank and First Search. Infotrak contains the following databases: General Business File ASAP, General Reference Center (Magazine Index), PsycINFO (information on psychology, pharmacology, physiology, linguistics, law, social work, anthropology), Health Reference Center—Academic, Expanded Academic ASAP (information on astronomy, law, religion, history, psychology, humanities, current events, sociology, communications, and general sciences), Predicast PROMT (Predicasts Overview of Markets and Technology), Kid's Edition (information designed for schools), Books in Print, National Newspaper Index, LegalTrac, etc. The Expanded Academic ASAP is an excellent database for undergraduate research.

First Search contains general databases, such as WorldCat (information on books and materials in worldwide libraries), ArticleFirst (article index), ContentsFirst (periodical's table of contents), ECO (full-text scholarly articles), FastDoc (index of articles on-line or by e-mail), NetFirst (Internet resources), Union Lists (periodical list), etc., and specialized databases, such as AGRICOLA (agriculture information), CINAHL (Cumulative Index to Nursing and Allied Health), ERIC (education information), Fact Search, GPA Monthly Catalog (government publications), MEDLINE, MLA (Modern Language Association), PapersFirst (index of conference papers), ProceedingsFirst (index of conference publications), World Almanac, etc.

LIBRARIANS

Librarians know everything. Well, that is not quite true. Librarians can find out anything. And that is true. A librarian by training knows where to look to find odd, unusual, or specialized subjects. A librarian by nature is curious and tenacious.

When you need help,
ask a librarian!

MECHANICS

This large section titled "Mechanics" is concerned with the technical aspects of writing, those picky "English things" like punctuation, grammar, spelling, etc., that make papers easier to read and, thus, life easier to live.

USAGE

Choosing which words to use depends largely on the situation in which you find yourself. Some forms of usage are not appropriate when formal written or spoken English is required but may be acceptable at another time or place.

Formal English is that form of the language that is appropriate in all situations (except maybe a party with the Hell's Angels). Formal English follows certain usage conventions, that is, some ways to speak and write are acceptable and some are not. Formal English is usually required in college speaking and writing.

Colloquialisms are expressions acceptable in informal use only. An example of a colloquialism is referring to a father as "pa."

Regionalisms are usages known only in certain areas. In Mississippi, people "carry" their grandmothers to the market instead of taking them. In Louisiana, people "make" groceries at Safeway instead of buying them. In Maine, people drink "tonic" instead of "pop," "soda," or "Coke."

Slang is a form of language used only among certain groups and is usually of short duration. Slang labels people as "in" or "out" of certain groups, depending on their use of the terms. Those who belonged to the drug culture of the fifties talked knowledgeably and esoterically about "grass" (not Bermuda) so that eavesdroppers or casual overhearers would not be aware of the subject under discussion. Of course, soon slang becomes outdated when "everyone" can use the terms and know the meaning. Then slang changes. Outdated slang sounds very strange.

Non-standard or illiterate usages are below the standard for use by even minimally educated people. Saying "He done gone to the store; I seen him go" is non-standard.

Informal English is English used between friends or on occasions when it is not necessary to be especially formal. It is much like a sweat suit, which is fun and comfortable, but which would not be worn to a job interview.

Non-idiomatic English is English that is used improperly, not because it is incorrect by the rules of grammar but because English speakers do not use the language in that manner. A non-idiomatic expression would be to say someone "went at" the store instead of "went to" because "at" is usually not used after the word "went."

Archaic or obsolete words or phrases are no longer used but appeared in earlier writing and speaking. People no longer appear "betimes"; they now appear quickly.

Poetic usage is found in poetry or poetic prose. Using "o'er" instead of "over" is poetic.

Dialect is a continuing pattern (including pronunciation, grammar and vocabulary) of speech or writing used in particular areas. It is related to regionalism but is not restricted to one or two words in a conversation. It is a pattern that is used overwhelmingly in the area or by the group.

Professional or occupational dialects include specialized terms, abbreviations, etc., applicable mainly to certain jobs or occupations.

SENTENCE STRUCTURE

Effective sentences reflect clear thinking. Clumsy or ill-structured sentences imply that the idea has not been clearly thought out. Thus, you must know not only what you think you want to say, but you must also decide how to say it so that the reader has a clear idea of what you mean.

Following are common errors.

1. A sentence fragment or incomplete sentence is a sentence that does not contain all the necessary parts (subject and verb) or that does not make complete sense when standing alone.

EXAMPLE INCOMPLETE SENTENCE: I went to the store. Following the marvelous lesson on sentence structure in my English class.

- The first part of this example "I went to the store" is complete because it has a subject and a verb and it makes complete sense when read alone. The second part does not have a subject and a verb, and it does not make sense when read without the preceding sentence.

EXAMPLE COMPLETE SENTENCE: I went to the store following the marvelous lesson on sentence structure in my English class.

2. A run-on sentence runs two or more sentences together without proper terminal punctuation or beginning capitalization. A comma splice, which is a kind of run-on sentence, hangs two or more sentences together with a comma between them.

EXAMPLE RUN-ON SENTENCE: When we go to the zoo, we hope to see the baby elephant its mother died from a twisted intestine and the baby is orphaned.

EXAMPLE COMMA SPLICE: The baby elephant is very small, it is not as big as a pony yet.

EXAMPLE CORRECT SENTENCES: When we go to the zoo, we hope to see the baby elephant. Its mother died from a twisted intestine, and the baby is orphaned. The baby elephant is very small. It is not as big as a pony yet.

PARALLEL CONSTRUCTION

The use of parallel construction enhances writing because it lends clarity, elegance, and symmetry. Wonderful! So what is parallel construction?

Parallel construction is using words, phrases, or clauses in series in a similar fashion, both grammatically and logically. Parallelism, as parallel construction is also called, coordinates words, phrases, or statements in similar grammatical construction. This means paralleling noun with noun, verb with verb, phrase with phrase, and statement with statement.

Consider the following famous quotation by Julius Caesar: "I came; I saw; I conquered." Caesar uses three simple verbs, in parallel construction, to tell about the things he did. The parallel construction makes what he said memorable. Suppose he had said, "I came to Gaul. I saw all those barbarians sitting around on all that undefended land. So I decided to conquer them and did." In that case, what he did may have been remembered, but hardly what he said about it.

When you have two or more items in a list, a series, a contrast, a choice, a statement of equivalence, a formal definition, a statement of evaluation, or a comparison, you should put all of the items into the same grammatical form.

EXAMPLE (parallel construction):

- **LIST**
  "I have nothing to offer but blood, toil, tears, and sweat."
  —Winston Churchill (four nouns)

- **SERIES**
  "Let every nation know, whether it wishes us well or ill, that we shall pay any price, bear any burden, meet any hardship, support any friend, oppose any foe to assure the survival and success of liberty." —John F. Kennedy (five object-verb combinations)

- **CONTRAST**
  "On all these shores there are echoes of past and future: of the flow of time, obliterating yet containing all that has gone before." —Rachel Carson (two participles)

- **SERIES PLUS CONTRAST**
  "Rather than love, than money, than fame, give me truth." —Henry D. Thoreau (four nouns)

- **CHOICE**
  "We must indeed all hang together, or most assuredly, we shall all hang separately." —Benjamin Franklin (two clauses)

- **COMPARISON**
  "A living dog is better than a dead lion." —Ecclesiastes 9.4 (two noun phrases)

Conjunctions play a part in the formation of parallel construction. Correlative conjunctions are defined as words or phrases used in pairs to join words, phrases or clauses. Correlatives include *both/and*, *not only/but also*, *either/or*, *neither/nor*, and *whether/or*.

When using a pair of correlatives, be sure that the word or word group following the first member of the pair is parallel with the word or word group following the second.

EXAMPLE (parallel construction):

Janet Rostek not only got the leading role of Fanny Brice, but also played the part brilliantly.
Windsurfing is both exciting and dangerous.
Janie could not decide whether to start college right after high school or to get a job first.

AGREEMENT

Agreement of subject and verb and of pronoun with antecedent noun is a common problem.

The two general rules are

- to make every verb agree with its subject in both person and number and
- to make every pronoun agree with its noun antecedent in person and number.

The difficulty is to follow the rules. Following are the specifics that make it possible to follow those rules.

VERB/SUBJECT

1. When two or more subjects are joined by *or* or *nor*, the verb agrees with the nearer subject.

   EXAMPLE: Neither you nor (she is) going to go.

2. When two or more subjects are joined by *and*, use a plural verb unless the two subjects are considered a unit.

EXAMPLE:	(You and she) (are) going to go.
BUT	(Milk and cereal) (is) his favorite breakfast.

3. When a verb is separated from its subject, ignore the words of separation.

EXAMPLE:	(One) of the four boys (is) going to get selected.

4. A linking verb agrees with the subject, not the subject complement.

EXAMPLE:	The most interesting (item is) the bridles.
AND	(It is) miles to the next town.

5. Singular pronouns and collective nouns both take singular verbs unless the members of the collective noun group are acting or are considered as individuals or individual items.

EXAMPLE:	(Everyone is) trying for a scholarship.
	The (board of directors has) voted yes to the merger.
	(Four dollars is) all I have.
BUT	The (dollars are) on the table.
	The (board of directors are) arguing over the merger outcome.

6. Singular nouns that look plural still take a singular verb.
Literary titles and words as words take singular verbs.

EXAMPLE:	(Mumps is) a disease for which there is now a vaccine.
AND	(*Christmas Stories* is) an edition of Dickens's short stories about Christmas.
AND	(Mass is) a word with different meanings in different areas.

7. *There* is never a subject.

EXAMPLE:	There (is) one (way) to do this project.
AND	There (are) two (ways) to do this project.

8. Verbs after words like *who*, *which*, and *that* agree with the antecedent noun.

EXAMPLE:	He is one (person) who (has) the list.
AND	He is one of the (people) who (have) the list.

PRONOUN

1. A word like *this, that, these* and *those* agrees with the nouns it modifies.

EXAMPLE: This sort of class is helpful.
AND These sorts of classes are helpful.

2. Following the same logic as subject/verb rule 5, pronouns agree with the sense of the antecedent noun.

EXAMPLE: The (board of directors has) made its vote.
AND The (board of directors have) not finished their argument.

3. Keep pronouns in person agreement; do not shift to *you.*

EXAMPLE: I like films when I get interested in the action.
NOT I like films when you get interested in the action.

4. Singular pronouns agree with singular nouns, such as

person woman	everybody everyone		neither either
somebody someone	anybody	man one	each anyone

EXAMPLE: The man has his own desk.
AND Somebody has taken his pencil.

When a singular antecedent may be either masculine or feminine, you may use the masculine pronoun (because it has been considered to be neuter–but it is not neuter politically), so the best alternative is to use both pronouns or change the entire sentence to plural in order to avoid using "sexist language."

EXAMPLE: A person has his own desk.
OR A person has his or her own desk.
OR People have their own desks.

5. Using the same logic as verb/subject rules 1 and 2 above, for antecedent nouns joined by *and*, use a plural pronoun; for antecedent nouns joined by *or*, use a pronoun agreeing with the nearest antecedent noun.

EXAMPLE: The (cat and the dog are) eating (their) food.
AND The (cat and the dogs are) eating (their) food.
AND George or the (boys are) bringing (their) car.
AND The boys or (George is) bringing (his) car.

CAPITALIZATION

1. Capitalize the first word of every sentence, including a quoted sentence. If the quotation is interrupted, do not capitalize the second part unless it is also a complete quoted sentence.

   EXAMPLE: The boy wailed, "A dog has bitten me!"
   AND "A dog," the boy wailed, "has bitten me!"

   a. Do NOT capitalize the first word of indirect quotations.

   EXAMPLE: The boy wailed that the dog had bitten him.

   b. Do NOT capitalize the first word of a fragmentary quotation unless it is capitalized in the original text.

   EXAMPLE: Although the Carpenter told the Oysters to go on home, they could not go because the Carpenter and the Walrus had "eaten every one."

   c. Do NOT capitalize the first word of a sentence in parentheses within another sentence.

   EXAMPLE: Alice (did you know her?) did not appreciate the story about the oysters.

2. Capitalize the first word of a line of poetry (unless, as in some modern poetry, the poet has not capitalized the first word of the line).

   EXAMPLE:

   "It seems a shame," the Walrus said,
   "To play them such a trick,
   After we've brought them out so far,
   And made them trot so quick!"
   The Carpenter said nothing but
   "The butter's spread too thick!"
   —Lewis Carroll,
   "The Walrus and the Carpenter"

3. Capitalize first word of phrases or words used as sentences.

   EXAMPLE: Not on your life. Yes, of course. Certainly.

4. Do not capitalize the first word of a formal question or statement following a colon unless the formal question or statement is quoted or unless the colon introduces a series of sentences.

   EXAMPLE: The problem is simple: we haven't the money.
   AND Because the Oysters were tired, the Walrus was sad: "The Carpenter said nothing. . . ."
   AND Discuss the following items: How do the Oysters travel? Who are the other characters? When does the meal take place? What is its accompaniment?

5. Capitalize the first word of numbered enumerations that form complete sentences and of phrasal lists and enumerations below texts. Do not capitalize phrasal lists or enumerations that are seen as part of the text.

   EXAMPLE: Be sure to ask these questions: (1) When did the patient last eat? (2) What was eaten? (3) What quantity was ingested? (4) What effect was first noticed?
   AND A short story has these elements:
   Character
   Setting
   Plot
   Point of view
   Theme
   AND A short story has these elements: (1) character, (2) setting, (3) plot, (4) point of view, and (5) theme.

6. Capitalize the first word, the last word, and all important words in a title, including *is*.

   EXAMPLE: "The Walrus and the Carpenter" *One Is Gone* *Alice in Wonderland*

7. Capitalize the first word of each item in a formal outline.

   EXAMPLE: I. Capitalization
   A. First word of a sentence
   B. First word of a title
   C. Last word of a title

8. Capitalize the first word of a letter salutation and the first word of the complimentary close.

   EXAMPLE: Dear Mary, Dear Sir: Love, Sincerely, Very unhappily,

9. Capitalize proper nouns and all words made from them. Do NOT capitalize common nouns.

EXAMPLE: Mary woman Tulsa city David man May month
Lion's Club club Great Dane dog Rogers State College college

a. Capitalize abbreviations if the full form is capitalized.

EXAMPLE: Dec. December Capt. Captain

b. Do NOT capitalize general terms referring to degrees. Capitalize names of academic degrees following a person's name. Capitalize abbreviations for degrees.

EXAMPLE: Martin Shawn, Doctor of Divinity Dr. James Fotinblach
Julia Sheppard, M.S.W. working for an associate's degree
received an A.A. degree

c. Do NOT capitalize names of academic disciplines unless they are part of course titles or are proper nouns.

EXAMPLE: He did especially well in math and English.
AND That course is Humanities 1223, the first humanities course.

d. Do NOT capitalize directions unless they refer to a specific section of the country.

EXAMPLE: Reporters traveled south on I-20 to cover primaries in the South.

e. Do NOT capitalize words of family relationship unless they are used as a name or part of a name.

EXAMPLE: I call my grandfather on my father's side Grandfather Ames and my grandfather on my mother's side Grandpa.

f. Capitalize a title or position only when it is used preceding a person's name.

EXAMPLE: The president of the United States was President Reagan; the queen of England was Queen Elizabeth.

10. Capitalize words in a memorandum following a heading as if the words appeared in a title.

EXAMPLE: SUBJECT: The Writing of Memos
TO: All Memo Writers

NUMBERS

1. With certain exceptions, exact numbers *ninety-nine* and below should be written as words. Exact numbers 100 and above should be written as numbers. **EXCEPTIONS**: Dates, addresses (except for *one*), highway route numbers, etc., are written as numbers.

EXAMPLE: She owns forty horses and 176 sheep.
AND The farm is on U.S. 40 at Exit 11-A, and the address is P.O. Box 1177, Clinton, OK, until May 11, 1999, when it will become One Bayshore Road, Arapaho, OK.

2. Approximate or round numbers should be written out.

EXAMPLE: Almost five thousand people attended the play.

3. Numbers that begin a sentence should be written out. (If the sentence looks odd or awkward with the number written out, restructure the sentence so that the number appears internally.)

EXAMPLE: Four thousand ninety attended.
OR The group numbered 4,090 people.

4. Hyphens are used in written-out numbers between *twenty-one* and *ninety-nine*.

5. Hyphens are used in written-out fractions used as modifiers.

EXAMPLE: When he cut the slices, each child got one-eighth pie.

6. Numbers are not divided at the end of a line.

7. Roman numerals should appear as uppercase letters (except for the designation of a scene in a play) unless an original quoted source uses lower case letters for the numerals.

EXAMPLE: Richard has "an ironic speech in Richard II, Act I, scene i, lines 139-141," according to critic Don DeLoon in the forward to his book Shakespeare's Great Shakes (VII).

8. With some exceptions (year dates, check numbers, binary numbers, telephone numbers, etc.), whole numbers of five or more digits are punctuated with commas in groups of three, counting from the right. Punctuation of whole numbers of four digits is optional.

EXAMPLE:	A.D. 1255	Check No. 135667	line 8
	command 11011	population of 1,233,544,651	
OR	population of 1,333		
OR	population of 1333	10,876 cans of spaghetti sauce	(918) 555-1345

PUNCTUATION

In the past, writing was characterized by full and detailed punctuation. Today we realize that, as a speaker who hems and haws and pauses too long is hard to understand, too much punctuation interferes with the flow of reading. You will have few punctuation problems if you use a mark of punctuation for only two reasons:

- because meaning demands it or
- because conventional usage requires it.

If a sentence is not clear, punctuation will not help it. If you find yourself struggling with the punctuation of a sentence, ask yourself if the problem is your arrangement of phrases or choice of words. The problem can often be eliminated by rephrasing the sentence.

END MARKS

1. A statement is followed by a period.

EXAMPLE: A statement is followed by a period.

2. An initial is followed by a period. An abbreviation may be followed by a period.

EXAMPLE: Mr. A. B. Cloe, born 1925 A. D., has entered college.

3. A question is followed by a question mark.

EXAMPLE: What is a person like you doing in a place like this?

a. Use the question mark after a direct question only: do not use the question mark after a declarative sentence containing an indirect question.

EXAMPLE: Did she enroll in the summer, fall, or spring?
AND He asked if she went to school too.

b. Orders and requests are often put in the form of a question, even when no real question is intended. Such a question may be followed by a question mark or a period.

EXAMPLE: Will you please turn that report in now.
OR Will you please turn that report in now?

c. A question mark should be placed inside quotation marks when the quotation is a question. If the whole item is a question, the question mark should be placed outside the quotation marks.

EXAMPLE: She asked, "Is that biology lab?"
AND Did she ask, "Is that lab"?

4. An exclamation is followed by an exclamation mark.

EXAMPLE: Of course I made an *A* on the exam!

a. An interjection at the beginning of a sentence is almost always followed by a comma.

EXAMPLE: Yes, I will get the scholarship!

b. An exclamation mark should be placed inside quotation marks when the quotation itself is an exclamation. Otherwise, it should be placed outside the quotation marks.

EXAMPLE: The burglar said, "Hands up!"
AND Someone is yelling, "Hands up"!

c. Do not use an exclamation mark unless a statement is obviously emphatic.

EXAMPLE: What a party!
NOT The party was a little fun!

COMMAS

Next to end marks, the comma is the most frequently used mark of punctuation, grouping words that belong together and separating those that do not. It is also used in conventional ways that have little to do with meaning.

1. Use commas to separate items in a series. Under circumstances where the meaning of the phrase can not be misunderstood, it is not necessary (but it is advisable) to put a comma before the last *and* in a series. It is never wrong to include the comma prior to the last *and* in the series.

   EXAMPLE: RSC offers programs in accounting, education and business.
   BUT The meeting included speeches by elementary and secondary education majors, business, and accounting of present funds.

2. Use commas to separate two or more adjectives that modify the same item.
   HINT: If you can say *and* between the two adjectives, put in the comma.

   EXAMPLE: A course of study leading to an associate's degree will enable a studious, interested student to more easily achieve lifetime goals.

3. Use a comma before *and, but, or, nor, for, yet, so* when they join independent clauses.

   EXAMPLE: We came to party, but we stayed to study.

4. Use a comma to set off non-essential clauses and non-essential participial phrases.

   EXAMPLE: The radio station, which is staffed by college students seeking broadcast experience, has become a vital part of the community experience.

5. Use a comma after certain introductory elements:

   a. After words such as *well, yes, no, why,* etc., when they begin a sentence.

   EXAMPLE: Yes, you can get an excellent background for engineering and science courses at this university.

   b. After an introductory participial phrase.

   EXAMPLE: Watching the viewers carefully, the art student was pleased that her exhibit was such a success.

   c. After a succession of introductory prepositional phrases.

   EXAMPLE: In the building at the edge of the campus, RSU houses the horse management facilities.

   d. After an introductory adverb clause.

   EXAMPLE: As the end of the play approached, the actors gave even better performances.

6. Use commas to set off expressions that interrupt the sentence:

   a. Appositives.

   EXAMPLE: The junior college, a community-based college offering the first two years of study, is the ideal place to begin college.

   b. Words in direct address.

   EXAMPLE: Gene, you need to see your advisor before enrolling.

   c. Parenthetical expressions.

   EXAMPLE: I believe, even though the course may not be required, that you need to take typing.

7. Use a comma in certain conventional situations:

   a. To separate items in dates and addresses.

   EXAMPLE: She was born in Guy, Oklahoma, on May 8, 1950, in the local hospital.

   b. After the salutation of a friendly letter and after the closing of any letter.

   EXAMPLE:

   > Dear Mom,
   > Thank you for the money! Now I can buy a Valentine in the bookstore and eat dessert.
   > Love,
   > Jim

   c. After expressions that introduce direct quotations.

   EXAMPLE: Thoreau said, "Rescue the drowning and tie your shoestrings."
   AND "Rescue the drowning," Thoreau said, "and tie your shoestrings."

8. Do not use unnecessary commas.

   EXAMPLE: Do, not, put, commas, just, anywhere.

COLONS

1. Use a colon to mean "note what follows."

   a. Use a colon before a list of items, unless the list immediately follows a verb or preposition.

EXAMPLE: RSU offers these options: Associate of Arts, Associate of Science, Certificate of Achievement, and Associate of Applied Science.
NOT RSU offers: Associate of Arts, Associate of Science. . . .
NOT RSU has options in: Associate of Arts, Associate of. . . .

   b. Use a colon before a long, formal statement or quotation **except** when the quotation follows immediately after a verb or preposition.

EXAMPLE: In "The Bear" Faulkner unites man, bear, and wilderness:

> He had left the gun; of his own will and relinquishment he had accepted not a gambit, not a choice, but a condition in which not only the bear's heretofore inviolable anonymity but all the old rules and balances of hunter and hunted had been abrogated. (157)

NOT Faulkner says:

> He had left the gun; of his own. . . .

NOT In "The Bear" Faulkner unites man and wilderness in:

> not a gambit, not a choice, but. . . .

   c. Use a colon between independent clauses when the second clause explains or restates the idea of the first.

EXAMPLE: A student makes a choice: he chooses to study or not to study.

2. Use a colon in certain conventional situations:

   a. Use a colon between the hour and the minute in the time.

EXAMPLE: It is 5:45 p.m.

   b. When writing a sentence, you **may** use a colon between the chapter and verse in referring to passages in the Bible. Otherwise, use a period betweeen chapter and verse.

EXAMPLE: Read John 3:16 in the New Testament
OR Read John 3.16 in the New Testament.

   c. Use a colon after the salutation in a business letter.

EXAMPLE:

Dear Mr. James:
Your shipment dated Monday. . . .

SEMICOLONS

The semicolon has often been described as a weak period or a strong comma; in other words, it is part period and part comma. The most common use of the semicolon is to indicate a close relationship between two independent clauses.

1. Use a semicolon between independent clauses not joined by *and, but, for, or, nor, yet.*

   EXAMPLE: Work turned in on time receives full credit; work turned in late receives partial credit; work not turned in at all receives no credit.

2. Use a semicolon between independent clauses joined by the words *accordingly, also, besides, consequently, furthermore, hence, however, indeed, instead, moreover, nevertheless, otherwise, similarly, still, therefore, thus, for example, for instance, that is, in fact.*

   EXAMPLE: I have taken only a few courses; nevertheless, I will finish my degree.

3. A semicolon (rather than a comma) may be needed to separate independent clauses if there are commas within the clauses.

   EXAMPLE: The humanities classes, although required, seem to be favorites of the students; and students often comment on how much they have learned.

4. Use a semicolon between items in a series when one or more of the items includes an internal comma.

   EXAMPLE: Important dates include Jan. 24, 2050; May 10, 1977; and April 21, 1979.

APOSTROPHES

1. To form the possessive of singular and plural nouns and indefinite pronouns, use an apostrophe.

   a. To form the possessive case of a singular noun, add an apostrophe and *s.*

   EXAMPLE: cat cat's dish car car's bumper Cass Cass's car

   b. To form the possessive case of a plural noun ending in *s,* add only the apostrophe.

   EXAMPLE: horses horses' manger helpers helpers' apron
   commanders commanders' batons heroes heroes' tales

   c. Indefinite pronouns in the possessive case require an apostrophe and *s.*

   EXAMPLE: anybody anybody's guess somebody somebody's book

d. In hyphenated words, names of organizations and business firms, and words showing joint possession, only the last word is possessive in form.

EXAMPLE: John and Mary — John and Mary's boat
son-in-law — son-in-law's talent
Rogers State University — Rogers State University's class

e. When two or more persons possess something individually, each of their names takes the possessive form.

EXAMPLE: John and Mary — John's and Mary's clothes
Tom and Jerry — Tom's and Jerry's traps

f. The words *minute, hour, day, week, month, year*, etc., when used as possessive adjectives, require apostrophes. Words indicating amount in cents or dollars, used as possessive adjectives, require apostrophes.

EXAMPLE: year — year's end — cent — cent's worth

g. Use the apostrophe and *s* to form the plural of letters, numbers, and signs, and of words referred to as words.

EXAMPLE: one *l* — two *l*'s — one * — three *'s — one *3* — four *3*'s
one *you* — seven *you*'s

2. Personal pronouns in the possessive case do not require an apostrophe.

EXAMPLE: her — her job — his — his class — its — its claws
their — their car

3. Use an apostrophe to show where letters have been omitted in a contraction or in dialect.

EXAMPLE: can not — can't — you are — you're
"She'll be comin' 'round the mountain. . . ."

HYPHENS

1. Use a hyphen to divide a word at the end of a line.

EXAMPLE: Sheila has found it almost impossible to become a published author this year.

2. Use a hyphen with compound numbers from *twenty-one* to *ninety-nine* and with fractions used as adjectives.

   EXAMPLE: Only the forty-first draft was acceptable.

3. Use a hyphen with the prefixes *ex-*, *self-*, *all-*; with the suffix *-elect*; and with all prefixes before a proper name or proper adjective.

   EXAMPLE: Ex-President Jones is the president-elect of his bridge club; he will take office in mid-October.

4. Hyphenate a compound adjective when it precedes the word it modifies.

   EXAMPLE: That well-dressed woman swatted the best-known actor here with her umbrella.

5. Use a hyphen to prevent confusion or awkwardness.

   EXAMPLE: semi-invalid re-cover a floor re-form a line re-mark a paper

QUOTATION MARKS

1. Use quotation marks to enclose a direct quotation–a person's exact words.

   a. A direct quotation begins with a capital letter unless the quoted material is only a phrase.

   EXAMPLE: My grandmother used to say, "You children don't pay any more attention to me than to the wind a-blowing."

   AND Faulkner said Boon had "the heart of a horse."

   b. When a quoted sentence is divided into two parts by an interrupting expression such as *she said* or *I asked*, the second part begins with a small letter unless the second part begins another complete sentence.

   EXAMPLE: "Boon was four inches over six feet," William Faulkner wrote, "and he had the mind of a child and the heart of a horse and the ugliest face I ever saw."

c. A direct quotation is set off from the rest of the sentence by commas (or by a question mark or an exclamation mark) unless the quoted material is only a phrase.

EXAMPLE: She asked, "Have you already fulfilled the General Education requirements?"
AND She felt she was looking "through a glass darkly."

d. When used with quotation marks, other marks of punctuation are placed according to the following rules in American English:

(1.) Commas and periods are always placed inside the closing quotation marks.

EXAMPLE: "I want to take biology," he said, "because it will be useful to me in understanding both myself and my ecology."

(2.) Semicolons and colons are always placed outside the closing quotation marks.

EXAMPLE: She said, "Yes, I'll go to the Scholar's Dance with you"; however, that was before she caught the flu.
Some companies understand "rush order": they begin order processing upon receiving the invoice.

(3.) Question marks and exclamation marks are placed inside the closing quotation marks if they belong with the quotation; otherwise they are placed outside.

EXAMPLE: She asked, "Did he go?"
AND Did she ask, "Did he go"?

e. When a quoted passage consists of more than one paragraph, place quotation marks at the beginning of each paragraph and at the end of the entire passage. Do not put quotation marks at the end of any paragraph except the last.

f. Use single quotation marks to enclose a quotation within a quotation.

EXAMPLE: Faulkner writes about "a little dog, nameless and mongrel and many-fathered, grown, yet weighing less than six pounds, saying as if to itself, 'I can't be dangerous, because there's nothing much smaller than I am.'"

g. When you write **dialogue** (two or more persons carrying on a conversation), begin a new paragraph every time the speaker changes.

EXAMPLE: Beauty and the Beast might well have had this conversation:

"I liked you even as the Beast," said Beauty.

"I know," replied the Beast.

"But you have changed only in appearance."

"Yes, am I not better to look at?"

"You're not only better to look at; you'll be easier to take out in public."

2. Use quotation marks to enclose titles of chapters, articles, other parts of books or magazines, short poems, short stories, and songs.

EXAMPLE: "Lion: A Dog" is one of Faulkner's short stories.

AND "Amazing Grace" is both a hymn and a folk song.

3. Use quotation marks to enclose slang words, technical terms, and other expressions that are unusual in standard English.

EXAMPLE: In the past some students referred to courses as "Mickey Mouse" if the courses were easy.

UNDERLINING

- **NOTE: When writing MLA-format academic papers, use underlining instead of italics,** even if you are using a word processor that is capable of creating italic font.

1. Use underlining (italics) for titles of books, periodicals, newspapers, works of art, ships, etc.

EXAMPLE:

Claremore Daily Progress (newspaper)
Sports Illustrated (magazine)
Bolero (musical selection)
the *Challenger* (shuttle)
the *Congressional Limited* (train)
Pieta (sculpture)
the *Nautilus* (ship)
Mona Lisa (painting)
The Shining (book)

2. Use underlining (italics) for words and letters referred to as such and for foreign words.

EXAMPLE: She would choose only the *crème de la crème*.

AND In formal writing, avoid contractions such as *isn't* and *doesn't*.

3. Use underlining (italics) to emphasize words or phrases.

   EXAMPLE: Notify the employee <u>in writing</u> if his job performance is not satisfactory.

4. Use underlining (italics) to indicate a word that re-creates a sound.

   EXAMPLE: The students scream <u>whee</u> when escaping from a classroom.

PARENTHESES

Use parentheses to enclose informative or explanatory matter that is added to a sentence but is not considered of major importance. Be sure any material contained in the parentheses can be omitted from the sentence without changing the meaning and construction of the sentence.

EXAMPLE: That school year (1987-88) was my first year on my own.

1. Punctuation marks belong outside the parentheses unless the material punctuated lies entirely within the parentheses.

   EXAMPLE: In the cartoon the only dialogue of the lavender moose ("He went that way!") serves to accent his character.

   AND The years when they were away "(1986-1988), although financially difficult," were almost a relief.

BRACKETS

1. Use brackets to enclose explanations within parentheses.

   EXAMPLE: Many traitors (Ullum Oak Meenen [named for his grandfather] among them) were hanged from this tree.

2. Use brackets in quoted material when the explanation is not part of the quotation.

   EXAMPLE: In his discussion, the author states that "any year, and especially that year [1514], would have been difficult for the peasants of Royolan."

ELLIPSIS

1. Use an ellipsis (three spaced periods) to designate omitted material in a direct quotation.

EXAMPLE: The quoted material as stands reads like this:
"If we place a penny on a bottle edge (and any bottle edge will do) and it falls, what will we do?"

The quotation in the writer's text in MLA format might read like this:
"If we place a penny on a bottle edge . . . and it falls, what will we do?"

2. If the material includes more than one sentence, or if the material includes the end of a sentence, the ellipsis mark will consist of four spaced periods–the ellipsis and the final period.

EXAMPLE: The quoted material reads like this:
"I wanted a dog, a dog of surpassing strength, ugliness, and power, a dog that would slay on command, a dog that would slay on my command. Dog. Yes, a real dog."

The quotation in the writer's text might read like this:
"I wanted a dog, a dog of surpassing strength, ugliness, and power, a dog that would slay on command. . . . Yes, a real dog."

3. If the quoted material begins in the middle of a sentence, it is not necessary to use the ellipsis at the beginning of the quoted material unless the beginning word starts with a capital letter.

EXAMPLE: The quoted material reads like this:
"A necessary list of Roman numerals is included."

The writer's text in MLA might read as follows:
The book says a "list of Roman numerals is included."

OR The book says that a table of ". . . Roman numerals is included."

DASHES

1. Use the dash to indicate an abrupt break in thought.

   EXAMPLE: How many classes—how many people—have failed because they would not work to fulfill their expectations?

2. Use a dash to set off parenthetical material.

   EXAMPLE: Only one person—the student—can determine what was learned.

3. Use a dash to mean *namely, in other words, that is,* and similar expressions that precede explanations.

   EXAMPLE: I want a horse—I want to take horsemanship classes.

SPELLING

Inaccurate spelling is a common problem. It is not one with which you have to live. Spelling skills can be improved. You need to be aware of whether you have difficulty with spelling and be willing to work on this problem. Getting a good dictionary and being willing to use it is one technique; having other people check your work is another.

The following are some simple techniques for improving your spelling skills.

1. Try to visualize how the word looks on the page. See if the visualization agrees with the word.
2. Practice pronouncing and spelling troublesome words that you commonly use.
3. Take care to distinguish between words that are similar in sound and/or spelling. Be conscious of these as you are writing.

   EXAMPLE: its/it's lose/loose to/too/two your/you're
   cote/coat idea/ideal whose/who's reign/rain
   there/their/they're

4. Use any memory devices that can help you remember words.

   EXAMPLE: Emma is in a dilemma.
   Always put a dent in the superintendent.
   The principal should be your pal; a principle never can be.

5. Memorize these spelling rules (remembering, of course, that they will not apply in all cases and that you will just have to remember those exceptions).

a. Remember this old, old–but still useful–little rhyme:

When the sound is like *EE*,
Put *i* before *e*–
Except after *c*.

EXAMPLE:

- <u>*i* before *e*</u>: chief grief relief belief field niece
- <u>except after *c*</u>: receive conceit deceive ceiling
- <u>unless the word doesn't sound *EE*</u>: eight their veil counterfeit foreign

b. When adding a suffix, drop a final silent *e* if the suffix begins with a vowel or with *y*.

EXAMPLE: type+ing = typing hope+ed=hoped
fame+ous = famous scare + y = scary

b-1. Keep the *e* when the suffix does not begin with a vowel.

EXAMPLE: grate + ful = grateful force + ful = forceful
safe + ty = safety love + less = loveless
lone + ly = lonely

b-2. Keep *e* if *e* comes after *c* or *g* in the base word and the added suffix begins with *a* or *o*.

EXAMPLE: notice+able = noticeable courage+ous = courageous

b-3. Keep the *e* to avoid confusion with other words.

EXAMPLE: singe+ing = singeing (to avoid confusion with singing)
dye+ing = dyeing (to avoid confusion with dying)

c. Change a final *y* to *i* before any suffix except *ing*.

EXAMPLE: happy + ness = happiness cry + ed = cried
BUT cry + ing = crying

d. Double a final consonant before a suffix beginning with a vowel (including *y*) if the consonant ends a word of one syllable and is preceded by a single vowel or if the consonant ends an accented syllable of the root word and is preceded by a single vowel.

EXAMPLE: hop+ed = hopped occur+ed = occurred control+ed = controlled
BUT hoop+ed = hooped boat+er = boater offer+ed = offered

e. To form most plurals add *s* to the singular word.

EXAMPLE: dog dogs textbook textbooks

e-1. When making a word plural creates a new syllable, add *es* to the singular word.

EXAMPLE: fox foxes church churches

e-2. When the final *y* rule (See Rule c) applies, add *es*.

EXAMPLE: fly flies fraternity fraternities

e-3. For a few nouns, change the final *f* or *fe* to *v* and add *es*.

EXAMPLE: calf calves knife knives

e-4. For a few nouns ending in *o* add *es*.

EXAMPLE: hero heroes potato potatoes

e-5. To make a singular compound noun plural, add *s* or *es* to the end if the word has no hyphen. If the word is a hyphenated word, add the *s* or *es* to the noun portion.

EXAMPLE: cupful cupfuls strongbox strongboxes son-in-law sons-in-law

e-6. For some nouns of foreign origin, use the foreign plural.

EXAMPLE: alumnus alumni stimulus stimuli datum data
synopsis synopses crisis crises
axis axes hypothesis hypotheses

WHEN IN DOUBT, LOOK IT UP!

SPACING PUNCTUATION MARKS

1. A dash as a sign of a break in thought is typed as two hyphens with no spaces between. Those two hyphens will become a dash in some word processing programs when you space after the word following the two hypens.

EXAMPLE: This is a dash--a kind of interruption.

2. A dash in place of an omitted word is four unspaced hyphens. This is the only kind of dash that is preceded, and followed, by a space.

   EXAMPLE: To fill the blank, place the word ---- there.

3. An ellipsis is three spaced periods, with spaces before and after the first period. A four-period ellipsis (signifying the omission of quoted material that includes at least one mark of end punctuation) begins with an unspaced mark.

   EXAMPLE: The quoted text reads like this:
   "A baby mouse in a tree in the woods lay quietly in the nest of cotton balls, newsprint, shredded Styrofoam and lace."

   The replicated text reads like this:
   "A baby mouse . . . lay . . . in the nest. . . ."

4. When a slash separates two quoted lines of poetry, leave a space before and after.

   EXAMPLE: One child's verse begins, "Jack and Jill went up the hill / To fetch a pail of water."

5. When a slash joins two words in an alternative or as a span of time, use no space before or after the slash.

   EXAMPLE: It's a case of *either/or* not *and/or*.

6. Leave one space after a period, question mark, exclamation mark, colon, four-dot ellipsis, comma, semicolon, closing quotation mark, closing parenthesis, or closing bracket.

   EXAMPLE: This is a sentence. Yes! One space after question mark, period, colon. . . . One, two, what do we do? We act; we write. "Create," we say. We (quietly) scream.

7. Leave no space before or after a dash, hyphen, or an apostrophe within a word.

   EXAMPLE: A dash--a mark of punctuation--is used by Fea-Smith when he's writing informally.

8. When an apostrophe ends a word, leave no space before any following punctuation.

   EXAMPLE: When singing "We're Goin'; We're Gone," remember to drop the final *g* in *goin'*.

9. Do not begin a line with any punctuation from the preceding line. Do not leave punctuation from a following line on the previous line.

WRONG EXAMPLE: It is WRONG to say and mean the lines I'll go
NEVER DO THIS! → , I'll follow, under any circumstances.

WRONG EXAMPLE: It is also WRONG to say anything that can be
misconstrued by a listener who overhears (← **NEVER DO THIS!**
and this is the truth).

10. Do not carry an ellipsis from one line to the next.

WRONG EXAMPLE: When you write and leave out words in a
quotation from a text or other written work. . ← **NEVER DO THIS!**
., don't do this.

COMMON MISTAKES NEVER TO MAKE!

NEVER	ALWAYS	NEVER	ALWAYS
grammer	grammar	gonna	going to
thier	their	could of	could have
haf to	have to	alot	a lot
suppose to	supposed to	writting	writing
theirself	themselves	hisself	himself
off of	off		

ALWAYS
In titles, "is" is an important word and must be capitalized.

NEVER SAY	SAY INSTEAD
He is prejudice.	He is prejudiced.

IMPORTANT DISTINCTIONS			
loose = not tight lose = to misplace	choose = to select chose = selected	except = excluding accept = to receive	they're = they are their = belonging to them there = a place
you're = you are your = belonging to you	it's = it is its = belonging to it		

REMEMBER: DO NOT USE CONTRACTIONS IN FORMAL WRITING.

SYMBOLS USED ON GRADED AND MARKED PAPERS

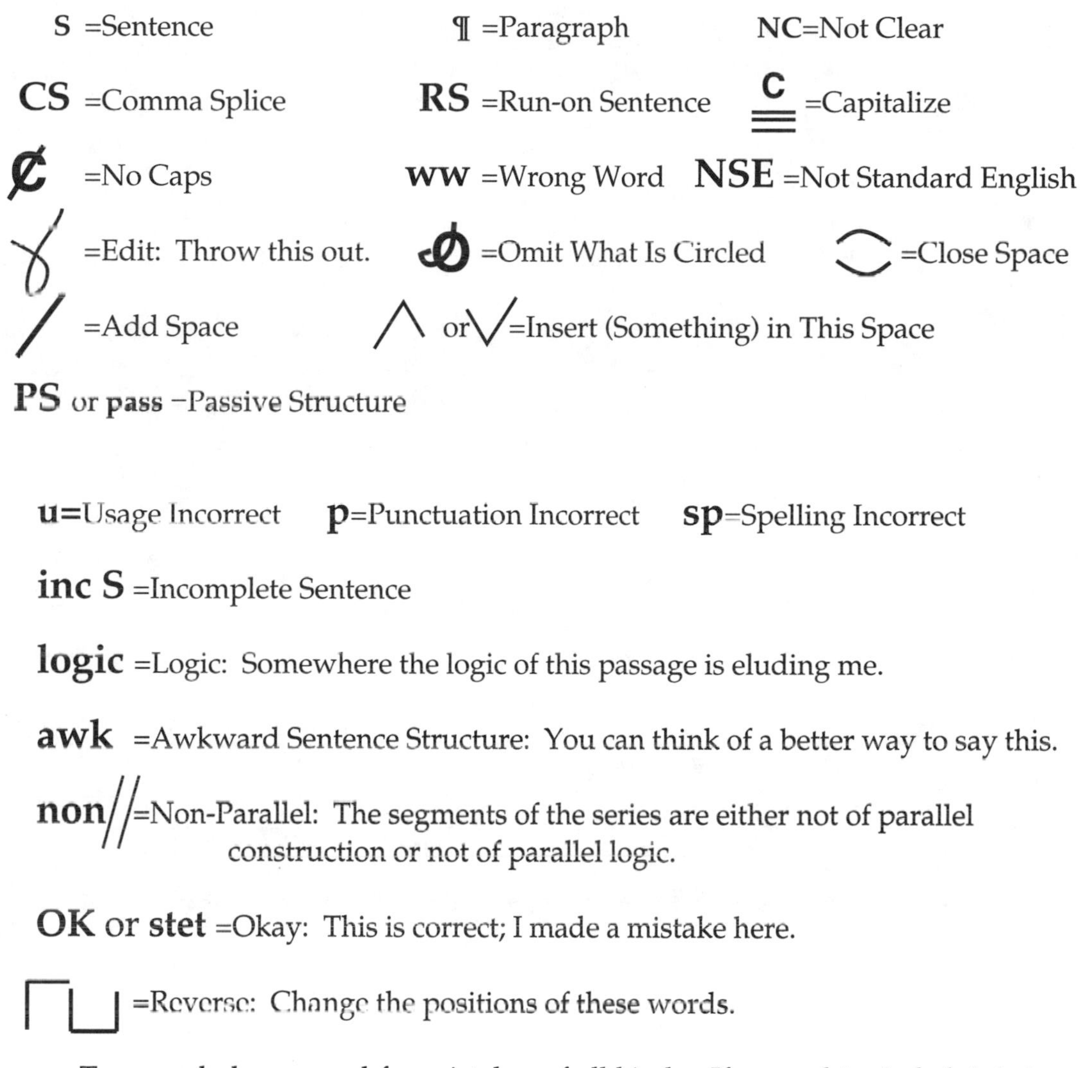

S =Sentence ¶ =Paragraph NC=Not Clear

CS =Comma Splice RS =Run-on Sentence C =Capitalize

¢ =No Caps WW =Wrong Word NSE =Not Standard English

=Edit: Throw this out. =Omit What Is Circled =Close Space

/ =Add Space ∧ or √ =Insert (Something) in This Space

PS or pass –Passive Structure

u=Usage Incorrect p=Punctuation Incorrect sp=Spelling Incorrect

inc S =Incomplete Sentence

logic =Logic: Somewhere the logic of this passage is eluding me.

awk =Awkward Sentence Structure: You can think of a better way to say this.

non// =Non-Parallel: The segments of the series are either not of parallel construction or not of parallel logic.

OK or stet =Okay: This is correct; I made a mistake here.

=Reverse: Change the positions of these words.

- Two symbols are used for mistakes of all kinds. If a word is circled, it is incorrect somehow: incorrect spelling, incorrect tense, etc. If a line is checked, there is a mistake in it somewhere. Just find it. If you cannot find your mistake or do not understand it, ask and the instructor will explain.
- **REMEMBER:** You cannot do better if you do not know what you have done right or wrong on a paper. So, if in doubt about what is marked or said, **ASK!**

STUDENT MODELS

The following model student papers are in different documentation formats. These models are above-average papers, but may or may not represent "A" work.

Papers in **MLA format** are shaded, like this:

Papers in **APA format** are surrounded by dashed lines, like this:

Papers with endnotes are surrounded by a smaller dash, dashed line.

If the paper is **APA formatted** with **endnotes**, the paper looks like this:

If the paper is formatted with **MLA endnotes**, the paper looks like this:

Documented Essays

- **NOTE: This paper is written in MLA format. Papers in MLA format have a blue background.**

Martin 1

Jane Martin

Dr. Exe

Comp II

18 Feb. 1998

The Subtle Fist

Nora Helmer of Henrik Ibsen's "A Doll House" is no stranger to me. For some, she may seem too accommodating and naïve to be believed; but, for me, she is all too real. When I think of her, I am filled with feelings of pity, shame, and disgust. I feel pity for the way that her own innocence is used against her, shame at her willingness to be so easily manipulated, and disgust at the reflection I see when I look at Nora. For when I am forced to look at her, it is my own reflection that I see; then I am forced to admit that I, too, was the victim of a subtle fist.

Innocence can be a pitiful thing indeed. Nora proves this by willingly giving up any notion of self to be her beloved Torvald's wife. At first, she probably does not see the harm in giving in to her husband's demands for control. She might even think that Torvald's controlling manner is sweet and thoughtful, that he has a touching conviction to take care of her. She could not know in the infancy of their relationship how much this eagerness to compromise would cost her. Just as Nora, I went straight from being my father's daughter to being my first husband's wife. I never felt as though I were in control of my own life as my parents were strict and protective. Therefore, my relationship with my boyfriend did not seem unnatural when he began asserting his authority over me. I did not know until after my ten-year marriage ended that I, as an individual human being, did have this thing called power.

After a time, however, innocence does wane. Nora begins realizing that she has a right to make some choices for herself. The first endeavor on her own is to secretly acquire a loan to take Torvald on an extended vacation for his health. Torvald would never allow such an action as he feels going into debt reduces one's status in life. Nora keeps this secret for years before she gets the courage to defy again. She begins sneaking macaroons, telling little white lies, and fantasizing about telling Torvald "to hell and be damned!" (Ibsen 1079). Her bravery, however, is quite confined, as only a couple of people know of her little acts of defiance. I must admit, though, that her concealed courage is greater than any I ever possessed under the control of my captor. I spent every day of ten years living as if I were walking on eggs. I was always so afraid that I would do or say something to offend or upset my first husband that I could never even entertain thoughts of rebellion. I was afraid that if I angered him, he might leave; and how could I ever live without him?

One can finally see a husband as he truly is. Upon this revelation, Nora realizes that she must begin to find herself and make her own way in this life. She does not yet realize that leaving is the easy part. When people wrap so much of themselves into another human being, they do not realize how little of a person exists without the other. My first husband's manipulation was so complete that I became a mirror image of him. I did only the things he liked to do. I associated only with the people that he found suitable. I worked only at jobs that received his consent. I readily changed my clothes if he, for any reason, did not approve. Obviously, this was not a happy way to live, but I thought that it was easier than the alternative of leaving the man I loved so dearly. When after more than ten years of marriage, my first husband left me, I was utterly lost. I had committed every particle of my being to this man and this marriage, so much so that without it, I threw only the shadow of a person. I had no identity, no substance, without him.

My memory of this time is still so painful that even now, five years and what seems a lifetime later, I rarely can speak his name. I refer to him only as "What's-his-name." Some may think this a bit childish and bitter; but, when I speak his name, I feel as if a part of the power that I suffered so to gain is compromised by his memory. Only one who has felt the kind of devastation and humiliation that was my life, and was Nora Helmer's life, can understand the vehemence with which I protect this priceless treasure that is called independence.

NOTE: The Works Cited page is generally a separate page from the rest of the paper, and is paginated as the next page in the series.

Works Cited

Ibsen, Henrik. "A Doll House." The Compact Bedford Introduction to Literature: Reading, Thinking, and Writing. 4th ed. Ed. Michael Meyer. Boston: St. Martin's, 1997. 1069-75.

Bradshaw 1

Earlene Bradshaw

Comp II

Dr. Ewe

17 Feb. 2005

Candide

In his novel Candide, Voltaire takes readers on a fast-paced, action-filled trip from castles to slave quarters, from great riches to abject poverty, from ugliness and death to the wealth and beauty of mystical Eldorado. There is humor, sarcasm, love, hate, lust, hypocrisy, and all the other emotions that human beings experience. However, in writing Candide, Voltaire addresses more serious issues than the story would indicate at first reading. Voltaire uses sarcasm and wit to express his dislike for accepted religious practices of Jews and Christians, his opposition of Leibniz's philosophical teachings, and his questions concerning God's love, the creation of man, and mankind's sinfulness.

Voltaire sees Christians and Jews alike as being hypocritical and evil, outwardly untouched by the evil of the world, but in actuality as lustful and greedy as those who profess no religious belief at all. That Don Issachar, a Jew, and a Catholic called "The Grand Inquisitor" (Voltaire 15) would share Cunegonde sexually reveals the lustfulness of men of both religions. The fact that they quarrel about "whether the night from Saturday to Sunday belonged to the old or the new dispensation" (Voltaire 15) shows the absurdity of the situation. Throughout Candide, Voltaire describes Jesuits, friars, in fact all religious men, as despicably greedy and lustful, with desires for riches and power and sexual desires for woman and men alike.

Voltaire opposes many of the philosophers, one in particular whose name is Leibniz. In Candide, the character Pangloss' teachings mirror Leibniz's philosophy. Pangloss "proved . . . that there cannot possibly be an effect without a cause. . . . 'It is clear,' said he, 'that things cannot be otherwise than they are, for since everything is made to serve an end, everything necessarily serves the best end'" (Voltaire 1-2). Voltaire continues throughout the novel to show the absurdity of these teachings. In the conclusion, Pangloss asserts "that he had always suffered horribly; but having once declared that everything was marvelously well, he continued to repeat the opinion, and didn't believe a word of it" (Voltaire 73). In this way Voltaire speaks his contempt of Leibniz's entire philosophical basis.

Throughout the novel are situations that raise questions concerning God and his love for man, mankind's disobedience to God's laws, and divine punishment. In Chapter Eight, Cunegonde refers to the earthquake in Lisbon as "divine punishment" (Voltaire 15), while Candide calls it "the Last Judgment" (Voltaire 10). Characters are hung, burned alive, and torn apart in the name of God. In the conclusion of the novel, Candide and his friends visit a Turkish philosopher to ask, "why such a strange animal as man was created" (Voltaire 73). Candide respectfully reminds him, "there's a horrible lot of evil on the face of the earth" (Voltaire 73). Pangloss says to the philosopher, "I had hoped . . . to reason a while with you concerning effects and causes, the best of possible worlds, the origin of evil. . ." (Voltaire 73). Obviously not having an answer, the Turk closes the door "in their faces" (Voltaire 73).

Voltaire raises questions concerning of philosophy of life, religious practices and beliefs, indeed questions concerning God himself. Candide and the many people he meets in his travels struggle to find answers to these questions, but are unable to find anyone who can answer them satisfactorily. These questions were not answered to everyone's satisfaction before Voltaire wrote Candide, nor have they been answered satisfactorily since. It seems doubtful that these questions will be answered in this life. Just as the characters in the novel struggle to do, people today must find a philosophy of life they can live with and do so.

NOTE: The Works Cited page is generally a separate page from the rest of the paper, and is paginated as the next page in the series.

Works Cited

Voltaire. Candide. c. 1755. Trans and Ed. Robert M. Adams. New York: W.W. Norton and Company, 1991.

Gay 1

Rick W. Gay

Prof. Sesso

Comp II

6 Apr. 1998

To Serve Man

As mankind's quest for power takes him ever deeper into the realm of the unknown, the danger of unforeseen consequences grows ever greater. As the protagonist in Mary Shelley's Frankenstein learns, some knowledge is best left unknown. An endeavor being possible does not guarantee it being ethical (Kreyche 82). Even eminent scientist Freeman J. Dyson worries that the growing use of high-technology will only exacerbate friction between upper and lower social classes, thereby creating greater problems than the ones it solves (Pennar 84). As Orlin Damyanov puts it, "We have unparalleled knowledge and power over nature and yet this faces us with moral dilemmas and responsibilities for which we are ill-prepared." It seems that with each solution that people produce to improve lives, a vast number of new problems occur. Problem begets solution. Solutions beget new problems. Thus, technology perpetuates and guarantees its own necessity. But, if technology cannot advance the whole of humanity, then it is only creating more social strife (Kreyche 82). Like Frankenstein's monster, technology has become a colossal entity with dangerous and unforeseen powers.

Technology's basic mandate is to raise the quality of life, but each step forward is both wondrous and frightening. While medical science makes people healthier, it creates a higher level of stress, anxiety, and worry. Alcohol consumption is down; smoking is down; careful diet and exercise are up. However, despite all medical statistics, Americans do not see themselves as healthier (Tenner 26). Political scientist Aaron Wildavsky describes it as "doing better but feeling worse" (Tenner 26). In short, progress in medical technology has created a great anxiety about personal health.

Advances in medicine have made treatments generally less invasive, but this has not brought peace of mind to the populace. As medical techniques become more complicated, they demand a higher degree of skill and education from the operator. This increases the possibility of mistakes and miscalculations due to human error. And, of course, the high cost of sophisticated equipment and technical training is passed on to the patient (Tenner 27). This adds to the general feeling of worry associated with any major medical procedure. Giant medical centers, with darkened rooms full of impersonal machines used to test every pore of the human body, give rise to visions of a mad scientist's laboratory.

Technological breakthroughs have certainly raised the standard of living around the world, but this too produces an unfortunate consequence (Tobias, Popcorn, and Celente 41). As modern science lengthens the average lifespan, mortality rates fall and birth rates continue. The population becomes larger, which contributes to increasing levels of mental illness, depression, and anti-social behavior: "Humans are designed to function best psychologically in the open, grassy spaces our ancestors inhabited. Stark, stony urban landscapes, replete with an ever-present backdrop of traffic and airplane noise, stress our psyches in subtle but real ways" (Tobias, Popcorn, and Celente 41). It is not surprising that Los Angeles, one of the most densely populated cities in the U.S., has approximately two thousand practicing psychologists per square mile (Tobias, Popcorn, and Celente 41).

Overpopulation places great stress not only on society but on the environment. Technological progress allows more people to survive, but it does not provide their sustenance. The growing crowd exacerbates the problem of depleting natural resources. The exponentially-multiplying populace demands an ever-increasing amount of food and energy, but it also takes up more land that would be used to generate these products (Tobias, Popcorn, and Celente 40). It is simple arithmetic. The amount of arable farmland decreases each year. Grassland for stock diminishes as well. The oceans provide a finite number of fish. As demand continues to rise, greater strain is placed on supply. Agriculture still manages to increase output by approximately one percent per year, but this is clearly a precarious situation (Tobias, Popcorn, and Celente 41). Through increased pollution, overcrowding, food and water shortages, and, of course, traffic, this technologically-induced population explosion will ultimately reduce the quality of human life.

Technology has helped give the world peace, but this too is not without consequence. The world's arsenal has evolved from weapons to doomsday devices. As weapons have increased in destructive power, world leaders have become less likely to actually use them. The threat remains that a nuclear incident could be instigated by terrorists or some country's irrational leader even if global thermonuclear war is unlikely. Today's technology has relegated warfare to conventional skirmishes in small politically-unstable areas. Technology creates peace; peace leads to overpopulation. Man's proclivity to war has always been a primary means of population control but technology has limited its effectiveness. The most highly-populated countries are hesitant to instigate conflict with each other for fear that a limited engagement could escalate to a nuclear confrontation. Thus, millions of deaths may have been avoided: "One might even argue that the misery that would have resulted from these unfought wars is less than the suffering from prolonged, worldwide famine" (Tobias, Popcorn, and Celente 41).

Man's quest for knowledge is not always beneficial to society. Technology has certainly brought great wonders, but it has created a complicated society. Science has given humans a life less physically demanding and more mentally stressful. In endeavoring to cure the world's ills, people have produced over-crowding, anxiety, and the possibility of famine. The same technology that made humanity more powerful erodes social ties. The world has not improved; it has gained a new set of problems.

In fact, we can learn an important lesson from Frankenstein. The social and psychological problems attributed to technology are a product of people's experimentation. Technology is a monster that carries its own curses. Some believe the monster is truly benign, but even they harbor a few fears. People have a deep and innate concern about the vast power unleased as compared to their own mortality. This speaks of an ancient fear, fear not of technology itself but of people's ability to control it. In the end, Shelley's protagonist pays the ultimate price for his lack of foresight when his own creation destroys him. One can only hope the same fate does not befall humanity.

NOTE: The Works Cited page is generally a separate page from the rest of the paper, and is paginated as the next page in the series.

Works Cited

Damyanov, Orlin. "Technology and Its Dangerous Effects on Nature and Human Life as Perceived in Mary Shelley's Frankenstein and William Gibson's Necromancer." 9 Mar. 1998 <http://www.geocities.com/ Paris/5972/gibson.html>.

Kreyche, Gerald. F. "Does the Future Have a Future?" USA Today Magazine Nov. 1996: 82.

Pennar, Karen. "Science's Great Dream-Spinner." Business Week 20 Oct. 1997: 84-92.

Tenner, Edward. Why Things Bite Back: Technology and the Revenge of Unintended Circumstances. New York: Knopf, 1996.

Tobias, Michael, Faith Popcorn, and Gerald Celente. "What's Next?" Psychology Today Feb. 1995: 34-42.

Bradshaw 1

Earlene Bradshaw

Prof. Bear

Composition II

15 Dec. 2002

Midwifery in the United States

For as long as women have been having babies, there have undoubtedly been other women caring for them and encouraging them during the birth process. Midwives have been mentioned in literature since recorded history. In the second book of the Bible, possibly written during the reign of Rameses II in the thirteenth century B.C., we read, "the king of Egypt spoke to the Hebrew midwives . . ." (Ex. 2.12). Even today, those involved in the occupation known as "midwifery" continue to play important roles in women's healthcare in much of the world.

As people migrated from Europe to the colonies, midwives were kept busy delivering babies for the settlers. The use of midwives as primary caretakers of pregnant women continued from the time Pilgrims settled in Plymouth Rock until the latter part of the 1800s, when a shift in healthcare began: "Between 1750 and 1852, women in the United States had four choices for childbirth: physicians, Indian doctors, herbalists, and midwives. A review of deliveries during the Colonial period showed that 2% of urban physicians had obstetrical cases and rural doctors had none" (Ament 2). Journals and other records indicate that most women chose midwives to deliver their babies. During the latter part of the 1800s more men began to train as physicians; their training included obstetrics; they began to deliver babies that would ordinarily have been delivered by midwives: "In the early years of this century, midwives attended about 40% of births in the United States, but by the early 1950s, that proportion had fallen to just over 3%" (Gabay 12). I am training for a career in midwifery; as a Certified-Nurse Midwife, I will be part of the group of healthcare professionals that will raise the percentage of midwife-attended births in the United States. Even though training for midwives has greatly improved, and even though there is a multitude of proof that midwives continue to have excellent birth results and patient satisfaction, there are many barriers to midwifery in the United States today.

In the early years in the United States, midwives had little or no formal training. Instead, they learned by watching and assisting experienced midwives called "grannies" or "lay midwives." These types of midwives, grannies and lay midwives, "existed in the United States, but . . . are virtually nonexistent today" (Hyder 5). While there are still people who do not feel they need formal training to become midwives, more women and men are realizing the necessity for quality training. During the past three decades, training for midwives is on the rise. Currently, "there are 43 major colleges and universities across the country offering a certificate or masters [sic] degree in nurse-midwifery. In addition, a community-based program allows students flexibility in graduate education, utilizing independent study and community resources" (U.S. Department of Health 12).

Today, training is intense, and licensing is based on graduation from the training as well as passing a national examination similar to that of Registered Nurses: "Certified Nurse-Midwives (CNMs) are Registered Nurses (RNs) who complete training to become certified in nurse-midwifery by the American College of Nurse-Midwifery. In the US, CNMs care for 5% of all births and 95% of all births delivered by midwives" (Hyder 5).

There are many reasons why women who have used midwives are satisfied with the results: personal care, excellent birth outcomes, and cost, to name a few. As early as 1925, a ". . . White House Conference on Child Health reported . . . the record of midwives surpasses the record of physicians for normal deliveries. . . . Midwives took better care of the expectant mothers because they waited patiently and let nature take its course" (Ulrich 108). According to the Congressional Office of Technology in 1986,

> these health care professionals managed routine pregnancies safely and as well as or better than physicians. Midwives were less likely to prescribe drugs or rely on technology. They had more interactions with the patients, who spent less time in the waiting room and had shorter hospital stays. Also, the patients receiving care from nurse-midwives tended to be more satisfied with their care. (Ulrich 108)

Another reason for patient satisfaction is that Nurse-Midwives usually know their patients and the patients' families well. They spend time teaching expectant mothers how to care for a newborn: how to bathe a baby, how to get the home ready for baby, how to use birthing techniques and positions, how to breast feed, and so on. They are available to answer questions and, therefore, ease stress and worry before and after the baby is born.

The majority of Nurse-Midwives have excellent records in birth outcomes. Detailed records are kept on many aspects of childbirth, including cesareans (C-sections) and Low Birth Weight (LBW) infants: "Many retrospective studies have shown that CNMs have a lower C-section rate than physicians . . . [for example] the C-section rate for six nurse-midwife services in Minnesota in 1982-1983 was 8.6% compared with the state's rate of 14.6%" (Ulrich 108). Those types of comparisons are reflected in many states over several years' studies. Concerning LBW infants: "Women who receive insufficient prenatal care are twice as likely to have LBW infants. They are also more likely to have premature infants, stillborn deliveries, or babies who die in the first year of life" (Ulrich 106). Because of the personalized, diligent care given by midwives, expectant mothers are more apt to take vitamins, eat well, and get sufficient rest. This in turn produces babies who are generally healthier, more likely to be carried to full term, have higher birth weights, and have fewer troubles during delivery.

Cost is an extremely important consideration when monitoring birth outcomes. In the issue of LBW infants, "The National Committee to Prevent Infant Mortality . . . estimated the lifetime cost of caring for a LBW infant to be $400,000. Avoiding one LBW infant would save between $14,000 and $30,000 a year" (Ulrich 106). Another startling statistic concerns unnecessary C-sections: "We estimate that 473,000 of the 966,000 cesareans performed in 1991 (49.0 percent) were unnecessary, costing American society more than $1.3 billion" (Gabay 30). A growing number of professionals see the benefits of a return to midwife-attended births in the United States: for mothers, for infants, and for America's pocketbook.

In spite of the many positive results, there are several formidable barriers to midwifery in the United States. These include public perception, physician opposition, and lack of training programs. Negative perception concerning midwifery can be traced back to Europe; there were times when the very lives of midwives were in danger:

> In 1484, Pope Innocent VIII made an official declaration against the crime of midwifery, which was codified in a volume called Malleus Maleficarium. This book became expert testimony and was utilized by European judges and magistrates for over 300 years. Women were tried and executed as directed by this book. . . . Witch hunters of the middle ages referred to midwives as "crones", [sic] and "hags". [sic] Not coincidentally, American physicians of the 19th and 20th centuries use these same terms when discussing this continent's midwives. Comments made . . . include: "[She] is pestiferous . . . the typical old hag, gin-fingering, gin-drinking . . . her mouth full of snuff and her fingers full of dirt." (Granju 2-3)

These stereotypical remarks have plagued midwives through the years; it has proven a difficult task to overcome the perception these remarks generate.

Professional jealousy over clients is another barrier in the physician/nurse-midwife struggle for power: "Unfortunately, physicians often view CNMs as competition for clients. If CNMs . . . assist with the care of private physicians' clients, there is a potential for real competition" (Ament 9). Often when a patient realizes the quality of care the midwife gives, she will request the midwife to assist her in delivery rather than the physician. This raises a green-eyed monster in the hearts of the doctors, who use it as "proof" that midwives are out to steal their reputation, as well as their clients. There are reported cases of physicians taking midwives to court, attempting to rid the country of these troublemakers: "The obstetrical community deemed out-of-hospital birth 'child abuse' at one point. . ." (Murray 10).

Training for midwives, or the lack of it, is another challenge facing women and men who desire to become Certified Nurse-Midwives. Because public perception of midwives is still somewhat negative, physicians continue to be in greater demand than midwives. It is difficult for students desiring financial aid to receive grants or loans to attend training schools.

Despite the barriers, there is a growing number of physicians who see the value of midwives in obstetrics. Patients are demanding that the medical profession legitimize midwives as healthcare professionals. Many women are choosing the services of midwives rather than physicians for care during pregnancy and delivery. These women appreciate the complete, personalized healthcare they receive from the CNMs. Accredited schools of midwifery are beginning to receive federal funding.

I have attended the births of four of my grandchildren. It has been wonderful for me to be included in the process. I held my daughter and daughters-in-law as they gave birth to their precious babies. As a trained birthing coach, I was able to comfort, encourage, and even scold these new mothers as the babies were born. Upon completion of the training I am now taking, I will be a Certified Nurse-Midwife and will be able to help many other young women during their pregnancies. I will help them prepare for their new babies; I will teach them how to keep healthy during and after pregnancy, and I will help during the actual delivery of their little ones.

The reputation of Certified Nurse-Midwives is definitely on the rise. Should this trend continue, it will be considered on honor to be a nurse-midwife, even in the United States.

NOTE: The Works Cited page is generally a separate page from the rest of the paper, and is paginated as the next page in the series.

Works Cited

Ament, Lynette A., and Lisa Hanson. "A Model for the Future: Certified Nurse-Midwives Replace Residents and House Staff in Hospitals." Nursing and Health Care Perspectives 19.1 (Jan.-Feb. 1998): 26-34. Academic Search Premier. EBSCO. Rogers State University, Stratton Taylor Library. 24 Feb. 2000 <http://www.epnet.com/>.

King James Version Study Bible. Nashville: Thomas Nelson, 2002.

Gabay, Mary, and Sidney M. Wolfe. "Nurse-Midwifery: The Beneficial Alternative." Public Health Reports 112.5 (Sep.-Oct. 1997): 386-45. Academic Search Premier. EBSCO. Rogers State University, Stratton Taylor Library. 24 Feb. 2000 <http://www.epnet.com/>.

Granju, Katie A. "Midwives Under Fire." Special Delivery 22.2 (Summer 1999): 1-8. 24 Feb. 2000. Academic Search Premier. EBSCO. Rogers State University, Stratton Taylor

Library. 24 Feb. 2000 <http://www.epnet.com/>.

Hyder, Leah. "Routine Midwifery Care: Why Not Here?" The Network News 23.4 (July 1998): 1-6. Academic Search Premier. EBSCO. Rogers State University, Stratton Taylor Library. 24 Feb. 2000 <http://www.epnet.com/>.

Murray, Elisa. "Birth Rights." Eastsideweek 19 Nov. 1997: 10-11.

Ulrich, Susan. "Revisiting an 'Old' Solution to the High Costs of Maternity Care." Medical Interface Oct. 1994: 106-18.

United States Department of Health and Human Services. Office of Inspector General. A Survey of Certified Nurse-Midwives Washington: GPO, 1992.

Brezina 1

Susan Brezina

Dr. Doubleu

Art Appreciation

20 April 2002

Leonardo da Vinci

Leonardo da Vinci was an Italian painter, sculptor, draftsman, architect, composer, and engineer whose genius epitomized the humanist Renaissance ideal more than any other artisan. He was the illegitimate son of a twenty-five year old notary and a peasant girl in Anchiano, Italy, born in 1452. He moved to Vinci in 1457 and began his apprenticeship at the age of fourteen in Florence at the workshop of Verrocchio. His spirit was one of contradictions. He had a brilliant scientific mind and made important scientific discoveries but yet never published any of them (Leonardo). He was one of the greatest painters of the Italian Renaissance but he left only a few paintings. Among his most widely popular and influential paintings were the Last Supper and the Mona Lisa.

The portrait of Mona Lisa (1503-06), also known as La Gioconda, the wife of Francesco del Giocondo, is full of secrets and mysteries. It is a 77 x 53 cm. large oil on wood, "the most famous painting in the history of the world" (Mona, Mona!). Many of the details in the painting cannot been seen today because the painting has been damaged and some parts of have been painted over. In spite of the alterations and damage, we can still appreciate the essence.

The Florentine woman is seated in front of a misty backdrop set in front of a mountainous landscape. The technique of gradually dissolving the forms, continuous interaction between light and shade, and an uncertain time of day create the mysterious, soft, and heavily shaded modeling that is called sfumato. Da Vinci believed that the expression in a model's face rests in the depiction of the corners of the mouth and the corners of the eyes. The model's hypnotic and enigmatic smile that is both alluring and aloof is the characteristic that has given this picture its universal fame. Gombrich asserts that the appeal is precisely these parts which da Vinci has left deliberately indistinct, by letting them merge into a soft shadow. That is why we are never quite certain in what mood Mona Lisa is really looking at us. Her expression always seems just to elude us. It is not only vagueness, of course, which produces this effect. If we look carefully at the picture, we see that the two sides do not quite match. This is most obvious in the fantastic dream landscape in the background. The horizon on the left side seems to lie much lower than the one on the right. Consequently, when we focus on the left side of the picture, the woman looks somehow taller or more erect than if we focus on the right side. And her face, too, seems to change with this change of position, because, even here, the two sides do not quite match (Gombrich 311). Another unusual aspect of the eyes in this portrait is the way that "eyes seem to follow you as you move in different directions; she returns your gaze" (Tamier).

It was Francesco di Bartolommeo di Zanobi del Giocondo, one of the noblest citizens of Florence, who commissioned da Vinci to paint a portrait of his third wife, Lisa di Antonio Maria di Noldo Gherardini. Da Vinci started working on this painting in 1503 when Mona Lisa was twenty-four years old, and he worked on it the next four years. There is much speculation over the reason that da Vinci left Florence in 1507 without selling the painting. Some believe it is because he did not finish the work. Others believe that he loved the painting so much that he was unable to part with it. He always carried the portrait with him; and, when he arrived in France in 1516 with the painting in his baggage, he sold it to King Francis I, who displayed it in his castle in Amboise. Over time the Mona Lisa was displayed at Fontainbleau, Paris, Versailles, and in the collection of Ludwig XIV. The Louvre obtained the painting after the French revolution, until Napoleon took it to hang in his bedroom. After Napoleon's banishment, the Mona Lisa returned to the Louvre in Paris (Mona, Mona!).

The painting was stolen on August 21, 1911; and two years later it was recovered in a hotel room in Florence and eventually returned to Paris. Acid damaged the lower half of the painting in 1956; it took years to restore the painting. During the 1960s and 1970s, the painting was displayed in New York, Moscow, and Tokyo. There are now international terms prohibiting the painting from travel, and it is kept behind bulletproof glass at the Louvre in Paris. It is considered the prototype of the Renaissance portrait (Stokstad).

Leonardo da Vinci's second most famous work is his rendition of the Last Supper, "one of the defining moments of Renaissance art" (Stokstad 690). It was painted during a four-year period from 1495 to 1498. Da Vinci was considered a rebel when it came to painting techniques. Over 500 years ago when da Vinci began The Last Supper he was experimenting with a new painting technique instead of the traditional method of buon fresco. Buon fresco is a "method of creating wall and ceiling murals with water colour on fresh lime-plaster so the resulting painting is an indestructible part of the wall, chemically integrated into the fabric of the building" (Bien). Instead of applying paint to wet plaster, da Vinci experimented with painting on drywall. The Last Supper was painted in the refectory of the church of Santa Maria delle Grazie in Milan, and at one point the painting almost completely deteriorated because of his inadequate fresco preparation (Stokstad).

The painting depicts one of the most dramatic episodes of Christ's life as recounted in the Gospel. The Last Supper is both a narrative study of emotions and a symbolic representation of the coming sacrifice that Christ would make for the salvation of mankind and for the institution of the traditional ritual of the Mass. There is an omnipresent sense of timelessness in this painting's perspective lines and geometrical and pyramidal forms. The use of "one-point perspective is defined by a coffered ceiling and four pairs of tapestries hanging on the walls. Its stagelike space recedes from a long table, placed parallel to the picture plane, to three windows on the back wall" (Stokstad 692). The pyramid at the center of the painting is created by Jesus' outstretched arms with a grouping of three disciples on either side. This is an emotional moment, frozen in time, as Christ announces that there is a traitor among them. Da Vinci depicts the emotional impact on each of the twelve disciples present. It is a "seated" drama which portrays the subjects' various degrees of surprise, anguish, and disquiet.

The subjects are divided into two groups. There are three on either side of Christ who are linked so as to indicate a certain continuity that is animated by a single movement. The impact of Christ's announcement rolls down the table like a wave. The subjects seated closest to him at the middle of the table are repelled and agitated as the wave undulates further down. The emotions of sorrow, indignation, denial, stupefaction, surprise, and vengeance are as important of the order of placement at the table. Judas being placed in the first triad, next to Christ, along with the John the Evangelist and Peter, indicates the important role that he would play in Jesus' mission. The groupings of three are evident in both the subjects and the architectural elements in the medieval tradition of numerical symbolism.

What sets this painting apart from all previous art is the variety of expression, the sincerity of the types and countenances, the power of the contrasts, and the depth of analysis. The countless studies that have been done of each figure are a testament to the ten years of preparation that da Vinci invested to summarize in a single picture such a totality of life. The hands have especially been singled out for their incomparable beauty and eloquence that contributed to a definitive historic painting. Leonardo da Vinci believed that in preserving the likeness of a subject, an artist could somehow preserve the soul of the person he portrayed. He not only knew what was required, he was among the first to instill life into the colors spread by his incredible brush strokes. In the words of Sigmund Freud, "Leonardo da Vinci was like a man who awoke too early in the darkness, while the others were all still asleep" (Leonardo).

NOTE: The Works Cited page is generally a separate page from the rest of the paper, and is paginated as the next page in the series.

Works Cited

Bien, Linda. Fresco Glossary. 10 Apr. 2002 <http:collections.ic.gc.ca/nincheri/en-fresco-gloss.html>.

Gombrich, E. H. The Story of Art. San Francisco: Chronicle Books, 1995.

Leonardo da Vinci: The Man, the Genius. 8 Apr. 2002 <http://starryskies.com/Artshtml/dln4-01/leonardo.html>.

Mona, Mona! 7 Apr. 2002. Montana State University. <http://www.montana.edu/4teachers/instcomp/hunts/art/owens/monalisa.htm>.

Stokstad, Marilyn. Art History. New York: Henry N. Abrams, 1999.

Tamier, Abraham. Mona Lisa, A Woman of Many Faces. Department of Chemical Engineering, Ben-Gurion University of the Negev, Beer-Sheva, Israel. 6 Apr. 2002 <http://www.tmoass.com/article3.htm>.

Shumaker 1

Stephanie Shumaker
Professor Hubble
American Literature I
26 Oct. 2001

The Crucible

The Salem witch trials have been written about fictionally and non-fictionally, as well as depicted in movies and plays. To compare one author to another or one trial to another is difficult at best. Arthur Miller chose to depict The Crucible in the form of a play. A review, "Witchcraft in The Crucible and The Witch of Blackbird Pond," states that

> The Crucible is quite clearly an artistic response to the political paranoia of McCarthyism. Miller uses his character introductions (whenever a new character first

> appears on the stage) to include political commentary. For example, when Rev. John Hale appears in Act I, his four page introduction compares the Salemites' belief in the awesome evil of the Devil with the 1950's fear of the awesome evil of Communism. (Shackleford Tise)

Arthur Miller is only one of many to use the religious fervor of the witch trials and their era as a literary basis.

Reading The Crucible as a play was rather difficult at first, though not impossible. Keeping each of the individual's responses and characteristics in line posed the most significant challenge. However, once the characters "take on a life of their own," the story becomes much easier to follow, and the structure is less imposing and practically seamless: "The story reminds its readers of an ugly blemish on human history. It reminds us that man is not perfect, and that we can make mistakes. However, even with these mistakes, we can cleanse ourselves and purify ourselves by making what is wrong right. The sufferings become to the sufferer like a crucible" (The Crucible). A "crucible" is "a place or situation in which concentrated forces interact to cause or influence change or development" ("Crucible"). Thus, considering the story, the play was appropriately named.

Fairly comparing the author Arthur Miller, and his style of writing, to Nathaniel Hawthorne would be difficult, considering that the latter never chose to publish a play. However, reading The House of the Seven Gables is cumbersome in that Hawthorne felt the need to express every emotion, color tone, temperature, and setting of each new "scene" to the greatest detail. He even advises the reader of the thoughts he believes the characters to be thinking . . . as if he knew. Such exacting descriptions may have been better served as a screenplay. Certainly, if one chose to act out the fictional events of The House of the Seven Gables, one would not be lacking in stage direction, or scene decoration. So detailed is he that lighting is even defined in the story line. Hawthorne seems to want to narrate the tale, and begs the reader to absorb the most minute concept, feeling, sound, or word, rather than write it for the reader to merely "read." It is as if he would prefer to sit with the reader and tell about all that he has seen and heard, rather than merely put it down on the page. Nathaniel Hawthorne was probably a very good storyteller in a social gathering, though reading his works, in my opinion, is neither relaxing nor enjoyable.

The Scarlet Letter, also written by Nathaniel Hawthorne, emphasizes the lack of rights women had in that day. They were expected to be submissive to their husbands, regardless of the heartless and uncaring treatment they were enduring from them. The bastard child, Pearl, of Hester Prynne in The Scarlet Letter, is born with a red birthmark on her stomach, which was, in those days, believed to be "the witches' mark": "The Scarlet Letter was based partly on his [Hawthorne's] experiences in Salem. The novel appeared in 1850 and told a story of the earliest victims of Puritan obsession and spiritual ferocity" (Liukkonen).

The Salem witch trials of The Crucible were just as capricious, based strictly on hearsay and the fears of the populace, wives tales, and nonsense with no facts or proof of damnable guilt. As men chose to treat women, they were so treated, regardless of the individual woman's status in the community. Editors of The Reader's Companion to American History claim, "Many colonists in late-seventeenth-century New England combined their Puritan faith with a belief in witchcraft, and charges that one or another person was one of Satan's agents, bent on bringing harm to the community, were common. By far the greatest concentration of these charges occurred in Salem Village, Massachusetts, in 1692" (Foner and Garraty).

The Puritan religion is the basis of the fears of Salem. The men believed one woman and her lies, which perpetrated the hangings of many innocent women and men. John Proctor, preacher and judge, ends his affair with Abigail Williams, who becomes obsessed and destructive, accusing many women of witchcraft, including Proctor's wife Elizabeth and subsequently Proctor himself. Elizabeth firmly declares in bitter triumph, "He have his goodness now. God forbid I take it from him," and the final curtain falls as John Proctor is hanged (Miller 91).

Another writer of the Puritan times, Cotton Mather, the minister of Boston's Old North church, was a true believer in witchcraft. In 1688, he had investigated the strange behavior of four children of a Boston mason named John Goodwin. The children had been complaining of sudden pains and crying out together in chorus. He concluded that witchcraft, specifically that practiced by an Irish washerwoman named Mary Glover, was responsible for the children's problems. He presented his findings and conclusions in one of the best known of his 382 works, Memorable Providences: ". . . Mather's experience caused him to vow that to 'never use but one grain of patience with any man that shall go to impose upon me a Denial of Devils, or of Witches'" (Linder).

The Puritan writer Anne Hutchinson, a midwife turned preacher, was unafraid of the Colony's stern male leaders. In 1638, Hutchinson was charged with heresy. Even though she was married to one of Boston's leading citizens, her charisma and learning was a threat to the Puritan leaders. So were her teachings, which can be summarized in her own words: "As I do understand it, laws, commands, rules and edicts are for those who have not the light which makes plain the pathway. He who has God's grace in his heart cannot go astray ("Mary Dyer"). Hutchinson was one of the women who stood for her beliefs and succeeded during a time when women were to be submissive to men and not have their words written, their thoughts known, or their beliefs heard.

The movie version of The Crucible remains relatively faithful to the play version. It does, however, divulge more of the sexual frustration than the McCarthy-era version. Abigail is portrayed in the movie as a girl obsessed with her sexual desires rather than a child who becomes enchanted by John Proctor. The movie holds true to the feigning of girls being ill and their ability to fool the court. However, differences exist in the play and movie versions as compared to the actual events of Salem in 1692. For instance, John Proctor's adultery with Abigail was not mentioned in the actual trials. His servant was actually twenty-year-old Mary Warren, who was believed to have "fits," which he would then beat out of her. John Proctor was the first male to be named as a witch. The story line of the movie had to be increased with sexual flirtations in 1996 to hold the attention of today's lustful audiences.

NOTE: The Works Cited page is generally a separate page from the rest of the paper, and is paginated as the next page in the series.

Works Cited

"Crucible." Merriam-Webster's Collegiate Dictionary. 1993 ed.

The Crucible. Dir. Nicholas Hytner. Perf. Daniel Day-Lewis and Wynona Ryder. 20th Century Fox, 2002.

The Crucible by Arthur Miller. 24 Oct. 2001 <http://summarycentral.tripod.com/thecrucible.htm>.

Foner, Eric, and John A. Garraty, eds. The Reader's Companion to American History. Boston: Houghton, 1991. Academic Search Premier. EBSCO. Rogers State University, Stratton Taylor Library. 23 Oct. 2001 <http://www.epnet.com/>.

Hawthorne, Nathaniel. The House of Seven Gables. New York: Bantam, 1981.

----. The Scarlet Letter. New York: Bantam, 1981.

Linder, Douglas. "Cotton Mather." Famous American Trials, Salem Witch Trials 1692. 23 Oct. 2001 <http://www.law.umkc.edu/faculty/projects/ftrials/salem/SAL_BMAT.HTM>.

Liukkonen, Petri "Nathaniel Hawthorne (1804-1864)." Books and Writers. 23 Oct. 2001 <http://www.kirjasto.sci.fi/hawthorn.htm>.

"Mary Dyer, Hung on Boston Common." Trials Without Justice. 23 Oct. 2001 <http://www.lawbuzz.com/justice/mary/banished.htm>.

Miller, Arthur. The Crucible. New York: Dramatists Play Service, Inc., 1980.

Shackleford Tise, Mary. "Witchcraft in The Crucible and The Witch of Blackbird Pond. 1998." 15 November 1998. 23 Oct. 2001 <http://www.delanet.com/~ftise/crucible.html>.

Harrison 1

Renetta Harrison

Prof. Sesso

Composition II/Cinema

30 Oct. 1998

A View Out a Rear Window

The film Rear Window is a voyeuristic suspense film starring James Stewart, Grace Kelly, Thelma Ritter, and Wendell Corey. James Stewart is the main character, Jeff, confined to his apartment with a broken leg. Grace Kelly portrays his girlfriend, Lisa. Thelma Ritter plays Stella, the nurse who comes to check on Jeff each day. Jeff is a travelling photographer who gazes out his apartment window to pass the time. He becomes obsessed with watching his neighbors, especially Mr. and Mrs. Thornwall. Lisa and Stella also develop interest in watching when Jeff explains the suspicious behavior of Mr. Thornwall. The remainder of the film deals with the three of them trying to prove their suspicions to Jeff's friend, Detective Doyle, played by Wendell Corey. Alfred Hitchcock is the brilliant and creative director of this film. Hitchcock is famous for his creative use of mise en scene in films of suspense and mystery. Rear Window is a perfect example of his creativity. This film consists of more than just a few mise en scene elements. The five most prominent elements in Rear Window are character proxemics, angles, shots and camera proxemics, lighting key, and framing.

First, character proxemics are useful tools in many of the scenes in Hitchcock's Rear Window. One example is the scene with Lisa and Stella gazing out the window while Jeff is on the phone with Mr. Thornwall, trying to get him to leave his apartment. Hitchcock places Lisa in the foreground, facing front, and Stella in the midground. This character placing shows the viewer that Lisa is the more important character of the two. Also, Lisa walks in front of Stella when leaving the room, blocking Stella from view. This action is meant to draw the viewer's attention to Lisa and possibly set up the importance of her in an upcoming scene. Another good example of Hitchcock's use of character proxemics to create a mood is the scene in which Mr. Thornwall leaves his apartment. In this particular scene, the viewer is watching through Jeff's camera lens and sees a medium shot of Mr. Thornwall walking from right to left and disappearing behind a brick wall. This action of walking right to left on screen denotes a conflict. The viewer later discovers that Mr. Thornwall is on his way to Jeff's apartment for a confrontation. Hitchcock uses character proxemics in almost every scene in this film to emphasize a point for the viewer.

Second, Hitchcock uses a variety of angles in Rear Window to place significance on an article or person. He mostly uses an eye-level angle when shooting scenes in which the viewer sees Jeff. For example, in the scene with Jeff talking on the phone to Mr. Thornwall, the viewer sees Jeff at eye level, as if the viewer were in the room with Jeff. This involves the viewer more intimately with Jeff. Hitchcock uses a high angle in the scene of Jeff watching Lisa and Stella dig in the flower bed below his window. This gives the viewer the feeling of being in the room beside Jeff and looking down at the girls with him. Another high angle shot is of Jeff in his wheelchair hiding in the shadows of his apartment listening to Mr. Thornwall approach his door. These instances are of high angle shots, one of Mr. Thornwall standing over Jeff before attacking him, and again when Jeff is struggling to get away from him. This creates a foreboding mood and depicts Mr. Thornwall as a menace. Hitchcock implements several different angles in this film in order to entangle the viewer in the action.

Third, shots and camera proxemics are very important aspects Hitchcock uses in this film. He uses extreme close-ups to emphasize the great importance of certain objects in Rear Window. An example of this is in the scene with Jeff watching Lisa and Stella digging. The viewer sees a shot through Jeff's camera lens of the girls' feet, panning to the empty hole dug. This places great importance on the fact that there is nothing in the hole. Next, the camera pans up to a close-up of Stella shaking her head, stressing the fact of there being nothing in the hole. Hitchcock uses full shots to long shots of Jeff's neighbors in their windows. These shots show that the neighbors are not directly involved or intimate with Jeff. Use of medium shots of Jeff, Lisa, and Stella creates a more friendly relationship between the three. Several shots of the three of them gazing out the window toward Mr. Thornwall's apartment are good examples. Hitchcock uses a very interesting long shot of both Lisa in Mr. Thornwall's apartment and the neighbor below, Ms. Lonely Heart, in her bedroom. In this shot, Lisa is snooping around Mr. Thornwall's apartment and Ms. Lonely Heart is about to attempt suicide. Jeff and Stella are watching out Jeff's window and are concerned about Ms. Lonely Heart, who is about to take a handful of sleeping pills. Jeff picks up his phone and dials the police department. At the same time, Mr. Thornwall arrives back home. Jeff and Stella have been concentrating on saving Ms. Lonely Heart and now do not have time to call and warn Lisa of the danger. This shot is meant to agitate the viewer and create an uncomfortable feeling of not being able to help Lisa escape. I found myself wanting to shout out to Lisa that Mr. Thornwall was back and to get out. Hitchcock frequently uses shots and camera proxemics to rivet the viewer's attention to the film.

Fourth, Hitchcock uses lighting to define the mood of a scene or film. In Rear Window, he uses low key lighting to emphasize a dark, foreboding atmosphere. The prime example of this use is in the scene of the conflict between Jeff and Mr. Thornwall. In this scene the viewer sees only silhouettes of Mr. Thornwall and Jeff. This use of low key lighting lends an eerie feeling to the scene. Another example of Hitchcock's use of lighting is the scene in which the viewer sees Jeff in the light as he wheels himself backwards into the shadows of his apartment. Seeing Jeff in the shadows of his apartment gives the viewer the illusion that Mr. Thornwall will not be able to see him. Also, it sets a mysterious, disorienting mood for the scene. Another lighting key Hitchcock uses is masking. In Rear Window he uses masking when the viewer sees shots of Jeff's view of his neighbor's windows at night. Their windows are brightly lit, but the surrounding building is blacked out. This allows the viewer to concentrate on what he or she sees through each window. Primarily, low key lighting is used throughout this film; however, other lighting aspects are occasionally implemented for effect.

Finally, framing is the major misc en scene element Hitchcock uses in Rear Window. He uses framing to include the viewer in the action of this film. In most of Rear Window Hitchcock utilizes a window for a framing effect. The window framing effect gives the viewer the feeling of actually looking out of or into a window. This film's setting is Jeff's apartment and the view out his window. Therefore, Hitchcock shows several scenes of Jeff in his window and then shows what he is seeing out of his window. One scene includes shots of Jeff by his window with his camera and binoculars, watching Lisa and Stella dig in the flower garden. Also, Hitchcock uses window framing in the shots of Lisa snooping in Mr. Thornwall's apartment. Another abundant framing aspect he uses in Rear Window is iris framing. This framing effect gives the viewer the feeling of actually looking through a camera or binocular lens. Iris framing is evident in the scene in which Jeff is looking out his window through his camera at the girls' digging. The viewer sees Jeff's actual view through his camera zoom lens, complete with the rounded-shadow effect around the edges of the shot. Hitchcock uses iris framing throughout this film as a transition to a close-up shot of an important person or item. In the scene of the girls digging, the camera pans a shot of their feet, the hole, and then finally Stella's face, using iris framing. This style of framing is Hitchcock's way of enabling the viewer to become much more involved and intimate in the film. He uses window and iris framing frequently in Rear Window to draw the viewer's total attention.

Rear Window is an excellent film in which to observe many mise en scene elements. Alfred Hitchcock is a director who uses many different elements in his films. The elements in Rear Window are abundant and usually easy to read. Hitchcock's use of character proxemics in this film allows the viewer to distinguish each character's importance. His uses of angles and shots lend emphasis to every scene. In addition, the lighting key defines the mood of the film, and framing personally involves the viewer. All of these elements create the suspense and mystery for which Hitchcock is so famous.

NOTE: The Works Cited page is generally a separate page from the rest of the paper, and is paginated as the next page in the series.

Works Cited

Rear Window. Dir. Alfred Hitchcock. Screenplay by John Michael Hayes. Perf. James Stewart and Grace Kelly. Paramount Pictures, 1954.

Gay 1

Rick W. Gay

Prof. Yee

Composition II

6 Mar. 1998

In the Name of Love

On its surface, Andre Dubus's "Killings" may look like just another tale of murder and revenge, but closer examination reveals a much deeper theme. The murders in this story are not incited by hatred or vengeance. They are brought on by emotion that is not usually considered malevolent. Both Richard and Matt are driven to extremes by their strong sense of family. These killers cite love as their motive.

With the statement "He was making it with my wife," Richard Strout believes he is justifying his murder of Frank (67). Despite legal separation, divorce proceedings, and his involvement with another woman, Richard still feels the obligation to protect his loved ones. This instinct to defend his territory causes him to perceive Frank as an interloper. Strout begins his defense on the civilized end of the spectrum, but when all attempts to warn off the intruder fail, he moves toward violence. Eventually he sees only one solution. To preserve his love of family, Richard Strout kills Frank.

Matt feels the same protective instincts. The love of a parent for a child is enormously strong but as the child matures, parents must make concessions. When Ruth complains of Frank's relationship with Mary Ann, Matt defends it saying, "She probably loves him. . . . Why can't we just leave it at that?" (65). He does not entirely approve of his son's liaison but his parental protectiveness is giving way to confidence in Frank's judgement. Matt believes that love justifies even questionable actions. Even his respect for the law is eventually overcome by this love for his family.

Matt cannot endure his wife's pain at seeing their son's murderer free on bail: "She sees him all the time. It makes her cry," he says, confiding his anguish to a friend (62). His inability to prevent Frank's death only intensifies his desire to shield his wife from further misery. Even the probability of Richard's eventual imprisonment is not enough to relieve Ruth's suffering. Matt is motivated to remove the source of her pain. His elaborate preparations for the murder are not for his own sake, but to protect Ruth from the misery she would surely endure if her husband were to be incarcerated. Matt murders Richard for love of family.

Both of these men take another human life for essentially the same reason. But the manifestation of love takes a decidedly different form with each killer. Richard loves his family, and yet he commits murder in the living room right before their very eyes. The repercussions of his action will undoubtedly have a profound effect on his entire family for the rest of their lives. Matt, on the other hand, goes to great lengths to limit his family's exposure to the unsavory event. With one outside party involved, and Ruth present in spirit only, Matt succeeds in shielding his family as much as possible. Richard's crime can be argued as a spur-of-the-moment decision, and thus would fall to the lesser charge of manslaughter. Conversely, Matt's crime is obviously premeditated, making it indisputably first degree murder. Despite the fact that Matt has committed the worse offense, his circumstances and distraught state of mind are more likely to elicit sympathy from a jury. In short, emotion can cause bizarre behavior.

The compelling force behind all criminal activity is nothing more than primitive human emotions. Although religious zealots would be quick to point out the Seven Deadly Sins as the source of all men's troubles, there is more to consider. Man is a hopelessly emotional creature, and his judgements are not always built on the foundation of right and wrong. Pride, lust, envy, anger, greed, gluttony, and sloth may be responsible for the bulk of mankind's problems, but another variable figures prominently into the equation. Criminal behavior is not exclusively generated by the dark side of man's psyche. Some crimes are motivated by love.

NOTE: The Works Cited page is generally a separate page from the rest of the paper, and is paginated as the next page in the series.

Works Cited

Dubus, Andre. "Killings." The Compact Bedford Introduction to Literature. 4th ed. Ed. Michael Meyer. Boston: Bedford Books, 1997. 61-73.

Lauderdale 1

Michael Lauderdale

Dr. Dial-Driver

Composition II

21 Apr. 1998

Where's the Beef?

Today's cattle ranchers are faced with ever-increasing production costs which erode their profits and make their jobs more difficult each day. The price of land, taxes, fuel, medical expenses, and general maintenance costs has risen steadily with inflation, yet the law of supply and demand causes the price of cattle to fluctuate drastically from one week to the next. In fact, cattle prices are lower today than they have been in ten years, even though the costs of production have increased. Many factors affect live cattle prices. For example, a flood or drought can drastically reduce the availability of grazing lands or destroy feed grain crops, thus increasing the cost of feeding cattle and, in turn, driving cattle prices down. Cattle ranchers are constantly at risk of losing money due to uncontrollable economic or environmental factors. One of the most important economic factors affecting cattle prices is that today's consumers are much more price and health conscious than consumers of past decades. Today's consumers are simply not eating as much beef as they did twenty years ago. Therefore, if cattle ranchers are to remain competitive in today's cattle industry, they must dispel myths concerning beef consumption while they also satisfy modern consumer demands for low cost and high quality by minimizing production costs and producing leaner beef, using technological advancements in heritability traits, Expected Progeny Differences, and artificial insemination practices.

Negative perceptions concerning the consumption of red meat have caused a severe decline in the amount of beef consumed by the American consumer: "Over the past 20 years Americans have steadily turned from beef to other meats such as chicken and turkey. Health-conscious consumers are worried about eating red meat; price-conscious ones note that beef costs more than chicken and pork" ("America's" A11). Because so many consumers feel that the consumption of red meat is unhealthy, a drastic reduction in the amount of beef consumed per average household has resulted. Today it is common to see the words "low-cholesterol," "low-fat," or "light" in the description of food products. As many Americans have became more health-conscious, so have many refused to pay higher prices per pound for beef than for other meat products. If beef is perceived as the least-healthy choice, in addition to being the most expensive of the meat products, consumers will simply bypass the red meat section in the grocery store, and thus lessen the demand for the beef the rancher must sell to maintain solvency.

The first item on the rancher's agenda should be to regain public confidence and dispute the prevailing myths concerning the consumption of beef. Many consumers believe that consumption of beef leads to an increase in blood cholesterol and fat build-up in the arteries. Are the concerns and beliefs of consumers well founded or not? According to a research article in the Drovers Journal,

> Scientists at Penn State University report that saturated fat in beef . . . may not be so bad after all. . . . Saturated fat actually may help lower "bad" cholesterol.
>
> Rat liver cells were treated with fatty acids from palm oil and coconut oil or with stearic acid from . . . meat. The stearic acid resulted in much lower levels of triglyceride, which is a precursor to bad cholesterol. ("Beef Fat" 14)

Another concern of consumers, in addition to fat content, is the link of the feared E. coli 0157:H7 bacteria to ground beef. It is common knowledge that increased cooking times and temperatures will eliminate the risk of the E. coli bacteria, but ranchers must show the consumer that they are willing to take the steps necessary to supply the public with a safe and healthy product. According to Ed Johnson, a cattle producer and veterinarian with Johnson Research of Parma, Idaho, "No one wants to put a product out there that is not safe. . . . However, contaminated beef does make its way through the production and processing to consumers. When that happens, their confidence in beef declines" (Watson 29). If today's ranchers encourage the beef industry to enforce stricter inspection requirements from the producer to the retailer, consumers may once again regain the confidence they once had in the safety of beef.

Today's ranchers have the ability to produce a leaner, more consumer-appealing beef by utilizing knowledge and information made available through biotechnological advances in the study of heritability traits: "Traits measured in beef cattle populations are each the sum of the genetic and environmental factors which have effect. Heritability indicates the proportion of the differences between individuals that is genetic" (Northcutt 1). Northcutt goes on to explain, "Probably the most practical use of heritability [traits] is that it indicates the ease with which we can make genetic improvement through selection" (1). Northcutt also reports, "Carcass traits as a group tend to be moderately to highly heritable. . ." (13). Carcass traits in beef cattle that can be improved are traits such as carcass weight, fat trim percentage, fat thickness, ribeye area, and marbling (Northcutt 13). To improve the quality of beef in the herd, the rancher can select cattle for breeding that exhibit proven and desirable carcass traits. By improving the carcass traits within the herd, the rancher supplies the consumer with a more desirable beef product from cattle that will grow to slaughter weight with maximum efficiency and therefore lessen the profit-to-cost ratio.

One of the latest advances in technology available to the cattle industry for improving the performance of beef cattle is the development of Expected Progeny Differences (EPD's):

> The EPD is simply the difference that is expected in the offspring of a particular individual relative to some base point. In most cases, the EPD is given as a positive or negative value in the units of measure for the particular traits. . . . The EPD values are most useful when two [cattle] individuals are being compared directly. (Buchanan and Northcutt 1)

EPD's values are available for traits such as birth weight, weaning weight, yearling weight, and milk production in female cattle. EPD values are an estimate of what the offspring of a particular sire can be expected to attain for each trait, over or under the existing breed average. For example, if the EPD weaning weight for a sire is shown as +20, then the progeny of that sire, under favorable conditions, can be expected to weigh approximately twenty pounds heavier at weaning than the breed average. Although EPDs for carcass traits are not available yet, the rancher can selectively use EPD values to breed cattle that will perform at optimal levels and therefore reduce production costs. This reduction in production cost should be reflected at the meat counter and thus provide the consumer with a reasonably-priced meat product.

If today's ranchers are to effectively utilize technological advancements in heritability traits and Expected Progeny Differences to raise cattle that contain less fat and perform more efficiently, ranchers should adopt an artificial insemination (AI) breeding program for his or her cattle herd. By using an AI program, the rancher can purchase the genetically high quality semen of bulls that would otherwise be too expensive to own. As research has shown, "Selection of bulls is very important to genetic improvement in the herd. Since 75-90 percent of all genetic progress will likely come from the sires used, it is difficult to overstate the importance of proper bull selection" (Northcutt 133). By using AI, the rancher can select a sire that will provide the genetics for high-quality offspring with emphasis given to selected carcass and performance traits. According to A. L. Neumann, "Artificial breeding has not been so widely practiced by beef cattle breeders as it has been by dairymen. This is changing rapidly. . ." (157). Even though natural reproduction is used far more, the increased use in AI proves that ranchers are making an effort to satisfy the American consumer by supplying a high-quality meat product.

Our nation's ranchers are faced with a few important and difficult decisions that must be made soon if the beef industry is to rebound from its current cellar position. The American consumer has over the past twenty years became much more health and value conscious. A decrease in the consumption of red meat has been stirred to some degree by medical information that is not yet complete. Much of the burden of the reduction in beef consumption falls on the shoulders of ranchers themselves. For many years, ranchers have refused to deviate from management practices learned from their fathers. The beef cattle industry has fallen behind in efficient production procedures and has not progressed at the same rate as other industries. Today, if ranchers are to remain solvent, they must attempt to regain their share of the food market lost to fish, poultry, and pork. Ranchers must first dispel the myths of beef consumption, allowing consumers to make more unbiased decisions concerning the consumption of red meat. Ranchers must also take advantage of the latest technological tools, such as the use of heritability traits, Expected Progeny Differences, and artificial insemination, to produce cattle of higher quality and quantity, with a lower fat content. By accepting these available tools, today's ranchers give themselves an opportunity to compete in a competitive economy. If ranchers are willing to make a diligent effort to use these available tools, they will be able to produce beef that will satisfy consumers' needs, as well as provide an increase in profit for themselves.

NOTE: The Works Cited page is generally a separate page from the rest of the paper, and is paginated as the next page in the series.

Works Cited

"America's Lean Beef Industry Says It's Getting a Bum Steer." Tulsa World 19 Mar. 1996: A11.

"Beef Fat May Be Good for You." Drovers Journal 123.5 (May 1995): 14.

Buchanan, David S., and Sally L. Northcutt. Unpublished research report Expected Progeny Difference (EPD). Animal Science Dept., Oklahoma State University, Stillwater, OK, n.d.

Neumann, A. L. Beef Cattle. New York: Wiley, 1977.

Northcutt, Sally L. Unpublished research report from Animal Science Dept., Oklahoma State University. Stillwater, OK, n.d. Genetic Tools for Designing Cattle-Size, Growth, Maternal, and Carcass. Oklahoma Beef Cattle Manual. Keith Lusby, Comm. Chair of the Okla. Beef Cattle Manual Comm., Stillwater, OK: Cooperative Extension Service Division of Agriculture Oklahoma State University, n.d.

Watson, Kim. "Food Safety Is Everybody's Concern." Drovers Journal 122.9 (Sep. 1994): 29-30.

Hastings 1

Laurie Hastings

Prof. Zee

Comp. II

25 July 2002

Similarities Between

"The Black Cat" and "The Tell-Tale Heart" by Edgar Allan Poe

Edgar Allan Poe went through different writing stages throughout his life, but he always followed the same formula. He felt that the writer should decide upon the effect a story or poem should create and write toward that effect (Herzberg 888). It seems evident that Poe must have had the same effect in mind when he wrote the stories "The Black Cat" and "The Tell-Tale Heart." The stories are similar in narrator, crime, and criminal discovery.

A brief summary of each story will help clarify the similarities between them. In "The Black Cat" a narrator cuts out the eye of his favorite cat and eventually hangs the animal. That night his house burns down, leaving only one wall standing, which seems to bear the outline of the dead cat. He replaces both the house and the cat. He obtains a second cat which is also black except for a small white patch which slowly comes to resemble a hangman's noose. The narrator attempts to kill the cat with an ax, but instead he kills his wife as she attempts to stop him. He walls her body up in the cellar. When the police who have come to investigate break down the wall, they discover the corpse standing erect, with the cat upon her head.

In "The Tell-Tale Heart" the narrator decides he must kill the old man he lives with because he hates the old man's eye. He devises a plan to kill the old man in his sleep and does so. He dismembers the corpse and hides it beneath the floor planks in the old man's room. The police come to search, and the narrator invites them into the old man's room. The narrator begins to hear the beating of the old man's heart from under the planks. When he can't stand to hear it any longer, he confesses.

Each story is narrated by a diseased madman attempting to convince the reader that he is not mad and proving just the opposite. Both of Poe's madmen refer to a disease, leading the reader to believe this is the cause of their madness. In "The Black Cat" the madman says, "But my disease grew upon me. . ." (64). In "The Tell-Tale Heart" the madman not only admits disease but believes it has helped him. He says, "The disease has sharpened my senses. . ." (9). In "The Black Cat" the madman tries to prove his sanity, saying, "I neither expect nor solicit your belief. Mad indeed I would be to expect it. . . . Yet, mad I am not. . ." (63). Similarly, the madman in "The Tell-Tale Heart" says, "True!--nervous--very, very dreadfully nervous I had been and am; but why will you say that I am mad?" (9). Each narrator attempts to make the reader believe that he is too clever to be mad. The narrator in "The Black Cat" states, "My immediate purpose is to place before the world plainly, succinctly and without comment, a series of mere household events. . . . I detail with awe, nothing more than an ordinary succession of very natural causes and effects" (63). The narrator in "The Tell-Tale Heart" states in a similar manner, "Hearken! and observe how healthily--how calmly I can tell you the whole story" (9).

Neither one of the narrators has a rational motive for the murder he commits. In "The Tell-Tale Heart" the madman says that he does not hate his intended victim but only his "Evil Eye"; in "The Black Cat" the narrator punishes the "evil" he imagines in a pet by cutting out one of its eyes. Both of the madmen seem to realize they have no sensible motive. In "The Tell-Tale Heart" the narrator describes his own feelings about why he killed the old man:

> Object there was none. Passion there was none. I loved the old man. He had never wronged me. He had never given me insult. For his gold I had no desire. I think it was his eye! Yes, it was this! One of his eyes resembled that of a vulture--a pale blue eye, with a film over it. (Poe 9)

In "The Black Cat" the narrator experiences very similar feelings about killing his cat: "One morning, in cold blood, I slipped a noose about its neck and hung it with the tears streaming from my eyes, and with the bitterest remorse at my heart;--hung it because I knew that it loved me, and because I felt it had given me no reason or offense" (Poe 65).

The reader comes to realize that the evil is not in the eye of the old man nor the eye of the cat. Just as in the old proverb "Beauty is in the eye of the beholder," in these stories evil is in the eye of the beholder narrator. Poe often puns on the words I and eye. In these stories the eye that causes the narrator disgust is really the qualities of himself, the I whom the narrator does not even recognize. Poe agreed with the Romantics that the Self assigns meaning to the world. However, instead of the positive qualities of human nature, Poe's characters transfer their own twisted desires and feelings to the people and animals around them (Howarth 19), feeling no shame for what they have done. In fact they seem quite proud of their deeds. They clearly know what has happened as a result of their irrational actions. In "The Tell-Tale Heart" the madman says the old man, whom he has killed, is "stone dead" (Poe 12). In "The Black Cat" the madman admits that, because of his action, his wife "fell dead upon the spot" (Poe 68).

Both madmen then set about accomplishing similar tasks by similar means. The madman in "The Tell-Tale Heart" describes what he does to hide his act; he says he

> worked hastily, but in silence. First of all I dismembered the corpse. I cut off the head and the arms and the legs. I then took up three planks from the flooring of the chamber, and deposited all between the scantlings. I then replaced the boards so cleverly, so cunningly, that no human eye--not even his, could have detected anything wrong. There was nothing to wash out--no stain of any kind--no blood whatever. I had been too wary for that. A tub had caught all--ha! ha! (Poe 12)

The madman in "The Black Cat" also describes his precautions in concealing the body: "This hideous murder accomplished, I set myself forthwith, and with entire deliberation, to the task of concealing the body" (Poe 68). He discusses several methods of disposing of the body, one of which is exactly what the madman in "The Tell-Tale Heart" uses. He then informs the reader he decides to wall up his wife's body:

> I determined to wall it up in the cellar. . . . By means of a crowbar I easily dislodged the bricks, and, having carefully deposited the body against the inner wall, I propped it in that position, while, with little trouble, I re-laid the whole structure as it originally stood. . . . I prepared a plaster which could not be distinguished from the old, and with this I very carefully went over the new brick work. . . . The wall did not present the slightest appearance of having been disturbed. (Poe 68-69)

The murderers apparently succeed in perfectly concealing all physical evidence of their crimes. It is not some overlooked detail but the murderers themselves who reveal their guilt. Neither story would be the same had an outsider discovered their hideous deeds. The madmen's consciences will not let them escape the judgment of God, the law, and their peers. Thus, the discovery of the crime results; that discovery is necessary: "Perhaps no aphorism has had such sanction in our society as 'Crime does not pay!' Our popular cultural forms have perennially shaped their material to dramatize this lesson. Anything else would seem to be, at least officially and as a serious proposal, unthinkable" (Martin 29).

The murderers have a great deal of confidence in their plans. When the doorbell sounds in "The Tell-Tale Heart," the madman says, "I went down to open it with a light heart" (Poe 12). Although it turns out to be the police at the door, the narrator still says, "I smiled, for what had I to fear? I bade the gentlemen welcome. . . . I took my visitors all over the house. I bade them search--search well. I led them at length to his chamber. . ." (Poe 12). Similarly the madman in "The Black Cat" does not panic when a party of police come to search the house. He says, "Secure, however, in the inscrutability of my place of concealment, I felt no embarrassment whatever" (Poe 6).

It is at this point in both stories that one could start to believe the madmen may escape justice. The madman in "The Tell-Tale Heart" knows "The officers were satisfied" (Poe 12). Likewise the madman in "The Black Cat" says, "The police were thoroughly satisfied and prepared to depart" (Poe 69). It is also at this point in each story that the madmen are both bursting with pride and over-confidence. From here on, nearly identical events happen within each story as the madmen are caught for their horrid deeds. Both refer to pacing the floor. The narrator in "The Black Cat" "roamed easily to and fro" (Poe 13). In "The Tell-Tale Heart" the narrator "paced the floor to and fro with heavy strides" (Poe 13). Both then seem to become ill. In "The Black Cat" the madman says, "Swooning, I staggered" (Poe 70), and in "The Tell-Tale

Heart" the madman says, "I felt myself getting Pale. . . . I gasped for breath" (Poe 12-13).

Subsequently, each narrator begins to hear a sound, either the beating of a heart or the wailing of a cat. The suspense leading to the ending builds as the sounds increase in intensity and clarity. The narrators believe that God may be punishing them. In "The Tell-Tale Heart" the narrator says, "Was it possible they [the police] heard not? Almighty God!" (Poe 13). In "The Black Cat" the narrator pleads, "But may God shield and deliver me from the hands of the Arch-Fiend!" (Poe 69). Likewise, in "The Tell-Tale Heart," the narrator says, "I fancied a ringing in my ears. . . . It continued and became more distinct. At length, I found that the noise was not within my ears . . . and yet the officers heard it not" (Poe 13). The narrator believes that what he hears is the increasingly loud beating of the old man's heart. However, the reader realizes that it is really the narrator's own conscience. Believing the police hear and are mocking his horror, he can take the torment no longer and confesses, "Villains! . . . dissemble no more! I admit the deed!--tear up the planks!--here, here--it is the beating of his hideous heart!" (Poe 13). In "The Black Cat" the increasing noise is also caused by the madman himself. He raps his cane where his wife is entombed. Then there is a sound from within the tomb which is muffled at first but steadily increases. He describes it as "quickly swelling into one long, loud, and continuous scream" (Poe 71). He is caught because he has unintentionally walled the cat up alive within the tomb.

In both stories the narrators, despite their protests, are quite obviously mad. The total effect in each story is one of controlled horror. In stepping over the fine line that divides sanity from insanity, each narrator creates an effect that at once frightens and fascinates the reader. In the end, the reader is relieved to find that crime does not, in fact, pay, because our own tormented consciences will not let us escape justice.

NOTE: The Works Cited page is generally a separate page from the rest of the paper, and is paginated as the next page in the series.

Works Cited

Herzberg, Max J., et al. The Reader's Encyclopedia of American Literature. New York: T. J. Crowell, 1962.

Howarth, William L., et al. Twentieth Century Interpretations of Poe's Tales. Englewood Cliffs: Prentice-Hall,1971.

Martin, Terence. The Imagination at Play. New York: Unk, 1966. 195-98.

Poe, Edgar Allan. "The Black Cat." Complete Stories of Edgar Allan Poe. New York: Doubleday, 1966. 63-70.

---. "The Tell-Tale Heart." Imaginative Literature: Fiction, Drama, Poetry. 4th ed. Ed. Alton C. Morris, Biron Walker, and Philip Bradshaw. New York: Harcourt Brace Javonovich, 1983. 9-13.

Rodgers 1

Anna Rodgers

Dr. Aye

Composition II

12 Nov. 2005

The Woman's Place

Throughout history, women's roles have been portrayed as inferior, if not downright subservient, to men's. Even in a story that has a heroine instead of a hero, there is usually a man around who has some measure of power over her, romantic or otherwise. These submissive roles are especially prevalent in literature written before the dawning of the women's liberation movement of the 1960's. The play by Susan Glaspell, "Trifles," and the short story "Boys and Girls" by Alice Munro both make a comment on how women tend to be portrayed and also give a glimpse into how that portrayal makes them feel. In both stories the point is made that anything a woman does is subject to an attitude of amused derision from a man, that the work women do is less important than the work men do, and that women are capable of only the most trifling of thoughts and emotions.

The words and actions of the women in these two stories receive amused, occasionally derisive, comments from the men. In Glaspell's play, there are several instances in which the men make fun of what the women are doing, such as looking at and discussing the quilt Mrs. Wright was working on (181). They also laugh at and "put down" some of the women's comments, especially when the women try to defend Mrs. Wright in any way (179). When the young girl in "Boys and Girls" lets Flora, the horse, escape, she does so out of strong feelings she has about the shooting of the horse. Rather than trying to understand her actions or praising her for acting on her convictions, her father simply demeans and dismisses her with the single comment, "Never mind. . . . She's only a girl" (Munro 835).

The work that the women do is regarded as unimportant compared to the work men do. Unfortunately, the women occasionally seem to share this opinion. There are several references in Glaspell's play to the unimportance and (men assume) easiness of the tasks women perform. The lawyer makes degrading remarks about the poor job Mrs. Wright seems to do of keeping her house up. He even kicks her pans around the kitchen floor, showing how little respect he has for the work she has done. When Mrs. Hale tries to defend her, he dismisses her reaction as the result of her simply being loyal to her own sex (179). Mrs. Peters, in an example of how women tend to accept the judgments of men, tries to explain away their rude behavior as due to the fact that "They've got awful important things on their minds" (181). The young girl in Munro's story describes her mother's work as "endless, dreary, and peculiarly depressing" while the work her father does is "ritualistically important" (828). The work that women are capable of is further demeaned when the mother and father discuss the fact that only after her little brother gets a little older and starts working with her father will he have "a real help" (827). In fact, the mother may be jealous of the freedom her daughter has to work at men's tasks instead of women's (829).

Not only is the work women do regarded as without merit, so is most of what they think and feel. In "Trifles" the men act as if the fact that Mrs. Wright is worried about her preserves is ridiculous compared to the fact that she is being held for the murder of her husband, the men saying, "Well, can you beat the women! Held for murder and worryin' about her preserves!" (Glaspell 178). It does not occur to them that Mrs. Wright worked hard to put them up and that, if she is not convicted, she will need them to get through the winter. The statement is also made that "women are used to worrying over trifles" (Glaspell 179). When the men overhear the ladies discussing how they think Mrs. Wright might be planning to finish her quilt, they speak to the women in a patronizing, amused tone. In fact, any time the men bother to bring their attention to the ladies at all it is as if they are "turning from serious things to little pleasantries" (Glaspell 183). The women, however, do not see anything amusing about spending their time "with little things" while they wait for the men to finish what they are doing (Glaspell 181). That women are considered incapable of deeper thoughts is evinced in the fact that the sheriff is not the least bit worried about what things they have gotten into and what they have chosen to take to Mrs. Wright in jail (Glaspell 185).

In both stories, men seem to regard the women as somehow less than men, based on things as irrelevant as the types of work women do, the topics that occupy the minds of women, and the fact they are women. This is probably the attitude that existed in society at the time the stories were written and is an attitude that even the raised consciousness of our current society has not lost. Both authors seem to be making a statement about how the attitude makes women feel. Both authors seem to think it is an incorrect way to regard women. In "Trifles" the men's disregard for the women's mental abilities turns against them in that the women basically solve the murder, but are able to hold back the damning evidence by using the men's attitude as a way to camouflage what they know (Glaspell 185). Conversely, in Munro's story of a young girl learning exactly what it means to be a girl, her reactions to how she is treated show how damaging to the girl's self esteem it can be to be forced into the small box of acceptable actions and behaviors men deemed as the woman's place in society.

NOTE: The Works Cited page is generally a separate page from the rest of the paper, and is paginated as the next page in the series.

Works Cited

Glaspell, Susan. "Trifles." Literature for Composition: Essays, Fiction, Poetry, and Drama. Ed. Sylvan Barnet, Morton Berman, William Burto, and Marcia Stubbs. New York: HarperCollins, 1992. 176-85.

Munro, Alice. "Boys and Girls." Literature for Composition: Essays, Fiction, Poetry, and Drama. Ed. Sylvan Barnet, Morton Berman, William Burto, and Marcia Stubbs. New York: HarperCollins, 1992. 825-35.

Ryan 1

Stephen Ryan

Dr. Emmons

Native American Literature

27 Nov. 2005

In the Reservation of My Mind: Exploring Sherman Alexie

Native American literature continues to explode on the popular consciousness, with such famous writers as Joy Harjo and Leslie Marmon Silko continuing to gain in popularity and notoriety as the years go by. One of the most popular and, in many ways, most controversial Native American authors writing today is Sherman Alexie. Sherman Alexie, most well known for his poetry, has branched out into the world of novel-length fiction and even into the realm of motion pictures. Obviously, for an artist to continue to stretch himself into various means and methods of story-telling speaks of a great passion for the art produced. Sherman Alexie is very obviously a passionate writer who believes in the things that he says and does. In the arena of art theory, Alexie has just as many strong ideas as he does in other areas; and, not surprisingly, he articulates them strongly and unflinchingly.

In his "General Commentary," Sherman Alexie talks about heroes. He states that he has always had as his heroes people who were "just decent people . . . my writing is somehow just about decency" (Caldwell 2). Great art, then, is about decency. Great art is about the people who, against all odds, continue to hold their ground against a tide of selfishness and degradation and maintain their decency. In "The Trial of Thomas Builds-the-Fire," Alexie tells the story of a single Indian man who stands his ground in a court of law and tells his stories, unwilling to be silenced. Though Thomas Builds-the-Fire is punished, sentenced to two concurrent life terms in prison for his stories, still he stands and refuses to change, as evidenced by the closing line of the story: "Thomas closed his eyes and told this story" (Alexie, Lone Ranger 103). In this way, Alexie's story helps, in his own words, to "even the score" (Caldwell 2), by showing the unflinching determination and rigid beliefs of one man.

Alexie also believes that Native American writers should write "about the way we live" (Caldwell 3). Alexie states that Native American writers, especially, should be true to their real lives, writing "from their own lived experiences, not some nostalgic and romanticized notion of what it means to be Indian" (Caldwell 3). Alexie fulfills this particular bit of his theory quite well, writing many poems that could certainly be autobiographical. In his ironically titled "An Unauthorized Autobiography of Me," Alexie tells of many events from his own childhood, such as a music class in school (One Stick Song 15) and a winter when, after failing to pay the electric bill, Alexie's family lived without heat (One Stick Song 14). Alexie does not restrict his writing to such extremely personal events, however, but also writes about larger events and ideas that can apply to all Native Americans, such as Alexie's Indian Killer, in which Alexie shows the plight of the modern day urban Indian in a story intended to represent true Indian experiences in a modern city. Alexie states that he believes Native American writers should write out of the experiences that they have gathered in their lives and it is certainly easy to see that Alexie practices what he preaches.

Sherman Alexie confronts many dangerously controversial issues in his works and he never shies away from that conflict. He does, however, hold that the author who dares to condemn something must make sure that his or her own life bears out the standard taken: "If you're writing about racism, I don't think you should be a racist. If you're going to write about sexism and exploitation, then I don't think you should be sleeping around. If you're going to write about violence and colonialism, then I don't think you should be doing it to your own family" (Caldwell 3). Alexie, then, speaks with a bitter sarcasm in "Open Books," when he writes, "Thank God he wrote love poems to his son / even as he beat the boy bloody into corners. / Let us now celebrate the poet who wrote odes / to her husband on the skin of her lover's back" (<u>One Stick Song</u> 31). Sincerity and honesty are important to Sherman Alexie, and Alexie reviles the artist who condemns with his mouth while partaking of the sin in private.

Alexie also discusses the dangers of art: "Part of the danger of being an artist of whatever color is that you fall in love with your wrinkles . . . then you don't want to get rid of them. . . . We can write about pain and anger without having it consume us" (Caldwell 4). Alexie certainly delves deeply into his own pain to find material for his writing. In "One Stick Song," Alexie enumerates the tragedies that have shaken his personal life: "and I will sing of my sister / asleep when her trailer burned / o, bright explosion, crimson and magenta / o, burned sister, scarlet skin and white ash" (<u>One Stick Song</u> 38). Alexie dwells, not only on his sister, but on a tremendous number of relatives: father, mother, grandfather, grandmother, aunts, uncles and cousins, all of whom gave pain when they passed from Alexie's life. In another poem, "Sugar Town," Alexie focuses page after page on his father and the struggle with diabetes. Alexie digs deeply into his own private pain and anger for his poetry. Whether or not Alexie has managed to walk the fine line of drawing on and using his pain without falling prey to the dangers of treading too closely to that pain and anger, only Alexie himself could say; and, on that point, he is very closemouthed.

Alexie believes the art of storytelling is tied very deeply to the art of lying, saying, "The nature, in my opinion, of storytelling in general . . . is that fiction blurs and nobody knows that the truth is" (West 6). Alexie explores this aspect of fiction and poetry writing and art in a poem already referenced once--"Open Books." Alexie tells in the opening section of reading a poem about a canyon and being impressed with the artist's descriptions. Upon talking with the artist's son, Alexie discovers the truth: "Hell, we never / even got close to the actual / canyon. . . . Later on, my mother and I went out / for hamburgers while my father sat in the room / and wrote that goddamn poem" (<u>One Stick Song</u> 29-30). It might be stretching the point to call a storyteller a glorified liar, but the point Alexie makes is well taken. In "Soon to be a National Geographic Special," Alexie pushes the boundaries of truth even farther in the opening lines, when he tells us, "All the Indian boys in the world / gathered into one red Toyota Celica / or perhaps it was just Steve, Tom and me / though, truthfully speaking, it wasn't Tom / at all" (<u>One</u>

<u>Stick Song</u> 62.) Sherman Alexie then recounts a true event from his youth, but only after he has lied twice in the first stanza. From claiming that all the Indian boys in the world occupy the car, he shifts quickly to give the reader three distinct names and then almost immediately retracts one of those names, only to finally reach the truth, or at least, what he finally says is the truth. This holds true in <u>Indian Killer</u> as well, in which Alexie, if he does not actively lie, at least withholds truth of any kind, leaving it up to the reader to draw his or her own conclusions about the identity of the killer. If "lying" is part of art, then Sherman Alexie is truly an artist for he has taken the method of "lying" to new stylistic heights.

Alexie certainly, however, sees art as a medium for uncovering the dark sides of society. Alexie discusses the recurring theme of the absent father within his writings and then springboards to a discussion of the problems that cross racial barriers: "Brown artists . . . write about fathers who physically leave and don't come back. White artists deal with fathers who leave emotionally, who sit in the chair in the living room but are gone" (West 7). Art, then, should illuminate the darker aspects of society that cross racial boundaries, not just those that are particular to a certain ethnic group. Alexie certainly does this with his theme of the absent father, as he states above, but he does not confine his cross-cultural writings to that theme. In <u>Indian Killer</u>, Alexie addresses the issue of adoption, not only with his Native American character, John Smith, but also with the white character, Jack Wilson. Alexie discusses the effects of not truly knowing origin in some detail. This is an issue that not only Native Americans face, but all people. Alexie might write from the perspective of the Native American, but he addresses issues that are larger than any single ethnic group, issues faced by all.

As an artist, Alexie also takes a stance somewhat reminiscent of Wagner's. When asked about his work on film, Alexie responds that he gave input on "everything—casting, costumes, sets, editing" (West 9). Much as Wagner did with his operas, Alexie attempts to keep his finger in every aspect of his storytelling. A true artist does not leave any aspect of his work up to outside influences, Alexie would say, but maintains creative control throughout the process. Alexie, having forged his theory while working alone on his poetry and fiction, does not let it go, even in the intricate and involved world of filmmaking.

A great deal of art theory can be derived by looking at those that Alexie credits as his major influences. Alexie names, as his five primary influences, "my father, for his nontraditional Indian stories, my grandmother for her traditional Indian stores, Stephen King, John Steinbeck and <u>The Brady Bunch</u>" (West 10). The first two influences, Alexie illuminates himself. His grandmother and father, respectively, taught Alexie that Native Americans are tied to a tradition of the past, but also that they can work with and tweak that tradition. Alexie lives up to their influences. In "A Drug Called Tradition," Alexie discusses the ways in which tradition influences the lives of Native Americans today, even as Native Americans adapt that tradition and change it to suit their own needs (<u>Lone Ranger</u> 12). This is also a theme in <u>Indian Killer</u>, which deals with some Native characters, such as Reggie Polatkin, who are non-traditional in some ways and yet traditional in others.

By referencing Stephen King and John Steinbeck, Alexie intimates that his theory is somehow tied to their writings. In the writings of Stephen King, one finds ordinary people thrust into extraordinary circumstances. In the writings of Steinbeck, everyday people struggle for life in the hard passages of the world. Both of these themes can be traced in Alexie's writings. In the previously mentioned "The Trial of Thomas Builds-the-Fire," Alexie paints a picture of a modern setting in a courtroom that quickly trades in the mundane for the bizarre, as the title character finds himself convicted for murders convicted over a century previous (Lone Ranger 93). Also, one could again turn to Indian Killer, in which Alexie approaches racial issues through the avenue of a serial killer who may or may not have supernatural powers, including wings and the ability to make himself or herself invisible.

Alexie, however, is not averse to showing simple and everyday struggles and portraying them as struggles so large and important as to be almost mythic. In "Tiny Treaties," Alexie presents a situation so simple as to be almost boring: a walk down a highway in the midst of snowstorm (First Indian 56). Yet, for Alexie, this simple walk becomes a symbol for racial understanding and tolerance and, in the final analysis, becomes a powerful statement about the state of society. Ordinary people in ordinary situations can become very important under the hand of the master, and Alexie is certainly the master at this aspect of writing.

Alexie also cites, as the fifth of his five great reference points, a television show. Specifically, Alexie gives credit to The Brady Bunch. As Alexie says later in the same interview, "I think a lot of Indian artists like to pretend that they're not influenced by pop culture or Western culture, but I am, and I'm happy to admit it" (West 10). Alexie acknowledges popular culture as his heritage, using it in many different ways to inform his art. Alexie's most intriguing foray into popular culture comes with "Reservation Drive-In," which features a paragraph of writings on five different films, ranging from Rocky ("Do you remember those Yakima Indian boys played the theme song from Rocky ninety times straight one summer day") to Enter the Dragon ("Suddenly the Indian boy is Bruce Lee. Maybe he's only the Bruce Lee of the reservation playground, kicking every other child aside on his climb to the top of the slide") (First Indian 16). Another tie to The Brady Bunch lies in Alexie's love for an almost obscenely large cast, such as occurs in Indian Killer.

Alexie states that his work should "bridge the cultural distance between the characters . . . and the non-Indian audience" (West 10). Despite the anger and pain inherent in much of Alexie's work, his final goal is to see the great gap between races and cultural groups bridged in some small way. In many ways, Alexie's work does do this, by using dominant popular culture as a touchstone and by addressing larger questions that cross boundaries of race, as mentioned before.

Alexie also wants to find a way to "speak to the audience through my characters in a way that will give them something to hold onto as they're hearing and seeing something brand new" (West 10). Great art, then, should communicate something new and different to the audiences and take it to places they have never been before and show them ways to think that they have never thought of before. In his poems, Alexie takes certain events and gives them a new spin, such as in "Split Decisions," in which Alexie dissects the Muhammad Ali-Joe Frazier fight and injects sociological statements and lines of thought into the event (First Indian 88). In "A Reservation Table of the Elements," Alexie shows that even tragic events are not immune to his new perspective: "Crazy Horse / never died. / Don't you know / he was the one / who climbed on top / of the Hindenburg / and lit / a match?" (First Indian 39). It is in these new perspectives that Alexie often offends the unprepared reader who finds in these statements simply inflammatory insults, rather than thought-provoking allegorical ramifications. As Alexie himself states, "I always want to be on the edge of offending somebody" (West 11). In this area, certainly, Alexie has succeeded with flying colors.

When discussing the uses of humor, Alexie states that humor is "really just about questioning the status quo" (West 11). Even a glance at the titles of some of Alexie's work can make this plain, as with his "An Unauthorized Autobiography of Me," which takes two opposing terms and puts them next to each other with no shame (Alexie, One Stick Song 13). That particular piece shows even more questioning:

> "Sherman," says the critic, "How does the oral tradition apply to your work?"
>
> "Well," I say, as I hold my latest book close to me, "It doesn't apply at all because I typed this. And when I'm typing, I'm very, very quiet." (Alexie, One Stick Song 16)

Alexie employs humor, in this way, to tweak the notion that all Native American literature ties directly to the oral tradition of ancient history. Humor, in Alexie's hands, is effective in the usual ways: it makes the reader laugh. Beyond that immediate response, however, lies a deeper purpose. The humor is often thought-provoking and significant, making statements about society and preconceived notions. Comedy often does not receive the recognition it deserves. In the hands of a talented individual, humor can be a powerful tool, just as it is in the hands of Alexie.

In a day when many artists are close-mouthed about the things they do and the reasons they have for doing them, Sherman Alexie stands as a great example of an artist who is not afraid to say what he believes in. His art theory is prominent in his interviews and can most often be seen directly in the art he produces. Alexie purports to be an artist to whom sincerity is very important. It is fitting then, that his art theory should coincide with his art as well as it does. The art of Sherman Alexie is easy to appreciate. Upon studying his art theory, however, it becomes even easier to understand the vision that drives Alexie and the means that he is willing to employ to see his vision come to life.

NOTE: The Works Cited page is generally a separate page from the rest of the paper, and is paginated as the next page in the series.

Works Cited

Alexie, Sherman. First Indian on the Moon. New York: Hanging Loose Press, 1993.

---. Indian Killer. New York: Warner Books, 1996.

---. The Lone Ranger and Tonto Fistfight in Heaven. New York: The Atlantic Monthly Press, 1993.

---. One Stick Song. New York: Hanging Loose Press, 2000.

"General Commentary by Sherman Alexie." Modern American Poetry: An Online Journal and Multimedia Companion to Anthology of Modern American Poetry. Oxford University Press, 2000. Ed. Cary Nelson. 28 June 1998. 15 Jan 2003 <http://www.english.uiuc.edu/ maps/poets/a_f/ alexie/general.htm>.

West, Dennis. Sending Cinematic Smoke Signals: An Interview with Sherman Alexie. 30 Sep 1999. Cineaste Publishers. 11 March 2003 <http://www.lib.berkeley.edu/MRC/alexie.html>.

- **NOTE: This paper is written in MLA format.**

Walker 1

Sherry Walker

Dr. Dee

Composition I

20 Nov. 1999

So . . . No Time to Read?

What would happen if everyone in our country only read material absolutely necessary to function in his or her job or to function in everyday life? We would flick on the TV each morning to get our half hour of condensed news, believing we've gotten the whole story when we have only seen bits and pieces rearranged to support the convenient viewpoint of the day. We would spend all our extra time sitting by the television, watching programs designed to tell us how to think and feel. We would then go to bed, only to start all over again the next morning. Starting to sound familiar? Actually, I believe many of us have almost reached that point now; and, if we are to change this frightening trend of television watching in place of reading, it must be soon.

What is so alarming about the idea of no one reading? Non-readers live in an amputated present tense, epitomized by the twenty-second news clip or the sixty-second paid political advertisement (Kozol 7). It is much easier for high-priced shills practicing manipulative arts to influence how we vote, what we buy, and how we think if we allow them to oversimplify issues and problems (thereby distorting them), to cynically use polls and media, and to make the assumption that nobody reads anymore (Crensen 3). When we rely on a variety of sources to confirm or deny the claims we hear made, then we increase our chances of getting at the truth and decrease the manipulators' chances of fooling us.

The rapidly growing number of non-readers is creating an ever-increasing group of apathetic people, and this apathy is seen by some as an invitation to take control of our lives: "The passive status of a third of all American adults is now addressed in full commission sessions by executives of advertising corporations, U.S. Army Specialists, and hard-nosed economic planners" (Kozol 7). These powerful people realize how easy it is to influence a passive public. By using television as our primary source of information and entertainment, we are making their jobs even easier. We are training ourselves and our children to be observers instead of doers. Not only that, we are providing these opportunists with the perfect media in which to use their influence to control events.

In order to increase citizen awareness, the eradication of illiteracy in our country has become a national goal. At first glance this appears to be an excellent way to solve our problem, but it actually screens it. First, we cannot agree on who is to be considered illiterate. Most agree a person is illiterate if unable to function in today's society, which seems fair, but we cannot agree on the level of reading ability required to be able to function: third grade, eighth grade, or twelfth grade (Crensen 3). And if everyone were to agree on this point, then what? Even if we manage to teach everyone we target as illiterate to read, should we believe they will spend any more time reading than the majority of people who currently know how? No, and this is where we risk hiding the larger problem. We must put the same effort we are putting into solving the illiteracy problem into inspiring citizens who can already read to do so more often. Far too many people are allowing world events to slip by without even blinking an eye, much less raising a question. After all, according to Gus Crensen, writer for the Baltimore Evening Sun,

> a reading public would not have tolerated the last presidential campaign. It would not have been possible to turn up jurors for the Oliver North trial who had no previous knowledge of the affair. It would not yield up the appalling ignorance we see from time to time in news stories--people who think Ronald Reagan is still president, the forty-two percent of college seniors who can not place the Civil War in the correct half-century, the many who have no idea where Nicaragua is. (Crensen 3)

What are we to do to solve this baffling problem? We must begin with our children, giving them a desire to spend more time reading. Of course, the best place to start is by setting a good example at home, but we can also do much by instituting more interesting reading programs throughout our schools. Children could be encouraged to read for pleasure by allowing extra credit for books read on their own time. Maybe more book reports at the grade school levels and requiring students to read books about the programs they are watching on television would help. By tying reading assignments to television programs and movies, teachers can show their students how much they are missing and how much more interesting their viewing experiences can be when reading is involved in the process. As Pauline Gough states, "Learning is produced by mutual participation in interesting activities" (346). If we want our children to want to read, we cannot continue to treat reading as a dull routine that must be struggled through only to find the answer to a question.

Wise teachers of reading will bear in mind the words of David Harman, a professor at Teachers College, Columbia University, who has studied illiteracy for almost two decades. According to Harman, "the largest literacy problem in the U.S. today is . . . the diminution of the value of reading as an activity" (Gough 346).

If we begin to view reading as an enjoyable responsibility instead of a nuisance to be avoided whenever possible, we may avoid the apathy that is tightening its grip on our society today. If not, we may become like Peter Sellers' character Chance in the movie Being There who watches television continuously and who often tells people, "I like to watch" (Being There). If we do not make changes soon, we may become a nation of watchers instead of doers.

NOTE: The Works Cited page is generally a separate page from the rest of the paper, and is paginated as the next page in the series.

Works Cited

Being There. Dir. Hal Ashby. Perf. Peter Sellers and Shirley MacLaine. United Artists, 1979.

Crensen, Gus. "Literates Who Don't Read Are Problem." Tulsa World 22 Oct. 1989: D3.

Gough, Pauline. "Literacy: Use It or Lose It." Phi Delta Kappa 70.5 (Jan. 1989): 346.

Kozol, Jonathan. "Dehumanizing the Humanities: Scholars and Adult Illiteracy." Education Digest 1.4 (Dec. 1985): 7.

- **NOTE: This paper is written in end-noted MLA format.**

Walker 1

Sherry Walker

Dr. Dee

Composition I

20 Nov. 1999

So . . . No Time to Read?

What would happen if everyone in our country only read material absolutely necessary to function in his or her job or to function in everyday life? We would flick on the TV each morning to get our half hour of condensed news, believing we've gotten the whole story when we have only seen bits and pieces rearranged to support the convenient viewpoint of the day. We would spend all our extra time sitting by the television watching programs designed to tell us how to think and feel. We would then go to bed, only to start all over again the next morning. Starting to sound familiar? Actually, I believe many of us have almost reached that point now; and, if we are to change this frightening trend of television watching in place of reading, it must be soon.

What is so alarming about the idea of no one reading? Non-readers live in an amputated present tense, epitomized by the twenty-second news clip or the sixty-second paid political advertisement.[1] It is much easier for high-priced shills practicing manipulative arts to influence how we vote, what we buy, and how we think if we allow them to oversimplify issues and problems (thereby distorting them), to cynically use polls and media, and to make the assumption that nobody reads anymore.[2] When we rely on a variety of sources to confirm or deny the claims we hear made, then we increase our chances of getting at the truth and decrease the manipulators' chances of fooling us.

The rapidly growing number of non-readers is creating an ever-increasing group of apathetic people, and this apathy is seen by some as an invitation to take control of our lives: "The passive status of a third of all American adults is now addressed in full commission sessions by executives of advertising corporations, U.S. Army Specialists, and hard-nosed economic planners."[3] These powerful people realize how easy it is to influence a passive public. By using television as our primary source of information and entertainment, we are making their jobs even easier. We are training ourselves and our children to be observers instead of doers. Not only that, we are providing these opportunists with the perfect media in which to use their influence to control events.

In order to increase citizen awareness, the eradication of illiteracy in our country has become a national goal. At first glance this appears to be an excellent way to solve our problem, but it actually screens it. First, we cannot agree on who is to be considered illiterate. Most agree a person is illiterate if unable to function in today's society, which seems fair, but we cannot agree on the level of reading ability required to be able to function: third grade, eighth grade, or twelfth grade.[4] And if everyone were to agree on this point, then what? Even if we manage to teach everyone we target as illiterate to read, should we believe they will spend any more time reading than the majority of people who currently know how? No, and this is where we risk hiding the larger problem. We must put the same effort we are putting into solving the illiteracy problem into inspiring citizens who can already read to do so more often. Far too many people are allowing world events to slip by without even blinking an eye, much less raising a question. After all, according to Gus Crensen, writer for the Baltimore Evening Sun,

> a reading public would not have tolerated the last presidential campaign. It would not have been possible to turn up jurors for the Oliver North trial who had no previous knowledge of the affair. It would not yield up the appalling ignorance we see from time to time in news stories--people who think Ronald Reagan is still president, the forty-two percent of college seniors who can not place the Civil War in the correct half-century, the many who have no idea where Nicaragua is.[5]

What are we to do to solve this baffling problem? We must begin with our children, giving them a desire to spend more time reading. Of course, the best place to start is by setting a good example at home, but we can also do much by instituting more interesting reading programs throughout our schools. Children could be encouraged to read for pleasure by allowing extra credit for books read on their own time. Maybe more book reports at the grade school levels and requiring students to read books about the programs they are watching on television would help. By tying reading assignments to television programs and movies, teachers can show their students how much they are missing and how much more interesting their viewing experiences can be when reading is involved in the process. As Pauline Gough states, "Learning is produced by mutual participation in interesting activities."[6] If we want our children to want to read, we cannot continue to treat reading as a dull routine that must be struggled through only to find the answer to a question.

Wise teachers of reading will bear in mind the words of David Harman, a professor at Teachers College, Columbia University, who has studied illiteracy for almost two decades. According to Harman, "the largest literacy problem in the U.S. today is . . . the diminution of the value of reading as an activity."[7]

If we begin to view reading as an enjoyable responsibility instead of a nuisance to be avoided whenever possible, we may avoid the apathy that is tightening its grip on our society today. If not, we may become like Peter Sellers' character Chance in the movie Being There who watches television continuously and who often tells people, "I like to watch."[8] If we do not make changes soon, we may become a nation of watchers instead of doers.

NOTE: The Notes page is generally a separate page from the rest of the paper, and is paginated as the next page in the series.

Notes

[1]Jonathan Kozol, "Dehumanizing the Humanities: Scholars and Adult Illiteracy," Education Digest 1.4 (Dec. 1985): 7.

[2]Gus Crensen, "Literates Who Don't Read Are Problem," Tulsa World 22 Oct. 1989: D3.

[3]Kozol 7.

[4]Crensen 3.

[5]Crensen 3.

[6]Pauline Gough, "Literacy: Use It or Lose It," Phi Delta Kappa 70.5 (Jan. 1989): 346.

[7]Gough 346.

[8]Being There, dir. Hal Ashby, perf. Peter Sellers, Shirley MacLaine, United Artists, 1979.

NOTE: The Works Cited page is generally a separate page from the rest of the paper, and is paginated as the next page in the series.

Works Cited

Being There. United Artists, 1979.

Crensen, Gus. "Literates Who Don't Read Are Problem." Tulsa World 22 Oct. 1989: D3.

Gough, Pauline. "Literacy: Use It or Lose It." Phi Delta Kappa 70.5 (Jan. 1989): 346.

Kozol, Jonathan. "Dehumanizing the Humanities: Scholars and Adult Illiteracy." Education Digest 1.4 (Dec. 1985): 7.

- **NOTE: This paper is formatted according to APA guidelines.** It is similar to MLA format, but does have some major differences.
  - Papers in APA format submitted for a class use a one-inch margin.
  - Pages are numbered consecutively, beginning with the title page.
  - Every page contains a running head, a shortened form of the title instead of the writer's last name.
  - An abstract (a short summary) of the paper may be required as the document's second page.
  - Quotations of less than forty words appear as part of the running text; quotations of more than forty words are inset five spaces and double-spaced, using no quotation marks.
  - Section headings may be appropriate. If so, they are centered; sub-section headings are justified left and underlined.
  - The Reference list (the APA equivalent of the Works Cited page) is a separate page of manuscript, numbered consecutively.

So . . . No Time 1

Running head: SO . . . NO TIME

So . . . No Time to Read?

Sherry Walker

Composition I

Research Essay

MW 1:00

November 20, 1999

NOTE: An abstract (short summary) may be required as the second page of the paper.

• **NOTE**: New page would begin here.

So . . . No Time 2

So . . . No Time to Read?

What would happen if everyone in our country only read material absolutely necessary to function in his or her job or to function in everyday life? We would flick on the TV each morning to get our half hour of condensed news, believing we've gotten the whole story when we have only seen bits and pieces rearranged to support the convenient viewpoint of the day. We would spend all our extra time sitting by the television watching programs designed to tell us how to think and feel. We would then go to bed, only to start all over again the next morning. Starting to sound familiar? Actually, I believe many of us have almost reached that point now; and, if we are to change this frightening trend of television watching in place of reading, it must be soon.

Problem

What is so alarming about the idea of no one reading? Non-readers live in an amputated present tense, epitomized by the twenty-second news clip or the sixty-second paid political advertisement (Kozol, 1985, p. 7). It is much easier for high-priced shills practicing manipulative arts to influence how we vote, what we buy, and how we think if we allow them to oversimplify issues and problems (thereby distorting them), to cynically use polls and media, and to make the assumption that nobody reads anymore (Crensen, 1989, p. 3). When we rely on a variety of sources to confirm or deny the claims we hear made, then we increase our chances of getting at the truth and decrease the manipulators' chances of fooling us.

The rapidly growing number of non-readers is creating an ever-increasing group of apathetic people, and this apathy is seen by some as an invitation to take control of our lives: "The passive status of a third of all American adults is now addressed in full commission sessions by executives of advertising corporations, U.S. Army Specialists, and hard-nosed economic planners" (Kozol, 1985, p. 7). These powerful people realize how easy it is to influence a passive public. By using television as our primary source of information and entertainment, we are making their jobs even easier. We are training ourselves and our children to be observers instead of doers. Not only that, we are providing these opportunists with the perfect media in which to use their influence to control events.

Solutions

In order to increase citizen awareness, the eradication of illiteracy in our country has become a national goal. At first glance this appears to be an excellent way to solve our problem, but it actually screens it. First, we cannot agree on who is to be considered illiterate. Most agree a person is illiterate if unable to function in today's society, which seems fair, but we cannot agree on the level of reading ability required to be able to function: third grade, eighth grade, or twelfth grade (Crensen, 1989, p. 3). And if everyone were to agree on this point, then what? Even if we manage to teach everyone we target as illiterate to read, should we believe they will spend any more time reading than the majority of people who currently know how? No, and this is where we risk hiding the larger problem. We must put the same effort we are putting into solving the illiteracy problem into inspiring citizens who can already read to do so more often. Far too many people are allowing world events to slip by without even blinking an eye, much less raising a question. After all, according to Gus Crensen (1989), writer for the *Baltimore Evening Sun*,

> a reading public would not have tolerated the last presidential campaign. It would not have been possible to turn up jurors for the Oliver North trial who had no previous knowledge of the affair. It would not yield up the appalling ignorance we see from time to time in news stories--people who think Ronald Reagan is still president, the forty-two percent of college seniors who can not place the Civil War in the correct half-century, the many who have no idea where Nicaragua is. (p. 3)

What are we to do to solve this baffling problem? We must begin with our children, giving them a desire to spend more time reading. Of course, the best place to start is by setting a good example at home, but we can also do much by instituting more interesting reading programs throughout our schools. Children could be encouraged to read for pleasure by allowing extra credit for books read on their own time. Maybe more book reports at the grade school levels and requiring students to read books about the programs they are watching on television would help. By tying reading assignments to television programs and movies, teachers can show their students how much they are missing and how much more interesting their viewing experiences can be when reading is involved in the process. As Pauline Gough (1989) states, "Learning is produced by mutual participation in interesting activities" (p. 346). If we want our children to want to read, we cannot continue to treat reading as a dull routine that must be struggled through only to find the answer to a question.

Wise teachers of reading will bear in mind the words of David Harman, a professor at Teachers College, Columbia University, who has studied illiteracy for almost two decades. According to Harman, "the largest literacy problem in the U.S. today is . . . the diminution of the value of reading as an activity" (Gough, 1989, p. 346).

Conclusion

If we begin to view reading as an enjoyable responsibility instead of a nuisance to be avoided whenever possible, we may avoid the apathy that is tightening its grip on our society today. If not, we may become like Peter Sellers' character Chance in the movie *Being There* who watches television continuously and who often tells people, "I like to watch" (*Being There*, 1979). If we do not make changes soon, we may become a nation of watchers instead of doers.

- ***NOTE***: *The References page is generally a separate page from the rest of the paper, although it is paginated as the next page in the series.*

References

Braunsberg, A. (Producer), & Ashby, H. (Director). (1979). *Being there* [Motion Picture]. United States: United Artists.

Crensen, G. (1989, October 22). Literates who don't read are problem. *Tulsa world*, p. D3.

Gough, P. (1989, January). Literacy: Use it or lose it. *Phi delta kappa, 70*(5), 346.

Kozol, J. (1985, December). Dehumanizing the humanities: Scholars and adult illiteracy. *Education digest*, *1*(4), 7.

- ***NOTE***: *This paper is written in APA format.*

Ironing Out 1

Running head: IRONING OUT

NOTE: *The author/title section is centered in the page.*

Ironing Out the Wrinkles:

Anti-Aging

Sallie Student

Sociology 1113

MTWR 7:30

November 29, 1996

- ***NOTE***: *New page would start here.*

Ironing Out 2

Abstract

The eternal quest for youth has led people to investigate externally applied skin creams, including Retin-A and aloe compounds, to be applied before or after exposure to sun. Researchers conclude that the best method of avoiding aging skin is avoiding exposure to the sun.

- ***NOTE:*** *New page would start here.*

Ironing Out 3

Ironing Out the Wrinkles:

Anti-Aging

> An old dermatologist once told me there are two groups who never get wrinkles: Buddhist monks and schizophrenics. That's because people who have been secluded in temples or institutions seldom see the sun. Therefore, their skin ages very little. But for us 76 million baby boomers, who have bagged a lot of rays en route to middle age, the horrible truth now greets us each morning in the mirror--wrinkles. (Moser, 1986, p. 72)

Today's baby boomers are aware of the ability to achieve goals unknown to the previous generation and yet they have found that success and money have not helped to obtain one thing which will separate them from all the generations past, the ageless complexion.

Background

Skin reveals age. The skin is the biggest organ of the body, about ten pounds of it. It is the body's first line of defense against disease, and it contains a vast network of senses which alert people to heat, cold, pain, and pressure. Yet despite its necessary versatility, people are constantly abusing skin in an effort to obtain a look of timeless beauty. Hardly anyone wants to admit that "loose skin, hanging jowls, and sagging eyebrows and eyelids can be blamed on gravity" (Fox, 1987, p. 42). Aging naturally causes a decline in the quality of collagen and elastin in skin tissue. Most pretend not to notice their skin beginning to give testimony to the passing of time, until one day they look in the mirror and see their mother's or father's face looking back.

Research Results

<u>Sun Damage</u>

In the past few years, research has led dermatologists to estimate that as much as 70 percent of skin damage comes from the sun: "Fine, creeping lines and irregular skin tone are due to sun exposure" (Fox, 1987, p. 42). This damage is caused by years of sun worship or working conditions requiring exposure to long periods of ultraviolet rays. Thus, much of what is considered an inevitable part of aging is preventable or can be reduced. Avoiding long periods in the sun, wearing a protective sunscreen of SPF (Sun Protection Factor) 15 or higher, and moisturizing the skin after exposure can help maintain the skin tissue.

<u>After-Sun Products</u>

Hundreds of "after-sun" products exist to choose from. They claim to reduce sunburn, prevent peeling, keep a tan from fading, and remove sun-induced wrinkles. These claims are not proved. One "after-sun" product ingredient is collagen, a protein in skin that keeps it elastic, which when smeared on the skin in a lotion or cream, does not do more than a moisturizer without collagen. The outer layer of skin is composed of dead cells, penetrable only by the smallest of molecules (such as water): "Collagen molecules are simply too big to get through," says Jennifer A. K. Patterson, M. D., Assistant Professor of Dermatology at New York University Medical Center ("The latest," 1988, April, p. 8). Collagen injections are a more widely-used and successful cosmetic treatment for patients who are prematurely wrinkled from chronic sun exposure. These injections hide blemishes for six months to a year (Freifeld, 1987, p. 6).

Another after-sun product ingredient is Vitamin E; but, like collagen, its molecules are too big to penetrate the skin. In some cases, too, it can cause allergic reactions.

Aloe vera, another ingredient in moisturizers, is supposed to heal wounded skin rapidly and rejuvenate it. Freifeld (1987) reports there is no solid evidence that this extract from the cactus plant has any special powers.

This year, Americans will buy about half-a-billion dollars' worth of products claiming anti-aging properties. Some members of the public think they will work; some members think they will not. The truth is hard to find because there is no authority validating anti-aging claims.

Product Safety

While people wonder if skin products are effective, few think about whether they are safe (Moser, 1986, p. 73). No one division of government has the responsibility for cosmetics. Even the Food and Drug Administration (FDA) is not responsible for most cosmetics. However, the anti-aging industry is fast changing the fact that the FDA has seldom taken action on cosmetic firms by banning ingredients. The FDA recently sent letters to twenty cosmetics manufacturers stating that because of claims the manufacturers have made in their advertising, their cosmetics are also drugs. When making anti-aging and related claims, many manufacturers have been implying that whatever miracle ointment they have developed can penetrate the epidermis and affect the function and structure of the body. Any such claim makes the product a drug under federal regulations: "In the U. S. all drugs must undergo extensive texts proving they're safe and effective. What the FDA is not saying, at least to the manufacturers, is that their tonics are bogus; rather the message is: prove that they work as claimed" (Moser, 1986, p. 73).

New Products: Retin-A

During the past two years, Ortho Pharmaceutical Corporation, a New Jersey-based subsidiary of Johnson and Johnson, has been trying to do just that by performing FDA trials on a drug called Retonic Acid (Retin-A), a derivative of Vitamin A. It is thought to counteract long-term damage to sun-ravaged skin. First introduced in 1971 as an acne medication, Retin-A reduced fine age lines, freckles, and blotches on older people. They reported not only that they had fewer problems with acne, but that their skin took on a rosy, youthful, healthy glow. Retin-A accelerated skin-cell turnover, stimulated blood-vessel growth, and boosted production of collagen and elastin fibers (Latest, 1988, p. 2). Tests were conducted by Ortho to prove these claims, and the researchers state that the results so far have been positive and that the company plans to submit their findings to the FDA.

Retin-A has already been FDA-approved for treating acne, but it cannot be promoted as an anti-aging cream without FDA clearance. Alerted by word of mouth, however, consumers and doctors have not been waiting. Prescribing Retin-A is perfectly legal. If a doctor wants to prescribe an approved drug for unproved purposes, that is what is called "accepted medical practice" (Toufexis, 1987, p. 91). This is reminiscent of doctors prescribing aspirin for thinning blood in heart patients, without testing having been completed and the FDA having given full approval. The medicated cream is used as often as every day for about six months, then less frequently after that. Some patients suffer from side effects, which usually last two to six weeks, including skin irritation, scaling, and peeling. Retin-A should never be used more often than prescribed because the results may be damaged tissue which will take weeks to heal. Retin-A leaves the skin more sensitive to sunlight than ever and is not an antidote to sun-worshipping (Toufexis, 1987). It is not the "fountain of youth" either. It will not make old people young, and it will not help very deep wrinkles. It will not help bags or sags in the skin. In persons over fifty years of age, the effect will be barely noticeable.

Conclusion

Many people are desperate to regain youthful appearance. Money and sometimes risks are not deterrents to the decision to try to look young. The baby-boomer generation is paying for its years of sun-worship with prematurely aging skin. That generation must teach the next to protect skin from the moment of birth, the only way to avoid premature wrinkling. However, it is never too late to begin new measures to protect skin and help it look its best. The best thing to do is to stay out of the sun or to use a sunscreen.

- ***NOTE:*** *The References page is generally a separate page from the rest of the paper; it is paginated as the next page in the series.*

References

Fox, M. (1987, September). Your skin's prime time. *Health*, 42.

Freifeld, K. (1987, July). Burned again. *Health*, 19-26.

Moser, P. W. (1986). An anti-aging cream with a new wrinkle. *Discover*, 72-76, 79.

The latest wrinkle. (1988, April). *University of California, Berkeley, wellness letter*, 7-12.

Toufexis, A. (1987, December 14). Antidote to all those wrinkles? *Time*, 90.

• *NOTE: This paper is written in a* **variation of APA format**.

ROGERS STATE COLLEGE

ASSOCIATE DEGREE NURSING PROGRAM

Delegation:

Effect On Nursing Care

In Partial Fulfillment

of the Requirements for

Nursing 2329

by

Sallie Student

Fall 1996

• ***NOTE:*** *New page would start here.*

Student--1

Delegation: Effect on Nursing Care

Introduction

Distributing work and getting things done through others should be as common as taking routine vital signs. However, some nurses are hesitant to let go of traditional tasks and accept help from others. These nurses need to be aware of delegation techniques and their effectiveness.

Problem

Bang! The shift begins and all the nurses are off running toward the finish line. The team for the eight (8) hour shift consists of two (2) registered nurses, two (2) licensed practical nurses, and two (2) nurses' assistants for thirty (30) patients. The nurses are faced with too many things to do and not enough staff to do them. One way for nurses to accomplish their tasks is through the skills of delegation.

Review of Literature

The act of delegation is an essential requirement for effective nursing management: "By definition delegation is the entrusting of power and authority to a person to act as one's agent or representative" (McAlvanah, 1989, p. 379). Delegation is used to get work done efficiently with optimal use of human resources. While nursing shortages continue, delegation is a tool to be used by nurses at all levels. Most sources agree that used wisely, delegation can prompt growth of others, decrease tension, and promote a smooth working environment.

Delegating tasks to others does not mean a nurse is good or bad: "Delegation lightens the nurses' workload, helps get the job done, and gives the staff member an opportunity for professional growth, achievement, and recognition" (Kroll, 1993, p. 23).

Pitfalls to delegation include lack of trust in others, low self-confidence, risk taking, inadequate information, and competition:

> Giving others the responsibility for the job and the authority to get it done is the only way to delegate work successfully. Nurses who feel a personal sense of power and satisfaction only when doing it themselves, experience mixed feelings over letting go of familiar work. (McMurray, 1991, p. 67)

Nurses can delegate more effectively by trusting their fellow team members, defining and identifying the work to be done, clarifying expectations of the job, and supervision. Beginning delegation may be difficult: "Successful delegation is habit-forming, [sic] the first step is usually the hardest" (Douglass, 1992, p. 128). Delegating successfully provides team members with the opportunity to demonstrate competency and the ability to expand their job capabilities: "Quality health care depends on the nurse's ability to delegate effectively" (Lane, 1990, p. 46).

Solutions

One solution to nursing shortages and, thus, overwork can be delegation. Delegation helps the nurse identify, plan, and implement the process of care.

Whether it is delegating administrative or clinical duties, nurses find it is not easy to let go. Nurses who are unsure of themselves are afraid to trust anyone else. Fear of mistakes or failures on the part of others may prompt nurses to handle everything themselves. Nurses think doing the job themselves will make sure it is done correctly. Nurses have to delegate and develop some guidelines, as they cannot possibly do everything themselves. The nurse's responsibility in delegation is matching the task to the appropriate team member. If the delegation is suitably done, risks of mistakes are minimized.

The significance of delegation is to pass along well-defined tasks and responsibilities to other team members. By passing these tasks and responsibilities to team members, nurses can free time for other important activities. Effective delegation of activities gives first priority to the patients and coordination among departments.

A key concept to effective delegation is for nurses to know themselves and to know their team members. It is important for nurses to know their own strengths and weaknesses. By identifying these strengths and weaknesses, nurses can feel more comfortable in delegating tasks.

The feelings that a nurse has about other team members may also block delegation. The nurse may think that the knowledge level, dependability, and level of experience of a team member are cause not to delegate responsibility to that person. This may be just the nurse's attitude toward the team member rather than actual limitations of appropriate delegations.

When delegating, the nurse must identify and define the work to be done. A nurse must have a clear definition of the work that is to be completed to help identify the likely candidate for the job. Doing this will facilitate the communication of the job to the proper individual: "It is important to keep in mind that an unclear definition or the incorrect choice of personnel will result in failure to accomplish the task" (McAlvanah, 1989, p. 379).

As stated before, a nurse must know his or her own strengths and weaknesses along with those of the team members. This is important for the nurse in order to delegate effectively. A few things for a nurse to look for in fellow team members are assertiveness and clear desire for advancement in their job. These persons will be the best candidates for the job or task because "The biggest mistake a nurse can make is to delegate to someone who does not really want responsibility" (Sumner, 1990, p. 104).

Once the nurse has identified the individual for the task, the nurse must describe precisely what expectations are and give directions on how to meet them. She or he might also find it helpful to identify the purpose and rationale for the task. By identifying the purpose and rationale for the task, the individual will not only understand what is to be done but why the task needs to be done: "Understanding job function fosters better work performance" (McAlvanah, 1989, p. 379).

The job or task a nurse delegates must be evaluated for accomplishment and effectiveness. The nurse should pre-arrange checkpoints on if and how the job is being done. The hospital policy and the state's nursing act will tell a nurse how closely supervision is needed when delegating. If it is the first time the individual has performed the task, the nurse must be present. After the individual has demonstrated competence in the task, supervision may not need to be direct. However, the nurse needs to be available for support and answers. The nurse is ultimately responsible for the work delegated; this is necessary to assure quality of care and completion of the delegated responsibility.

<u>Conclusion</u>

The busier nurses are, the more important it is for nurses to learn to delegate. A systematic approach and a healthy attitude will let nurses distribute work fairly and provide patients with the care they need in a timely fashion. Delegation can foster growth of workers, decrease tension, and facilitate smooth work operations. Delegation can be a cost-effective way to offset the nursing shortage. By practicing effective delegation, nurses can give first priority to the patients and provide efficiency and coordination among departments.

- ***NOTE**: The References page is generally a separate page from the rest of the paper; it is paginated as the next page in the series.*

References

Douglass, L. (1992). *The effective nurse: Leader and manager* (4th ed.). St. Louis: Mosby.

Kroll, B. (1993). A good manager has to delegate. *RN*, 23-26.

Lane, A. (1990). Refocusing on the art of delegation. *Journal of nursing management, 20*(5), 40-46.

McAlvanah, M. (1989). A guide to delegation. *Pediatric nursing, 15*(4), 379.

McMurray, C. (1991). The art of delegation. *Nursing management, 22*(2), 67-68.

Sumner, S. (1990). Delegate carefully. *Nursing*, 101.

PRINCIPLES OF READER RESPONSE AND REVIEW

Writers who are interested in a good product tend to revise extensively. In fact, it is possible to throw out an entire draft and start over. Revision is based on a number of factors. A writer might revise to include additional material. A writer might revise to make his/her audience and/or purpose more clear. A writer might revise to make the structure stronger. A writer might revise because, as he/she writes, his/her ideas change. Finally, a writer revises for correct grammar and mechanics and to make the document as elegant as possible.

As a peer reviewer, it is your job to help the writer determine what needs revision. You might want to help the writer brainstorm for more ideas or help the writer with clarification. If you disagree with the ideas expressed, help the writer with the areas of disagreement so the writer can strengthen the arguments.

A peer reviewer is a reader. It is the reviewer's job to function as a reader so the writer can determine what he/she needs to revise to make the points more clear.

ESSAY RESPONSE FORMS

During the semester, you may want to check your essays against a checklist before those essays are submitted in final copy for grading. Following are forms which you might use to aid you, or which you might ask others to use to aid you, in the review process.

ESSAY RESPONSE FORM

Subject
1. Is the subject sufficiently narrowed for an essay of the assigned length?
2. List two or three other narrowed topics that might be used for an essay on this general topic.

Introduction
1. Does the introduction sufficiently catch your attention and make you want to read the paper?
2. Does the introduction lead logically to the thesis?
3. What suggestions could you make for improving the introduction?

Thesis
1. Where is the thesis? Is it in the appropriate place?
2. Does it fit the requirements of a thesis?

Development
1. List the segments of the thesis that you are trying to develop.
2. What are the strongest segments?
3. What other segments within the range of the thesis could have been included?

Conclusion
1. What method of conclusion is used?
2. To what degree do you feel the discussion is "rounded off" by the conclusion paragraph or paragraphs?

Each Body Paragraph
1. What is the topic sentence?
2. What is the principle method of development?
3. What is the order in the paragraph, the logical connection between the sentences?
4. What other ordering of the sentences might work?
5. Evaluate the completeness of the paragraph. To what extent do you feel satisfied with the paragraph's development?
6. What one or more pieces of development might be included?
7. Are there transitional elements in the paragraph? List obvious attempts at transition. Are they successful and smooth?

Whole Essay
1. What is your level of interest in the essay as it is written?
2. Do the mechanics interfere with your reading of the essay?
3. Do you make unnecessary use of the indefinite "you"?
4. Is there careless shifting of tone?

ESSAY RESPONSE FORM

The answer to each section must be YES before you go to the next section.

1. Read the paper. Does the paper make sense? YES/NO If the answer is NO, where does the paper not make sense, and what is needed to make the paper make sense?
2. Find the thesis statement. Is it clear? YES/NO If the answer is NO, what do you need to know to make it clear?
3. Are there topic sentences in the paragraphs in the body of the paper? YES/NO If the answer is NO, what do you need to know to make a clear topic sentence for each paragraph in the body?

   Do the topic sentences support the thesis statement? YES/NO If the answer is NO, what would make the topic sentences support the thesis statement?

   Are the topic sentences supported by the information in the paragraph, such as three or more specific items of support or one long example? YES/NO If the answer is NO, what do you need to see in the paragraph to have a fully supported topic sentence?
4. Does the introduction of the paper lead up to the thesis statement? YES/NO If the answer is NO, what do you need to see in the introduction paragraph to lead up to the thesis?

   Does the conclusion of the paper summarize the main points, restate the thesis, state the significance of the information in the paper, or otherwise provide closure for the paper? YES/NO If the answer is NO, what do you need to see in the conclusion to really end the paper?
5. Are the mechanics accurate? YES/NO If the answer is NO, what corrections need to be made?

   If the paper is documented, is the documentation accurate in the paper and on the Works Cited page? YES/NO If the answer is NO, what corrections in documentation need to be made?

ESSAY RESPONSE FORM

The answer to each section must be YES before you go to the next section.

1. Read the paper. Does the paper make sense? YES/NO If the answer is NO, where does the paper not make sense, and what is needed to make the paper make sense?
2. Find the thesis statement. Is it clear? YES/NO If the answer is NO, what do you need to know to make it clear?
3. Are there topic sentences in the paragraphs in the body of the paper? YES/NO If the answer is NO, what do you need to know to make a clear topic sentence for each paragraph in the body?

   Do the topic sentences support the thesis statement? YES/NO If the answer is NO, what would make the topic sentences support the thesis statement?

   Are the topic sentences supported by the information in the paragraph, such as three or more specific items of support or one long example? YES/NO If the answer is NO, what do you need to see in the paragraph to have a fully supported topic sentence?
4. Does the introduction of the paper lead up to the thesis statement? YES/NO If the answer is NO, what do you need to see in the introduction paragraph to lead up to the thesis?

   Does the conclusion of the paper summarize the main points, restate the thesis, state the significance of the information in the paper, or otherwise provide closure for the paper? YES/NO If the answer is NO, what do you need to see in the conclusion to really end the paper?
5. Are the mechanics accurate? YES/NO If the answer is NO, what corrections need to be made?

   If the paper is documented, is the documentation accurate in the paper and on the Works Cited page? YES/NO If the answer is NO, what corrections in documentation need to be made?

ESSAY RESPONSE FORM

The answer to each section must be YES before you go to the next section.

1. Read the paper. Does the paper make sense? YES/NO If the answer is NO, where does the paper not make sense, and what is needed to make the paper make sense?
2. Find the thesis statement. Is it clear? YES/NO If the answer is NO, what do you need to know to make it clear?
3. Are there topic sentences in the paragraphs in the body of the paper? YES/NO If the answer is NO, what do you need to know to make a clear topic sentence for each paragraph in the body?

   Do the topic sentences support the thesis statement? YES/NO If the answer is NO, what would make the topic sentences support the thesis statement?

   Are the topic sentences supported by the information in the paragraph, such as three or more specific items of support or one long example? YES/NO If the answer is NO, what do you need to see in the paragraph to have a fully supported topic sentence?
4. Does the introduction of the paper lead up to the thesis statement? YES/NO If the answer is NO, what do you need to see in the introduction paragraph to lead up to the thesis?

   Does the conclusion of the paper summarize the main points, restate the thesis, state the significance of the information in the paper, or otherwise provide closure for the paper? YES/NO If the answer is NO, what do you need to see in the conclusion to really end the paper?
5. Are the mechanics accurate? YES/NO If the answer is NO, what corrections need to be made?

   If the paper is documented, is the documentation accurate in the paper and on the Works Cited page? YES/NO If the answer is NO, what corrections in documentation need to be made?

ESSAY RESPONSE FORM

The answer to each section must be YES before you go to the next section.

1. Read the paper. Does the paper make sense? YES/NO If the answer is NO, where does the paper not make sense, and what is needed to make the paper make sense?
2. Find the thesis statement. Is it clear? YES/NO If the answer is NO, what do you need to know to make it clear?
3. Are there topic sentences in the paragraphs in the body of the paper? YES/NO If the answer is NO, what do you need to know to make a clear topic sentence for each paragraph in the body?

   Do the topic sentences support the thesis statement? YES/NO If the answer is NO, what would make the topic sentences support the thesis statement?

   Are the topic sentences supported by the information in the paragraph, such as three or more specific items of support or one long example? YES/NO If the answer is NO, what do you need to see in the paragraph to have a fully supported topic sentence?
4. Does the introduction of the paper lead up to the thesis statement? YES/NO If the answer is NO, what do you need to see in the introduction paragraph to lead up to the thesis?

   Does the conclusion of the paper summarize the main points, restate the thesis, state the significance of the information in the paper, or otherwise provide closure for the paper? YES/NO If the answer is NO, what do you need to see in the conclusion to really end the paper?
5. Are the mechanics accurate? YES/NO If the answer is NO, what corrections need to be made?

   If the paper is documented, is the documentation accurate in the paper and on the Works Cited page? YES/NO If the answer is NO, what corrections in documentation need to be made?

ESSAY RESPONSE FORM

Subject
1. Is the subject sufficiently narrowed for an essay of the assigned length?
2. List two or three other narrowed topics which might be used for an essay on this general topic.

Introduction
1. Does the introduction sufficiently catch your attention and make you want to read the paper?
2. Does the introduction lead logically to the thesis?
3. What suggestions could you make for improving the introduction?

Thesis
1. Where is the thesis? Is it in the appropriate place?
2. Does it fit the requirements of a thesis?

Development
1. List the segments of the thesis that you are trying to develop.
2. What are the strongest segments?
3. What other segments within the range of the thesis could have been included?

Conclusion
1. What method of conclusion is used?
2. To what degree do you feel the discussion is "rounded off" by the conclusion paragraph or paragraphs?

Each Body Paragraph
1. What is the topic sentence?
2. What is the principle method of development?
3. What is the order in the paragraph, the logical connection between the sentences?
4. What other ordering of the sentences might work?
5. Evaluate the completeness of the paragraph. To what extent do you feel satisfied with the paragraph's development?
6. What one or more pieces of development might be included?
7. Are there transitional elements in the paragraph? List obvious attempts at transition. Are they successful and smooth?

Whole Essay
1. What is your level of interest in the essay as it is written?
2. Do the mechanics interfere with your reading of the essay?
3. Do you make unnecessary use of the indefinite "you"?
4. Is there careless shifting of tone?

RESPONSE SHEET FOR DOCUMENTED ESSAYS

Explain each "No" answer and mark the paper.

1. Does the paper support the thesis? Y N
2. Does the paper have logical sequencing? Y N
3. Does each topic sentence relate to the thesis? Y N
4. Are the topic sentences clearly defined in the paragraphs? Y N
5. Do the sentences in the paragraph all relate to the topic sentence? Y N
6. Does the paper have correct format? Y N
   a) Paragraphs Y N
   b) Documentation Y N
      Does the paper contain information from sources? Y/N
      Is this information in the form of paraphrases/summaries/quotations? Y/N
      Is each quotation connected to the text? (No quotation can stand without words from the essay writer to introduce it.) Y/N
      Has all information from sources been documented? Y/N
      Is the documentation exactly in accordance with MLA format? Y/N
      Is there a Works Cited page? Y/N
      Does the Works Cited page contain the number of sources required by the assignment/ subject/length of the paper? Y/N
      Do each of the Works Cited entries exactly correspond to MLA format requirements? Y/N
   c) Manuscript Y N
7. Are the sources appropriate to the topic of the paper? Y N
8. Do the citations in the paper correlate to the listing on the Works Cited page? Y N
   Does each Works Cited entry appear at least once cited in the text or as a parenthetical citation in the text?
9. Does the Works Cited page correlate to the citations in the paper? Y N
   Does each source which appears in the text or as parenthetical citation in the text appear as a Works Cited entry?
10. Does the tone fit the subject matter? Y N
11. Is the paper easy to read? interesting? Y N
12. How could the paper be improved?
13. Additional Comments

RESPONSE SHEET FOR DOCUMENTED ESSAYS

Explain each "No" answer and mark the paper.

1. Does the paper support the thesis? Y N
2. Does the paper have logical sequencing? Y N
3. Does each topic sentence relate to the thesis? Y N
4. Are the topic sentences clearly defined in the paragraphs? Y N
5. Do the sentences in the paragraph all relate to the topic sentence? Y N
6. Does the paper have correct format? Y N
   a) Paragraphs Y N
   b) Documentation Y N
      Does the paper contain information from sources? Y/N
      Is this information in the form of paraphrases/summaries/quotations? Y/N
      Is each quotation connected to the text? (No quotation can stand without words from the essay writer to introduce it.) Y/N
      Has all information from sources been documented? Y/N
      Is the documentation exactly in accordance with MLA format? Y/N
      Is there a Works Cited page? Y/N
      Does the Works Cited page contain the number of sources required by the assignment/ subject/length of the paper? Y/N
      Do each of the Works Cited entries exactly correspond to MLA format requirements? Y/N
   c) Manuscript Y N
7. Are the sources appropriate to the topic of the paper? Y N
8. Do the citations in the paper correlate to the listing on the Works Cited page? Y N
   Does each Works Cited entry appear at least once cited in the text or as a parenthetical citation in the text?
9. Does the Works Cited page correlate to the citations in the paper? Y N
   Does each source which appears in the text or as parenthetical citation in the text appear as a Works Cited entry?
10. Does the tone fit the subject matter? Y N
11. Is the paper easy to read? interesting? Y N
12. How could the paper be improved?
13. Additional Comments

RESPONSE SHEET FOR REPORTS

Explain each "No" answer and mark the paper.

1. Is the format correct for each section? Y N
   a. correct bibliographic data Y N
   b. title of the work in the first sentence of the summary paragraph Y N
   c. sufficient number of sentences to cover and develop the topic in each paragraph Y N
2. Does the summary convey the necessary information? Y N
3. Does the evaluation address the work and its strengths and weaknesses? Y N
4. Does the personal reaction reveal engagement with the work? Y N

RESPONSE SHEET FOR PARAGRAPHS
Each Expository Paragraph

1. The topic sentence is ______________________________
2. The principle method of development (the mode) is ______________________________
3. The development order is ______________________________
4. An alternative developmental ordering might be ______________________________
5. Evaluate the completeness of the paragraph. To what extent do you feel satisfied with the paragraph's development? ______________________________
6. What one or more pieces of development might be included?
7. Are there transitional elements in the paragraph? Yes/No Explain.
   List obvious attempts at transition.
   Are they successful and smooth? Yes/No Explain.
8. Does the paragraph interest you?
9. Is the manuscript prepared in accordance with manuscript guidelines? Yes/No Explain.

RESPONSE SHEET FOR REPORTS

Explain each "No" answer and mark the paper.

1. Is the format correct for each section? Y N
   a. correct bibliographic data Y N
   b. title of the work in the first sentence of the summary paragraph Y N
   c. sufficient number of sentences to cover and develop the topic in each paragraph Y N
2. Does the summary convey the necessary information? Y N
3. Does the evaluation address the work and its strengths and weaknesses? Y N
4. Does the personal reaction reveal engagement with the work? Y N

RESPONSE SHEET FOR PARAGRAPHS

Each Expository Paragraph

1. The topic sentence is ____________________
2. The principle method of development (the mode) is ____________________
3. The development order is ____________________
4. An alternative developmental ordering might be ____________________
5. Evaluate the completeness of the paragraph. To what extent do you feel satisfied with the paragraph's development? ____________________
6. What one or more pieces of development might be included?
7. Are there transitional elements in the paragraph? Yes/No Explain.
   List obvious attempts at transition.
   Are they successful and smooth? Yes/No Explain.
8. Does the paragraph interest you?
9. Is the manuscript prepared in accordance with manuscript guidelines? Yes/No Explain.

READER RESPONSE FORM

Writer: Prepare two or three questions for the respondent. You might ask about some aspect of the essay with which you want help or which you especially like or dislike.

Respondent

1. First read through the entire paper. Note in the margin "good" when you come across particularly strong or interesting writing. Place a question mark next to any item you find confusing, that needs more explanation, or that does not seem to fit.

2. Read through the paper again carefully and answer the following questions:
   a. Does the title catch your interest and tell you what the paper is about?
   b. Does the introduction engage your interest and lead you to the thesis?
   c. What kind of essay is the paper designed to be? Does the essay fulfill the requirements for that kind of essay? For example, does a descriptive essay appeal to all five senses? Does a classification essay divide the topic into categories and then define how those categories are limited? Does a cause and effect essay show you the clear cause/effect relationship? If the paper contains an analogy, is the analogy clear? Does an argument essay present an argument, address both sides, and appropriately prove the writer's side? Does an expository essay use examples on which to base the reader's view of the topic?
   d. What is the thesis of the paper? What does the thesis say that makes you want to read the rest of the paper? What is new or interesting about the thesis?
   e. Is the evidence sufficient to prove the writer's point? How could the evidence be improved? What additional evidence or material should the writer add? For each argument, are the lines of reasoning clear? Where could the reasoning be made clearer? Are alternate views addressed and then disproved?
   f. Does the writer seem knowledgeable? credible? trustworthy? Does the writer appeal to the audience's values, intelligence, imagination, emotion? How could that appeal be strengthened?
   g. What strategies could the writer use to improve the essay? What changes in words, sentences, sentence structure might the writer make to increase the effectiveness or to improve the accessibility of the essay?
   h. What points need clarification or expansion? Where might the writer improve the essay by explaining more or more clearly? Where might the writer add examples?

i. Is the essay organized appropriately for presentation of the topic? Might the writer move paragraphs or thoughts around to improve clarity or effectiveness?

j. Does the conclusion bring closure? Does it complete the essay? How might it be improved?

k. Sum up the strengths and weaknesses of the essay. Make at least one comment in each category.

3. Respond to the writer's questions. Carefully consider what the writer has asked and try to make helpful comments in response to that question.

4. Finally, read the paper again, carefully noting any problems in grammar, spelling, mechanics, documentation, etc. Place a check or bar in the margin for each problem you find, one check or bar per problem.

WRITER REFLECTION FORM

To improve as a writer, it is important to think critically about the process as well as the product that you have produced.

First, gather all the material that you used in creating the document: pre-writing, organizational plans, drafts, reader response or reaction forms, etc.

Then, write reflectively about the process you went through as you created the document.

1. Write one-half to one page about the process you used as you created the document.
2. Write one page about a problem you had while you worked on the essay. Tell how you solved that problem and what you learned while working on it.
    a. For example, if you were writing a descriptive essay, did you have trouble making sure you addressed all five senses? If you were writing an expository (informative) essay, did you have trouble finding examples to support your point? If you were writing a research essay, did you have trouble designing a thesis that was interesting and informative? Did you have trouble with the documentation or with the appropriate use of quotations?
    b. How did you find out you had the problem? Did you find it yourself by having difficulty originally or did a peer reviewer call it to your attention?
    c. How did you solve that problem? Did you work on wording? Did you go to a peer? a tutor? the instructor? How useful were the tactics you used to solve the problem?
    d. What did you learn from working on this problem?

WRITER REFLECTION FORM

To improve as a writer, it is important to think critically about the process as well as the product that you have produced.

First, gather all the material that you used in creating the document: pre-writing, organizational plans, drafts, reader response or reaction forms, etc.

Then, write reflectively about the process you went through as you created the document.

1. Write one-half to one page about the process you used as you created the document.

2. Ask yourself the following questions and answer them in approximately one page.

    a. What could you have improved in your paper?
    b. What worked?
    c. What did not work?
    d. What would you do differently, now that you have had the experience of writing this paper?
    e. What was the hardest part of the assignment for you?
    f. What was the easiest part of the assignment for you?
    g. What was the most satisfying part of the assignment for you?
    h. What was the least satisfying part of the assignment for you?

3. Finally, draw a conclusion from this process and the process of doing the original assignment: what did you learn from the original assignment and from the reflection?

WRITER REFLECTION FORM

As you look over a body of work, consider the following:

1. In which areas of writing do you consider you've shown most improvement? What are your strengths as a writer? What are your weaknesses?
2. Rate each essay or other work in the body according to the grading rubric that follows, using 1-5. Support the rating that you give each work.
3. Choose an item from the body of work which you believe you could revise most successfully. Plan a strategy for revision.
4. Choose one section (a paragraph, an introduction, etc.). Include the original and the revised versions and explain why you choose to make the revisions you did.
5. After completing 1-4 above, assemble the answers into a full document of approximately two pages (500 words). That means each of the four steps should be a paragraph or more.

GENERAL RUBRIC FOR PAPERS, SCALE OF 1-5 (Rubrics, scaled 1-5, furnished by Jim Ford.)

STUDENTS will demonstrate mastery of course material and stated goals under the following guidelines.

5 The paper displays mastery of communication skills. All work is rich, smooth, and significant; it is free of mechanical errors; and it shows stylistic finesse. The paper demonstrates excellence in all areas. The paper is intriguing and thought-provoking. Arguments are logical and persuasive. Ideas are well-articulated and presented in original ways.

4 The paper is significantly more than competent. The paper should be free of mechanical errors. The paper engages the reader and shows evidence of significant critical and creative thinking. The student displays excellence in critical analysis or artistic creation, if not both. Arguments show careful thought and are basically persuasive. Ideas are presented in original ways.

3 The paper is generally competent, with few errors. The paper shows evidence of significant progress, and as a whole gets the job done. The paper provides evidence of some critical and creative thought. The student may display excellence in either critical analysis or artistic creation. Arguments are present and show some thought. Ideas are present and developed, if not particularly original or well-articulated.

2 The paper is barely competent. The paper may have mechanical errors and/or lack significance. The paper may provide evidence of the student's ability to communicate but not reveal skill. Evidence of critical and creative thinking is marginal. The paper displays adequate critical and creative thinking, but not much more than that. Arguments and ideas are asserted without much critical thought. Little originality is evident. This is a rote or hasty paper.

1 The paper is inadequate. There are frequent errors. The paper is superficial and lacks organization. Evidence of critical and/or creative thinking is largely absent. The paper shows little or no method or planning. Work seems thrown together with minimal critical or creative thought.

GENERAL RUBRIC FOR PROJECTS, SCALE OF 1-5

STUDENTS will demonstrate mastery of course material and stated goals under the following guidelines.

5 The project displays mastery of communication skills. All work is rich, smooth, and significant; is free of mechanical errors; and shows stylistic finesse. The project demonstrates excellence in all areas. The project is intriguing and thought-provoking. Arguments are logical and persuasive. Ideas are well-articulated and presented in original ways.

4 The project is significantly more than competent. The project should be free of mechanical errors. The project engages the reader and shows evidence of significant critical and creative thinking. The student displays excellence in critical analysis or artistic creation, if not both. Arguments show careful thought and are basically persuasive. Ideas are presented in original ways.

3 The project is generally competent, with few errors. The project shows evidence of significant progress and, as a whole, gets the job done. The project provides evidence of some critical and creative thought. The student may display excellence in either critical analysis or artistic creation. Arguments are present and show some thought. Ideas are present and developed, if not particularly original or well-articulated.

2 The project is barely competent. The project may have mechanical errors and/or lack significance. The project may provide evidence of the student's ability to communicate but not reveal skill. Evidence of critical and creative thinking is marginal. The project displays adequate critical and creative thinking, but not much more than that. Arguments and ideas are asserted without much critical thought. Little originality is evident. This is a rote or hasty paper/project.

1 The project is inadequate. There are frequent errors. The project is superficial and lacks organization. Evidence of critical and/or creative thinking is largely absent. The project shows little or no method or planning. Work seems thrown together with minimal critical or creative thought.

RUBRIC FOR EVALUATING CAPSTONE PORTFOLIO AND PROJECT

Students will demonstrate, by portfolio and by capstone project, mastery of

Written, Oral, and Visual Communication

5 Both the project and the portfolio display mastery of some communication skills. All work is rich, smooth, and significant; free of mechanical errors; and shows stylistic finesse. The portfolio demonstrates strength in all three areas, and excellence in at least two of the three (written, oral, visual).

4 Both the project and the portfolio are significantly more than competent. The project should be free of mechanical errors. The portfolio demonstrates significant ability in all three areas, and excellence in at least one of the three (written, oral, visual).

3 Both the project and the portfolio are generally competent, with few errors. The portfolio shows evidence of significant progress, and as a whole gets the job done.

2 Both the project and the portfolio are barely competent. The project may have mechanical errors and/or lack significance. The portfolio may provide evidence of the student's ability to communicate in one of the three areas, but at least one other skill is not evident.

1 Either the project or the portfolio (or both) is inadequate. There are frequent errors. The project itself is superficial and lacks organization.

Critical and Creative Thinking

5 Both the project and the portfolio are intriguing and thought-provoking. Arguments are logical and persuasive. Ideas are well-articulated and presented in original ways.

4 Both the project and the portfolio engage the reader and show evidence of significant critical and creative thinking. The student displays excellence in either critical analysis, or artistic creation, if not both. Arguments show careful thought, and are basically persuasive. Ideas are presented in original ways.

3 Both the project and the portfolio provide evidence of some critical and creative thought. The student may display excellence in either critical analysis, or artistic creation, and are competent with both. Arguments are present and show some thought. Ideas are present and developed, if not particularly original or well-articulated.

2 Evidence of critical and creative thinking is marginal. The project and portfolio display adequate critical and creative thinking, but not much more than that. Arguments and ideas are asserted without much critical thought. Little originality is evident. This is a rote or hasty project and/or portfolio.

1 Evidence of critical and/or creative thinking is largely absent. Either the portfolio or the project (or both) shows little or no method or planning. Work seems thrown together with minimal critical or creative thought.

Ability to Critique Own Work

5 The reflective paper is insightful and nuanced. The student articulates a deep awareness of the strengths and limitations of both the portfolio and the project. The reflective paper critically examines the various works in the portfolio and the project. The student illuminates the key decisions that shaped the final version of the project and portfolio, weaving the entire work into a coherent narrative.

4 The reflective paper is coherent and engaging. The student articulates some awareness of the strengths and limitations of both the portfolio and the project. The reflective paper critically examines the various works in the portfolio and the project. The student discusses the key decisions that shaped the final version of the project and portfolio, and provides some narrative of the overall process.

3 The reflective paper is basically coherent. The student articulates some awareness of the strengths and limitations of either the portfolio, or the project, if not both. The reflective paper critically examines some aspects of the portfolio and the project. The student discusses the key decisions that shaped the final version of the project and portfolio; the larger narrative is present, although it is largely undeveloped and/or unpersuasive.

2 The reflective paper is problematic at best. The student articulates minimal awareness of the strengths and limitations of either the portfolio, or the project, but not both. The reflective paper fails to critically examine either the portfolio or the project. The student discusses the final version of the project and portfolio without providing much insight into the overall creative process. If a narrative is presented at all, it is unoriginal and poorly articulated.

1 The reflective paper is weak. The student fails to provide a meaningful discussion of the strengths or limitations of the portfolio and project. The reflective paper shows little or no method or planning. Work seems thrown together with minimal critical or creative thought.

Understanding of Western Cultural Heritage/Appreciation of Diversity of Perspectives on Human Condition

5 Based on one of the items in the portfolio and/or on the capstone project, the rater finds the item insightful and nuanced. The student articulates a deep awareness of western/world culture and an appreciation of varying perspectives on the human condition.

4 Based on one of the items in the portfolio and/or on the capstone project, the rater finds the item significantly more than competent. The student articulates some awareness of the western/world culture and an appreciation of varying perspectives on the human condition.

3 Based on one of the items in the portfolio and/or on the capstone project, the rater finds the item generally competent. The student articulates some awareness of the western/world culture and some appreciation of varying perspectives on the human condition, although they are largely undeveloped and/or unpersuasive.

2 Based on one of the items in the portfolio and/or capstone project, the rater finds the item barely competent. The item may lack significance, articulating only a narrow awareness and minimal insight into western/world culture and narrow or minimal appreciation of varying perspectives on the human condition.

1 Based on one of the items in the portfolio and/or capstone project, the rater finds the item fails to show even minimal awareness of western/world culture; the item fails to reveal even a narrow or minimal appreciation of varying perspectives on the human condition.

GRADING SHEET

CONTENT (0-25 points)		
Excellent	25 points	no improvement necessary
Very Good	24, 23	writer's own truth, original perception; narrow enough to be clearly and completely developed by specifics; appropriate to audience/purpose; substantive; thorough development of thesis; relevant to topic; creative; evidence of critical thinking; no logical flaws
Good	22, 21	has many of characteristics of truth/perception/appropriateness, development, relevance, but lacks thoroughness, freshness, creativity; has some evidence of critical thinking
Average	20, 19	some perception of subject; adequate range; limited development; mostly relevant to topic; lacks detail; reasonably well-developed, but lacking completeness; good content, but lacking organization
Fair-Poor	18, 17, 16	limited perception of topic; little substance; little development
Very Poor	15-11	little perception of the subject; non-substantive; not pertinent to subject; not enough to evaluate
ORGANIZATION (0-15)		
Excellent	15	no improvement necessary
Very Good	14, 13	fluent expression; ideas clearly stated/supported; succinct; well-organized; logical sequencing; cohesive
Good-Average	12, 11	organized but predictable; obvious/mechanical organization; occasional blurring of purpose
Fair	10	focus blurred; poor beginning/ending; weak movement, repetition, paragraphing, proportion; lacking transitions
Poor	9, 8	ideas confused/rambling; lacks logic/sequence; not focused/no main point
Very Poor	7, 6	does not communicate; no organization; too little to evaluate
VOICE, TONE, DICTION (0-15)		
Excellent	15	no improvement necessary
Very Good	14, 13	sophisticated range; precise word choice/usage; word form mastery; appropriate tone; effective figurative language
Good-Average	12, 11	adequate range; somewhat vague; occasional errors of word form, choice, use; clichés; slang; redundancies; little or no figurative language
Very Poor	8, 7	meaning confused or obscured; inappropriate use of language

SENTENCE STRUCTURE	(0-15)	
Excellent	15	no improvement necessary
Very Good	15, 14	sentence variety; mastery of compound-complex structure/tense/ parallelism/agreement/number/ word function/pronouns/prepositions
Good-Average	13, 12, 11	undistinguished; generally unified, correctly constructed, few slips in unity or clarity, some dull sentences; generally lacking in positive qualities
Fair/Poor	10, 9	occasional lack of unity/ clarity; sentences noticeably thin and immature, repetitious patterns, wordy structures
Poor	8, 7	marked lack of unity or clarity
Very Poor	6, 5	communication seriously impeded by lack of unity/ clarity
PUNCTUATION	(10-0)	One point deduction for each error
USAGE, MECHANICS	(10-0)	One point deduction for each error
SPELLING/READABILITY	(10-0)	One point deduction for each error: Manuscript form, carelessness, excessive errors also affect this area.

NOTE: DOCUMENTED PAPERS (papers assigned which should be documented) may lose additional points if incorrectly documented. For example, a paper might lose 10-20 points if it lacks correct Works Cited format and 10-20 points if it lacks internal, parenthetical documentation, etc.

NAME ____________________
CONTENT (0-25 points)
Excellent 25 points
Very Good 24, 23
Good 22, 21
Average 20, 19
Fair/Poor 18, 17, 16
Very Poor 15, 14, 13, 12, 11
ORGANIZATION (0-15)
Excellent to Very Good 15, 14, 13
Good to Average 12, 11
Fair 10
Poor 9, 8
Very Poor 7, 6
VOICE, TONE, DICTION (0-15 points)
Excellent to Very Good 15, 14, 13
Good to Average 12, 11
Very Poor 8, 7
SENTENCE STRUCTURE (0-15 points)
Excellent to very good 15, 14
Good to Average 13, 12, 11
Fair to Poor 10, 9
Poor 8, 7
Very Poor 6, 5
PUNCTUATION (10-0) _____
One point deduction for each error
USAGE, MECHANICS (10-0) _____
One point deduction for each error
SPELLING/READABILITY (10-0) __
One point deduction for each error
Manuscript form, carelessness,
excessive errors may also affect this area.

NAME ____________________
CONTENT (0-25 points)
Excellent 25 points
Very Good 24, 23
Good 22, 21
Average 20, 19
Fair/Poor 18, 17, 16
Very Poor 15, 14, 13, 12, 11
ORGANIZATION (0-15)
Excellent to Very Good 15, 14, 13
Good to Average 12, 11
Fair 10
Poor 9, 8
Very Poor 7, 6
VOICE, TONE, DICTION (0-15 points)
Excellent to Very Good 15, 14, 13
Good to Average 12, 11
Very Poor 8, 7
SENTENCE STRUCTURE (0-15 points)
Excellent to very good 15, 14
Good to Average 13, 12, 11
Fair to Poor 10, 9
Poor 8, 7
Very Poor 6, 5
PUNCTUATION (10-0) _____
One point deduction for each error
USAGE, MECHANICS (10-0) _____
One point deduction for each error
SPELLING/READABILITY (10-0) __
One point deduction for each error
Manuscript form, carelessness,
excessive errors may also affect this area.

NAME ____________________
CONTENT (0-25 points)
Excellent 25 points
Very Good 24, 23
Good 22, 21
Average 20, 19
Fair/Poor 18, 17, 16
Very Poor 15, 14, 13, 12, 11
ORGANIZATION (0-15)
Excellent to Very Good 15, 14, 13
Good to Average 12, 11
Fair 10
Poor 9, 8
Very Poor 7, 6
VOICE, TONE, DICTION (0-15 points)
Excellent to Very Good 15, 14, 13
Good to Average 12, 11
Very Poor 8, 7
SENTENCE STRUCTURE (0-15 points)
Excellent to very good 15, 14
Good to Average 13, 12, 11
Fair to Poor 10, 9
Poor 8, 7
Very Poor 6, 5
PUNCTUATION (10-0) _____
One point deduction for each error
USAGE, MECHANICS (10-0) _____
One point deduction for each error
SPELLING/READABILITY (10-0) __
One point deduction for each error
Manuscript form, carelessness,
excessive errors may also affect this area.

NAME ____________________
CONTENT (0-25 points)
Excellent 25 points
Very Good 24, 23
Good 22, 21
Average 20, 19
Fair/Poor 18, 17, 16
Very Poor 15, 14, 13, 12, 11
ORGANIZATION (0-15)
Excellent to Very Good 15, 14, 13
Good to Average 12, 11
Fair 10
Poor 9, 8
Very Poor 7, 6
VOICE, TONE, DICTION (0-15 points)
Excellent to Very Good 15, 14, 13
Good to Average 12, 11
Very Poor 8, 7
SENTENCE STRUCTURE (0-15 points)
Excellent to very good 15, 14
Good to Average 13, 12, 11
Fair to Poor 10, 9
Poor 8, 7
Very Poor 6, 5
PUNCTUATION (10-0) _____
One point deduction for each error
USAGE, MECHANICS (10-0) _____
One point deduction for each error
SPELLING/READABILITY (10-0) __
One point deduction for each error
Manuscript form, carelessness,
excessive errors may also affect this area.

NAME ______________________________
CONTENT (0-25 points)
Excellent 25 points
Very Good 24, 23
Good 22, 21
Average 20, 19
Fair/Poor 18, 17, 16
Very Poor 15, 14, 13, 12, 11
ORGANIZATION (0-15)
Excellent to Very Good 15, 14, 13
Good to Average 12, 11
Fair 10
Poor 9, 8
Very Poor 7, 6
VOICE, TONE, DICTION (0-15 points)
Excellent to Very Good 15, 14, 13
Good to Average 12, 11
Very Poor 8, 7
SENTENCE STRUCTURE (0-15 points)
Excellent to very good 15, 14
Good to Average 13, 12, 11
Fair to Poor 10, 9
Poor 8, 7
Very Poor 6, 5
PUNCTUATION (10-0) _____
One point deduction for each error
USAGE, MECHANICS (10-0) _____
One point deduction for each error
SPELLING/READABILITY (10-0) __
One point deduction for each error
Manuscript form, carelessness,
excessive errors may also affect this area.

NAME ______________________________
CONTENT (0-25 points)
Excellent 25 points
Very Good 24, 23
Good 22, 21
Average 20, 19
Fair/Poor 18, 17, 16
Very Poor 15, 14, 13, 12, 11
ORGANIZATION (0-15)
Excellent to Very Good 15, 14, 13
Good to Average 12, 11
Fair 10
Poor 9, 8
Very Poor 7, 6
VOICE, TONE, DICTION (0-15 points)
Excellent to Very Good 15, 14, 13
Good to Average 12, 11
Very Poor 8, 7
SENTENCE STRUCTURE (0-15 points)
Excellent to very good 15, 14
Good to Average 13, 12, 11
Fair to Poor 10, 9
Poor 8, 7
Very Poor 6, 5
PUNCTUATION (10-0) _____
One point deduction for each error
USAGE, MECHANICS (10-0) _____
One point deduction for each error
SPELLING/READABILITY (10-0) __
One point deduction for each error
Manuscript form, carelessness,
excessive errors may also affect this area.

NAME ______________________________
CONTENT (0-25 points)
Excellent 25 points
Very Good 24, 23
Good 22, 21
Average 20, 19
Fair/Poor 18, 17, 16
Very Poor 15, 14, 13, 12, 11
ORGANIZATION (0-15)
Excellent to Very Good 15, 14, 13
Good to Average 12, 11
Fair 10
Poor 9, 8
Very Poor 7, 6
VOICE, TONE, DICTION (0-15 points)
Excellent to Very Good 15, 14, 13
Good to Average 12, 11
Very Poor 8, 7
SENTENCE STRUCTURE (0-15 points)
Excellent to very good 15, 14
Good to Average 13, 12, 11
Fair to Poor 10, 9
Poor 8, 7
Very Poor 6, 5
PUNCTUATION (10-0) _____
One point deduction for each error
USAGE, MECHANICS (10-0) _____
One point deduction for each error
SPELLING/READABILITY (10-0) __
One point deduction for each error
Manuscript form, carelessness,
excessive errors may also affect this area.

NAME ______________________________
CONTENT (0-25 points)
Excellent 25 points
Very Good 24, 23
Good 22, 21
Average 20, 19
Fair/Poor 18, 17, 16
Very Poor 15, 14, 13, 12, 11
ORGANIZATION (0-15)
Excellent to Very Good 15, 14, 13
Good to Average 12, 11
Fair 10
Poor 9, 8
Very Poor 7, 6
VOICE, TONE, DICTION (0-15 points)
Excellent to Very Good 15, 14, 13
Good to Average 12, 11
Very Poor 8, 7
SENTENCE STRUCTURE (0-15 points)
Excellent to very good 15, 14
Good to Average 13, 12, 11
Fair to Poor 10, 9
Poor 8, 7
Very Poor 6, 5
PUNCTUATION (10-0) _____
One point deduction for each error
USAGE, MECHANICS (10-0) _____
One point deduction for each error
SPELLING/READABILITY (10-0) __
One point deduction for each error
Manuscript form, carelessness,
excessive errors may also affect this area.

Permission to Use Student Writing

We hope to include more student papers in each subsequent edition of the *Guide to College Writing*. Please let us see your essays! Include this form and submit the essay to

Dr. Dial-Driver, Dept. of English and Humanities
Rogers State University
1701 W. Will Rogers Blvd.
Claremore, OK 74017

Please initial each statement.

________ 1. All of the writing turned in by me to
____________ (Name of person to which paper is submitted)
____________ (Class and school in which the paper is submitted)
____________ (Address of school in which paper is submitted
____
____________ (Telephone number of school in which paper is submitted)
this semester is my writing.

________ 2. I agree to let the Writing Faculty of the Department of English and Humanities use my writing to help other students. This may include using my writing in handouts, in the publication the *Guide to College Writing*, or in other publication(s), etc.

________ 3. I agree to let the Writing Faculty make minor revisions in my writing.

________ 4. I do/do not want my name placed on any writing used. (Please circle the appropriate response.)

Student Signature: ____________________ Date: ____________

Student Contract for Class ________________________
Name: ____________________ Date:____________________

Initial each statement and turn this contract in. This contract must be on file for you to attend the class.

_____ I have read and understood the guidelines and requirements in the syllabus.

_____ I understand that this class is for ___ hours college credit; this implies ___ hours of class meeting per week.

_____ I understand that each hour of college credit usually requires two or more hours per week study time outside of class; this implies a total of ___ hours per week study time outside of class.

_____ I understand that attendance is required.

_____ I understand what plagiarism is, and I understand that strict penalties will incur if I plagiarize material.

_____ I understand that peer critiquing may be required in this class; this means that any work I do for this class may be subject to peer review by my classmates.

_____ I understand literary and/or academic selections for this class may contain controversial or "offensive" material; this is the nature of educational works.

(signature)____________________ (date) ____________________

OTHER DOCUMENTATION STYLES

In addition to APA and MLA documentation, other documentation styles and guides include the *ACS Style Guide* (for chemistry documents), the *Chicago Manual of Style* (for general documents), the *Columbia Guide to Online Style* (for on-line sources), the *Complete Guide to Citing Government Documents* (for citing government documents), the *Scientific Style and Format: The CBE Manual for Authors, Editors, and Publishers* (for documents in the biological sciences), and Turabian's *A Manual for Writers* (for general documents). In addition to these major style manuals, some fields have their own style guides. Always check with the person requesting the paper to determine which style is appropriate for the paper.

MLA ENDNOTE/FOOTNOTE FORMAT SAMPLE DOCUMENTATION EXAMPLES

Works Cited Page

- **Note:** For MLA-format Works Cited examples, see the main section on the research paper. For page set-up, see "Manuscript Preparation."

Endnotes or Footnotes

BOOK with one author.

[3] Charles Dickens, Great Expectations (New York: Rinehart, 1948), 134.

BOOK with more than three authors, with an edition after the first, with several volumes.

[8] Walter Blair, et al., The Literature of the United States, vol. 1, 3rd ed., 3 vols. (Glenview: Scott Foresman, 1969), 322.

ARTICLE, signed, appearing on only one page, in a magazine/journal with volume and issue number, with part of the title in quotation marks.

[13] Richard Wolkomir, "For the 'Tied Up' Businessman," Smithsonian 17.12 (March 1987): 192.

ARTICLE in a magazine/journal with no volume number, appearing on more than one page, inclusive pages, from a magazine/journal published bi-monthly.

[7] Daphne Gail Fautin, "The Anemone Is Not Its Enemy," National Wildlife Oct.-Nov. 1987, 22-25.

ON-LINE SOURCE.

[6] Erica Recomp, "Computers and Film Focuses," Computers in Film 1 May 1998 <http://www. millingu.edu/univnews/>. (15 Aug. 2005).

Subsequent References

[5] Dickens 136.

[9] Blair et al. 11.

[13] Wolkomir 192.

[19] Fautin 25.

[28] Recomp.

Rhetorical Appeals

Lori Butler and Frances Morris

When writing an argument, consider how to appeal to the audience. How will you persuade the readers to at least think about what you have said? What will it take to get them to listen? When and how do you develop a strong argument that appeals to an audience that typically believes the opposite of what you are writing? As a writer, you should use rhetorical appeals to make your argument strong and memorable. However, you need to understand how each of three appeals works before you consider using them. Rhetorical appeals fall into three categories: logos, ethos, and pathos.

Logos is the appeal to reason or the ability to think rationally about the topic. You may use inductive and deductive reasoning in logos. Deductive reasoning begins with a generalization and draws a specific conclusion; inductive reasoning begins with some specific statement and moves backward to the generalization. Logical appeals can be built by using induction, deduction, classification, cause and effect, comparison, definition, facts and statistics. (Look at "Where's the Beef?" in the student example section of this Guide.)

Ethos is an ethical appeal. Ethos is based on the character of the writer and the credibility of the argument being established by that writer. It is the writer's credibility and character that is under the microscope when considering ethos. Ethical appeals can be built by establishing the writer's credentials as an authority on the subject; however, especially for students, credibility is also built by including and correctly citing reliable sources, by using a respectful tone, by establishing common ground with the audience, and by adhering to the grammatical and mechanical standards of college writing. (Look at "Midwifery in the United States" in the student example section of this Guide.")

Pathos is an emotional appeal. It is how the writer pulls at the heart strings of the audience. Emotions are a strong part in making an argument from pathos. Most people are swayed to listen and act because of their emotions. Pathos is built by appealing to the audience's values, i.e. morals, beliefs, and feelings. Using figurative language and emotionally charged words become important tools in establishing an appeal using pathos. (Satire and irony may also be emotional appeals.) (See "The Doll" in the example section of this Guide; see also "A True Man" in the definition section of this Guide.)

Important factors to remember when using rhetorical appeals:

1. Be positive in the argument. Do not denigrate your opponent.
2. Watch your tone so that the audience does not feel as though you are talking down to them.
3. Be honest so that your audience can feel a sense of trust.
4. Select appeals that are open and honest. This helps build your character and credibility as a writer.

COMMON LOGICAL FALLACIES

Renèe Turk

Below are definitions of some of the common logical fallacies (errors in reasoning).

Circular reasoning: Restating the point rather than supporting it with reasonable evidence; this argument often contains a "begging-the-question" fallacy as well, a form of circular reasoning that assumes the certainty of a questionable statement.

(Example: That is a good movie; I liked it.)

Non sequitur ("it does not follow"): Drawing a onclusion that does not logically follow from the evidence presented; a conclusion that is based on irrelevant evidence.

(Example: A university that can afford to build a new football stadium does not need to raise tuition.)

False cause: Falsely assuming that because one thing happened after another, the first event was a cause of the second event. This is often called a "post hoc" argument.

(Example: How interesting that right after the November elections when that party took the majority, gas prices went down all over the nation. Obviously, politicians of that party determine gas prices.)

Stacking the deck: Slanting the evidence to support a position.

(Example: Ninety percent of Wal-Mart employees are satisfied with Wal-Mart's treat ment of women. [This may sound reasonable, but consider the following questions: Who was surveyed? Ninety percent of all Wal-Mart's employees nationwide or ninety percent of the ten who were actually interviewed in one store in one city? What was the gender of those interviewed--were they all males, for example?])

False authority: Presenting the testimony of an unqualified person to support a claim.

(Example: Bill O'Reilly, who is well known and respected, agrees with me. He stated on his talk show that the young boy must have enjoyed the circumstances of his life with his kidnapper, otherwise the boy would have tried to escape.)

False analogy/false comparison: Comparing two unlike things as if they were similar.

(Example: That university has a great sports program. Obviously, it would be a good place to get a degree in geophysics.)

Hasty generalization: Basing a conclusion on inadequate evidence.

(Example: I personally played video games for hours while I was a kid, and several of my friends did too, and none of us turned out to be violent. Playing video games does not influence teens to be violent.)

Red herring: An argument that diverts attention from the true issue by directing attention to or concentrating on something irrelevant.

(Example: Federal relief programs for Hurricane Katrina victims have failed because many dishonest people tried to take advantage of those programs.)

Oversimplification/black and white thinking: Taking a very complex issue and presenting it as a simple one. This fallacy also "chickens out" by refusing to acknowledge any gray area in an issue—often by presenting one side as purely good and the other side as purely bad.

(Example: Mothers who work are choosing money over the well-being of their own children.)

Straw man: Intentionally misrepresenting the reasoning and actions of the opposing side as extremely weak, dumb, evil, illogical, etc.

(Example: Insurance companies are charging young people with ridiculously high auto insurance rates just so the companies can make a ton of money off teens who do not know they are being taken advantage of.)

Guilt by association: Discrediting a person or group because of problems with that person's or group's associates, friends, families, challenges, etc.

(Example: It is well known that cops have power issues. My sister should avoid marrying her boyfriend, who is a cop; he will not treat her like an equal.)

Ad hominem: Attacking a person rather than that person's arguments or claims.

(Example: Queen Elizabeth II did not even seem to care when Princess Diana was killed, so how much could the queen really care about a British program to provide care for orphaned children?)

Either/or reasoning: Indicating that a complicated issue can be resolved by resorting to one of only two options when in reality there are additional possibilities. Also called the false dilemma fallacy, this fallacy generally depends on inspiring fear for its success—in which case the fallacy is also an appeal to fear.

(Example: Either we figure out how to monitor the activities of Muslims living in America, or we will face terrorist acts like September 11th daily.)

Slippery slope: Assuming that if one step is taken, a series of catastrophic events will inevitably follow. This fallacy, like the either-or fallacy, often manipulates with what is essentially a threat (an appeal to fear).

(Example: Once we allow birth control, marriage will fall out of the norm, and so will the natural reproduction of children. The result will be a much lower population in the United States, and our country will then be vulnerable to being taken over by a foreign power.)

Bandwagon mentality: An argument that depends on going along with the crowd; a false assumption that truth can be determined by which ideas are accepted by the most people. This fallacy manipulates by appealing to a desire to belong to a certain group. Rather than offer solid evidence, it appeals to the fundamental beliefs and prejudices of the audience in order to inspire a false feeling of solidarity.

(Example: People who do not support the war are against our troops.)

Appeal to ignorance: Attempting to get the audience to accept a claim as true, in the hopes that the audience in fact does not know any better (this fallacy succeeds if the audience is ignorant of the facts).

(Example: The revolution was fought and the Constitution was written and signed by men who were all devout, practicing Christians; this shows that the Unites States was meant to be a Christian nation.)

Appeal to pity: Using manipulation of the audience's feelings, rather than using solid or relevant evidence. An element of this fallacy is often that if you (the reader) do not accept the claim, then you are evil, mean, heartless, etc. The appeal to pity is usually used as a red herring.

(Example: That poor girl does not deserve to spend 45 days in jail for driving with a suspended license. People have to understand that she lives under tremendous pressure from the media and that sometimes people crack under that pressure. She is not a horrible person and she deserves for others to show her some compassion.)

RECOGNIZING LOGICAL FALLACIES

(or "What you should NEVER do when presenting an argument")

Read the essay below. Find and label the logical fallacies in the argument (the sentences are numbered for easy labeling). Discuss how the fallacies weaken the writer's claims and how the writer should have/could have presented a stronger, more logical case.

No Gun Control

1} The gun control debate is really just a matter of the right of the American people to defend themselves and defend their property. 2} But many people, who seem to have no sense of reality and no sense of what it means to be an American, are fine with the idea of guns being completely controlled by the government and being taken away from decent people.

3} Senator Scott Hayes, a Republican serving the state of Tennessee, understands this; he is a great sportsman and hunter and speaks against gun control several times a year in Washington. 4} On the other hand, Senator Daniel Chance has spoken in favor of gun control several times in the past decade, but considering the political party he serves, we should not be surprised. 5} However, since Senator Chance is the one who is now under investigation for hiring illegal aliens, I do not think we should take his opinions very seriously. 6} Thankfully, we have political watchdogs like Ridge Linton, who just two months ago on his late night radio show, made the following comment: "It's as simple as this, people. A government that would deny its own people the right to defend themselves is a government that echoes of fascist Germany, and I tell you I want no part of a nation like that." 7} Linton has been talking about political issues on the air for almost fifteen years; he knows what he is talking about.

8} Some people say they are OK with gun control as long as it is handled responsibly and as long as people's individual rights are not trampled on, but they need to realize there is no middle road—there is complete, absolute gun control, or there is no gun control at all. 9} The people who are in favor of gun control are in favor of seeing all American's civil rights revoked, including the right of self-defense. 10} They believe that guns kill people, but all they need to do is remember the bumper sticker: "guns don't kill people—people kill people." 11-14} And just because a person owns a gun does not mean he is going to go out and shoot somebody. My family has owned guns for our whole lives, and we have never shot anyone. I do not know a single person in my whole family or circle of friends who is violent or who is a threat because he has a gun. Just from my own personal experience, it is easy to see that owning guns does not make a person more likely to be violent.

15-16} But all this squawking and debating over gun control is not even necessary, because the United States Constitution solves everything. All the citizens of the United States are given the right to own handguns and hunting weapons in the Second Amendment, which was part of the Bill of Rights, ratified in December of 1791. 17} The fathers of our country knew that Americans deserved that right, and all true Americans believe that we still deserve it. 18} As for those who do not believe we deserve it, we should take a few minutes to imagine how the nation would be if gun control succeeds. 19} As the saying goes, "if guns are outlawed, only outlaws will have guns." 20-22} Innocent people will not have any way to stay safe from criminals who would kill them. Fathers and husbands will not be able to protect their wives from rapists. Men who do not make much money will not have the right to hunt and bring home food for their hungry children. 23-24} Is this really how we want life to be in our country? We have to stand up for our constitutional rights. 25} Either we find a way to keep gun control laws from being passed, or we lose everything.

Test/Exercise Banks

contributions by Lori Butler, Frances Morris, and Renèe Turk

Usage Test A

Cross out the inappropriate words or phrases and write in the appropriate formal words or phrases.

1. We carried our grandmother to the store to get groceries.
2. There are four kids in our family.
3. As we gone at the rodeo, we saw a car wreck.
4. Elizabeth deserves to marry Darcy because she is a total sweetheart.
5. Just as Barry was fixing to cast his vote, he forgot what he had read about the candidate.
6. People who are crackheads are not going to get high grades in college.
7. Spiderman 3 is the best of the Spiderman movies, and I seen it three times.
8. My grandmother learned me how to tie my shoes.
9. Pop took us fishing last weekend.
10. On the night of the performance, I could not find my ticket anywheres.

Usage Test B

Cross out the inappropriate words or phrases and write in the appropriate formal words or phrases.

1. My papa took us shopping for a Mother's Day gift.
2. Would you like another pop?
3. Our senior prom was slammin'.
4. Andrew seen the boys playing ball.
5. Lots of people smoked pot in college.
6. I graduated high school.
7. Kids have a tendency to make lots of noise in crowds.
8. John is fixing to move to Colorado.
9. I kinda learned my lesson.
10. Nohow will I ever stuff valuable tickets into the back pocket of my jeans.

Sentence Structure Test A

Correct each sentence so it is complete and correct.

1. Danny was learning to drive. Speeding along the highway.
2. I read to a kindergarten class today the book was about zoos.
3. Zoos are interesting places to see baby animals. In their habitats.
4. In the pond was a toad the toad was in the water.
5. One should avoid the appearance of misdoing. Even when the deed is innocent.
6. Attorneys suggesting difficulties with the qualitative and quantitative analysis of the evidence.
7. Although the circumstantial evidence overwhelmingly identified motive and opportunity.
8. The prosecutor decided to take the case to trial, however, he did not charge the defendant with first degree murder.
9. The judge sequestered the jury he cited the national interest in the case as the reason.
10. The jury deliberated for three weeks, finally, they found the defendant innocent.

Sentence Structure Test B

Correct each sentence so it is complete and correct.

1. When we go to the ranch, Lexi will ride the pony, he is so cute.
2. Tests will be given tomorrow. In the afternoon.
3. His mother died when he was very young, she had a car wreck.
4. John went to Rogers State University. During the time they changed from a community college to a four year university.
5. Destiny will graduate next year with a degree in psychology, she is then going to medical school.
6. Early diagnosis of breast cancer is often curable.
7. His mother didn't know that a convenience store manager could be a job that was life-threatening.
8. When battered and fried, I love sweet potatoes.
9. Watching in breathless horror, the tornado raced into our front yard.
10. Demonstrating a strong work ethic is necessary. For success at work and in college.

Parallel Construction Test A

Correct the sentence(s) so that each is complete and correctly phrased.

1. I buttered my toast, drank orange juice, and egg.
2. When shifting, go to first gear, second gear, and then put it in third.
3. I hate animated films, going to romances, and seeing action shows.
4. Too many people eat extra butter and sour cream and pour on salt on potatoes.
5. Reading e-mail, messages, and cruising the Internet make my day go fast.
6. My favorite sporting activities are water skiing, in-line skating, and to go rock climbing.
7. My new diet requires me to eat fruits, vegetables, and drinking eight glasses of water.
8. Readers rely on small town newspapers for local news, high school game scores, and predicting area weather forecasts.
9. Bulldogs like to play with their toys, eating, and sleeping.
10. The new teacher required the students to read three novels, to write three essays, and presenting a PowerPoint presentation.

Parallel Construction Test B

Correct the sentence(s) so that each is complete and correctly phrased.

1. Typically, we go camping, take a hike, swim and ran along the stream.
2. Riding a bicycle or to take a walk relaxes me.
3. Which is easier—babysitting or to send them to the movies?
4. To be a part of a team, win a tournament, and getting a trophy is a great feeling.
5. He applied for a job that required skill in managing inventory, placing supply orders, tagging new shipment arrivals and damaged product returns.
6. Hillary Clinton has been praised and criticized for her boldness and being very certain.
7. Queen Elizabeth I pacified her all-male parliament with careful consideration of all their views and is hesitant to make important state decisions without consulting them first.
8. Jacking the car up was hard, but to change the tire was not much easier.
9. I am against the war in Iraq because the American people have been lied to about the need to stay in the region, not enough money for the military equipment that is needed, and the unfairness to soldiers who have had to extend their service.
10. Everybody knows the Pledge of Allegiance, can sing "The Star-Spangled Banner," and "America the Beautiful."

Verb-Subject Agreement Test A

Correct each sentence.

1. Either Sandra or Margaret are going on the cruise.
2. She gone to the market.
3. He seen a giraffe at the zoo.
4. There is too many people in this room.
5. What are the implication of this data?
6. All the songs in the Beatles' repertoire was scheduled to be played at the convention.
7. Rudy Giuliani's vague position on women's privacy issues trouble some voters.
8. Reducing emissions from greenhouse gases were a Kyoto Treaty goal.
9. Each director, screenwriter, and actor deserve respect.
10. The audience for "new" versions of old TV series seem to be growing.

Verb-Subject Agreement Test B

Correct each sentence.

1. Peanut butter and jelly is good foods.
2. Neither George nor the boys is going camping with us next week.
3. Peanut butter and jelly are a great sandwich.
4. One of my friends are developing a new course.
5. Measles are a contagious disease.
6. The list of honor students were compiled by the instructors.
7. In the fall and spring catalogues are the list of requirements.
8. Every student listed are expected to attend the awards banquet.
9. The decision of which classes to take are difficult to make.
10. The instructor along with the students are going to attend the lecture tomorrow.

Exercises

Pronoun Test A

Correct each sentence.

1. The rabbit and her baby are sitting in her hutch.
2. The tame rabbit or the wild one is eating their lettuce.
3. The hung jury handed the foreman its votes.
4. Everybody has taken their seats.
5. The girl or the boy can pick up their own test.
6. Her and her husband should realize that their stinginess towards their family may backfire someday.
7. The gas price hike was devastating because no one wanted to give up their summer vacation plans.
8. Elizabeth and Jane Bennett corresponded regularly while she was in London with their relatives.
9. Every weekend, her parents bring toys for her children, and she puts them in the garage for safe keeping.
10. In many countries, like Switzerland for example, the government pays teachers as highly as they pay doctors.

Pronoun Test B

Correct each sentence.

1. Everybody needs to bring their books with them tomorrow.
2. I like to watch films when you get involved in the plot.
3. The boys' and girls' groups are developing his or her own programs.
4. That horses are the ones used to round up cattle.
5. A person should know their multiplication table.
6. Every student in the class completed their assignment on time.
7. Nobody wanted to voice their objections to the proposal.
8. The guide book makes traveling easy for we tourists.
9. The instructor gives special attention to whomever is in need.
10. He is as disappointed about her failure to call home as me.

Exercises

Capitalization and Numbers Test A

Correct each sentence.

1. I am taking English and Math this semester.
2. The short story is called "The Master is Coming."
3. She asked, "where is he?"
4. Unless there are 10 students enrolled, the class will be closed by the enrollment office.
5. There was a moment of silence at 9 o'clock in the morning to commemorate the lives lost.
6. 5,000 students attend the university.
7. A popular children's movie is One Hundred One Dalmations.
8. Only ¼ of the students passed the last test.
9. Many think that principal Robertson is a nice lady.
10. Even though he is the Mayor, he is inexperienced.

Capitalization and Numbers Test B

Correct each sentence.

1. We bought 1500 cans of apple juice for the campout.
2. I received a Bachelor's degree in 1996.
3. My Aunt said that she would bring the Tabbouleh.
4. Do you think, senator, that the law is just?
5. A Democracy needs educated voters in order to thrive.
6. The country had not held Presidential Elections in several years.
7. It was rumored that the celebrity had moved to 4th street in phoenix, Arizona.
8. One of the books discovered to be in Mcveigh's list of favorites was The Turner diaries.
9. Five thousand and eight dollars was the total of her winnings on The Price is right.
10. The costumer had made a mistake; she had bought 5/8 of a yard instead of seven-eighths of a yard.

Spelling Test A

Correct each sentence.

1. A tornado is lose here!
2. Each data reflects one person's height.
3. He will recieve an award tonight.
4. There is a dove coat on the top of the building.
5. Weather or not it is true is irrelevant
6. Voters in are country need to pay attention to the candidates who are running for office.
7. Chocolat is a story about a women named Vivien and the impact she has on a village in France.
8. Foster parents deserve to be paid more money for there efforts with children.
9. Compared to doctor and lawyer wages, firefighters and policemen receive wages that are unexceptable.
10. I will except your nomination for senior class president.

Spelling Test B

Correct each sentence.

1. Alot of the students are planning to skip school on the last day of classes.
2. I will be alright if I take all my medicine.
3. There are many reasons their not going on vacation.
4. I like to study the lifes of the Egyptian pharaohs.
5. Wilson was going ahead with his League of Nations plan, weather he had support for it or not.
6. The dog ate it's food quickly.
7. Many students lose there patience with boring classes.
8. Hypothesis are formed from research.
9. Often, fraternitys host outlandish parties.
10. Emily cryed over losing her kitten.

Punctuation Test A

Put the appropriate punctuation into the paragraph.

A liberal arts degree is a good choice of college major the degree that more Fortune 500 CEO's have than any other degree is in liberal arts However a student does not have to aspire to be a CEO to benefit from having a degree in liberal arts A liberal arts degree prepares students for a number of employment opportunities work for a magazine or newspaper work in business perhaps in human resources management or customer relations work in urban or engineering planning work in research analysis work as an artist a librarian a teacher work for the government state local or national perhaps even in the CIA A student could go to a professional school in law or medicine or to graduate school in English or humanities. The possibilities are endless. A liberal arts degree gives the skills that employers today want oral and written communication skills creative and critical thinking skills research skills ability to learn and adapt These are the skills that are needed to succeed in the world today in the work place and beyond.

Punctuation Test B

Put the appropriate punctuation into the paragraph.

The Day My Preppy Son Became a Real Cowboy

On a misty morning in April my two teenage sons, and I set out to corral the herd bull Maynard. First we called the cows up. The bull always the aggressive one charged into the open front gate. I yelled to Aaron to secure the rear gate. Instead, of walking around the corral he scaled the iron pipe, and walked tightrope style toward the back gate. Just, as I opened my mouth to caution him he slipped off the wet metal and landed straddling the massive muscled neck of the 2000 pound beast. I begged the 110 pound boy to hang on and I screamed for Clayton to get a bucket of feed. I could see Aaron's fists, gripping tight to Maynard's hair. His Nike tennis shoes, and Pepe jeans were pressed hard into the animal's hide. Aaron, had his eyes closed. Neither of us wanted to see the horrendous possibilities at hand. Finally Clayton returned, and rattled the bucket full of cattle, cake. The bull stopped his flailing around. His huge nostrils sniffed the air. Clayton, shoved the bucket toward the beast. Maynard stuffed his head down deep into the pail providing a slide for Aaron's safe dismount.

Editing Test A

Correct all the mistakes and insert the correct words, phrases, punctuation, and capitalization.

Liberal Arts is a Good Major

A liberal arts degree allows a student to study all kinds of human achievement. One can study everything from philosophy to literature to films to religion to music to theatre and more! From English to spanish, Shakespeare and Graphic Novels to Native American studies, majoring in the Liberal Arts opens a world of possibilities. The degree can be supplemented by an assortment of activities. A number of miners is offered to increase the value of your degree. A student also can find activities, clubs, and organizations of all kinds, including the International student organization and the Native American student association. If students have an interest in writing, he has access to several opportunities. A writing contest for various class essays and for creative efforts in the short story and poetry. Students can even submit their work to Cooweescoowee, a nationally-distributed literary magazine. If a student is interested in art, there are student shows of paintings, sculpture, and drawings can be submitted. Prizes are awarded for best entries. Some students even sell his or her works. If you're interested in music, one can play in the jazz band or the pep band, which perform at atheletic activities. If students are interested in theatre, he can perform in one of the many plays and/or musicals from Shakespeare to original student productions which ocurs every year. One can participate in theatre as a student director; as a scene builder; as playwright; as a member of cast or crew. Choosing a liberal arts degree mean choosing the world.

Editing Test B

Correct all the mistakes and insert the correct words, phrases, spelling, punctuation, and capitalization.

Why not Study

When ever the stress of taking tests and writing papers tempts me to giveup on college I remember my Fathers principal. My Dad a first generation immigrant had to dropout of Highschool so that he could work and earn money to help fed his 9 younger brothers' and sisters'. However his loss of formal schooling did not mean the end of his education for I remember each friday nite of the new school year I was suppose to bring home all of my textbooks so that Dad could study them. It use to anger me to lug all those heavy books home but I always did because I new my Dads principal: "In this country they give you the books, so why not study, study study". 5 years ago on a saturday nite my Dad past in his sleep but open on his nite table was my younger sisters Ancient History textbook. So when my hunger for knowledge needs a boost in honor of my Dad I brew a pot of Kenyan Coffee and study, study study.